Re〔barcode: D0777866〕**th**

"Run to pick up a copy of *Flight Path*. Reading it made me feel inspired, encouraged and better equipped to live life well. Very highly recommended!"

> — **Michael Stallard,** President, E Pluribus Partners, Author of *Connection Culture* and *Fired Up or Burned Out*

"Scott's humble patriotism and empathy are well-demonstrated in this unusual journey through wars, international relations, and many personal give-backs. His memoir portrays one of America's finest servant-leaders."

> — **Josh Weston,** Honorary Chairman, Automatic Data Processing Inc.

"Scott's first-person rendition of the Khobar Towers attack and the sleepless days that followed is riveting. You will feel the pain and anger we all felt with the cowardly attack—and the determination we all felt in getting on with America's mission. You'll also get a good sense of the integral part Scott played in the response."

> — **Terry Schwalier,** Brig Gen, USAF (Ret) Commander, 4404th Composite Wing (Provisional), 1995–96

"*Flight Path* tells the story of how General Scott Gration—honest, diplomatic, resilient, and focused on his plan—won the trust of the Sudanese and fulfilled his mission as the US Special Envoy to Sudan."

— **Dr. Ghazi Salahuddin Atabani**
Former minister and presidential adviser,
and chief interlocutor with the US Envoy,
Republic of the Sudan

"I grew up with Scott in the Belgian Congo. Scott's memoir is a fascinating and compelling glimpse into the intersection of the deeply personal and broader socio-political dimensions of history through the eyes of one who helped to shape significant global events. Margaret Mead observed that the course of history is influenced and changed primarily through the actions of thoughtful, committed, and passionate individuals. Scott Gration is one of those persons."

— **Dr. Paul W. Robinson**
Professor Emeritus, Wheaton College (Illinois)
and Senior Advisor, Congo Initiative USA

"Scott Gration captures his careers as a fighter pilot, special envoy, and ambassador to Kenya with exquisite detail, tracing their beginnings to those formative years of his African childhood. I enthusiastically recommend this book to anyone interested in Africa, military aviation, or American politics."

— **Shel Arensen**
Editor, *Old Africa* magazine

FLIGHT PATH

Son of Africa to Warrior-Diplomat

Ambassador

SCOTT GRATION

Major General, USAF (Ret)

Mulami Books
Winter Garden, Florida

Flight Path: Son of Africa to Warrior-Diplomat

Copyright © 2016 by Jonathan Scott Gration

The Library of Congress has catalogued the paperback edition as follows:

Flight Path: Son of Africa to Warrior-Diplomat / Scott Gration—1st ed.
p. cm.
ISBN: 978-0-9976516-0-7
eBook ISBN: 978-0-9976516-1-4
Library of Congress Control Number: 2016908989

Cover design by Blake Arensen and Saija Autrand
Cover photos: Personal
Book design by Saija Autrand
All pictures used by permission

Published by Mulami Books Limited

www.scottgration.com

Printed in the United States of America

Contents

Foreword
by
Jimmy Carter

Exactly one year before the referendum on the independence
of Southern Sudan, Kofi Annan, Rosalynn, and I sat around a dining table
at the American Consulate's guest quarters in Juba discussing Sudan's
upcoming national election with Scott Gration and his team. Throughout
his tenure as the President's Special Envoy to Sudan, Scott and I exchanged
views regularly by telephone and in person.

When I was a member of The Elders, I invited Scott to spend a day
in Istanbul, Turkey, to give our group of eminent global leaders the latest
information on the Darfur peace efforts and the negotiations between
Khartoum and Juba on the Comprehensive Peace Agreement (CPA). He
not only understood the complex dynamics in Sudan and the surrounding
countries, but he had a solid plan to influence the outcome. My interactions
with Scott gave me the perfect window to observe his servant spirit, warrior tenacity, and negotiating prowess.

Raised in Africa as the son of missionary parents, Scott learned at
an early age about appreciating diverse cultures, communicating across
multiple boundaries, and succeeding in difficult situations. Losing all the
family's possessions in the 1964 Congo rebellion and living as a refugee in
Kenya gave Scott a genuine compassion for those who were displaced in
Darfur and Southern Sudan. His core value of "service before self" is clearly demonstrated in his volunteer efforts in Uganda following the scourge
of Idi Amin, his service as the community barber for the less fortunate in
Virginia, and his venture to start a company in East Africa to create jobs.

A strategic thinker and military planner, Scott needed his warrior
credentials and practical problem-solving approach to devise and execute
a plan that would achieve a free, fair, and credible referendum on Southern

Scott (left) with President Jimmy Carter (2010).

Sudan's independence by the January 9, 2011, deadline. Failure in this mission would likely see Sudan plunge back into the fighting and unrest that characterized the previous four decades. In addition to shepherding the CPA negotiations, assisting the national election process, and pushing the peace talks on Darfur, he had to orchestrate international diplomatic efforts in Sudan and to keep Sudan-focused constituencies in the United States informed and satisfied.

Scott's years of diplomatic experience and negotiating background were needed every day in Sudan. Representatives of the North and South brought forty years of enmity and distrust to the CPA negotiations. He brought them to consensus. Concerns of twenty-nine rebel groups had to be merged into a single voice when negotiating the Darfur Peace Agreement with Khartoum. His team fostered the required unity. At the same time, Scott and his colleagues successfully negotiated an end to the conflict between Chad and Sudan. They brought more security to Darfur.

This dynamic memoir tells more than the Sudan story. It also includes accounts of developing the Predator drone, conducting the 2003 "Scud hunt" in Iraq, and accompanying then-Senator Obama to Africa in 2006. The book tells about piloting an F-16 fighter in combat, surviving the 1996 Khobar Towers bombing in Saudi Arabia, protecting the Kurds in Iraq, and speaking at the 2008 Democratic National Convention. Finally, Scott answers the question of why the State Department pushed him out of his position as US Ambassador to Kenya without due process.

The last chapter is one of my favorites. Scott has had a unique career flight path as a warrior and diplomat. Each story in the book contributes to twelve lessons, which he compiles in the last chapter. Scott believes God has had a hand on his life from an early age. So do I.

— Jimmy Carter
39th President of the United States of America

This book is dedicated to my father,

Dr. John Alexander Gration,

who insisted until his last days
that I keep a diary and notes because
he believed I would one day write this book.

He was a man of vision,
a great communicator, a model of integrity,
and passionate about Africa.

I desire to be like him.

Preface

IN NOVEMBER 2012, I registered a company in Kenya. I was excited about a new career as a businessman seeking to bring international investment and development to Africa. But the long holiday season and an all-consuming country-wide political campaign were causing a pervasive economic paralysis that would not end until the new national government was in place. I used the slow period to begin to record my life's unlikely journey—what I only half-jokingly call my flight path.

This memoir traces that path: the story of a warrior who acted as a diplomat, a diplomat who was not afraid to think like a warrior, and an entrepreneur who continues to both fight for good and do so diplomatically. Service to God, my country, and my fellow global citizens is a dominant and connecting theme. As is timing.

Who would have thought this missionary kid who spent his early childhood in the Belgian Congo, fled to Kenya as a refugee, and struggled in school would become a fighter pilot, a general officer, a presidential envoy, a US ambassador, and a friend to two American presidents? But looking back, I realize that so much of my success came from being in the right place at the right time, with the right skills and experiences with which to serve. To say that I have been blessed is not a cliché; it is the truth.

Take, for example, my friendship with President Barack Obama. When the then freshman senator from Illinois requested in 2006 that I be his guide to the land of his father as he was ramping up a run for the presidency, I was honored—but it also made sense. I considered myself a son of Africa. I spoke Kiswahili and understood the history and cultures of Africa; I'd been a White House Fellow; I had spent over ten years as a senior officer in the US Air Force dealing with geopolitical and national security issues; I'd negotiated with heads of state and top political leaders and was versed in the ways of statesmanship. I would be able to draw on all this to advise the next president of the United States.

The relationship led to participating in Mr. Obama's 2008 presidential campaign, which led to working as a presidential assistant in the early stage of the Obama administration, which led to being chosen in 2009 to serve as the Special Envoy to Sudan—and gaining the mentorship of another president, Jimmy Carter.

But not everything has been smooth flying.

My life prior to May 2011 seemed to be perfect preparation for what my wife, Judy, and I viewed as the culmination of our experiences and our love for Africa: the appointment to become the US Ambassador to Kenya. But, like a deceptive cold front forcing a jet pilot to abandon the planned flight route and set down in uncharted territory, what happened in Nairobi broke our hearts and raised questions we will probably never have answered.

Nevertheless, as you read this narrative you may notice several themes. One is how God has had His hand on my life from an early age and how, even during hard times and dark days, I felt humbled and in awe to see how things generally worked together for good over time. Another is how leadership opportunities gave me openings to practice integrity, fairness, and doing the "right things right." Finally, while I wrestled with priorities and balance throughout my career, I finally realized that only relationships are enduring—spiritual, family, and friends. Some might say the patterns in my life are just coincidences. I choose to see them as evidence of a heavenly Flight Commander—a merciful and loving God behind my life's flight path.

The content of this memoir is limited to those issues, events, and stories that were unclassified or have since been released in open sources. Unfortunately, some of my most compelling experiences and interesting stories, being classified and confidential in nature, will have to follow me to my grave. The text of this manuscript received full security reviews from the Pentagon, the State Department, the Central Intelligence Agency, and the White House. The opinions and characterizations in the book are exclusively mine, of course, and do not necessarily represent the official positions of the United States Government.

Most of the quotations in this book come from the detailed diaries I have kept throughout my life. Others are from individuals who recounted stories to me, from individuals who witnessed certain events, or from my distinct memory of a specific experience. Where dialogue uses a non-verbatim quotation, the conversation remains true to the context of the event as I remember it or as it was recorded in my personal journal.

Every effort has been made to contact copyright holders for material used in this book. I would be pleased to rectify any omissions in future editions if notified by the copyright holder.

I hope you enjoy the journey.

— Scott Gration
Mombasa, Kenya

Timeline

US Air Force Officer Ranks and Scott Gration's Promotion Dates

Rank	Abbreviation	Pay Scale	Gration's Promotion Date
General	Gen	O-10	---
Lieutenant General	Lt Gen	O-9	---
Major General	Maj Gen	O-8	April 1, 2003
Brigadier General	Brig Gen	O-7	October 1, 1999
Colonel	Col	O-6	January 1, 1995
Lieutenant Colonel	Lt Col	O-5	June 1, 1988
Major	Maj	O-4	May 1, 1985
Captain	Capt	O-3	July 24, 1978
First Lieutenant	1st Lt	O-2	July 24, 1976
Second Lieutenant	2nd Lt	O-1	January 24, 1974

Biographical Timeline

Date	Location	Title/Activity
Jul 14, 1951	St. Charles, Illinois	Birth, Delnor Hospital
1951–1952	Peapack, New Jersey	Parents interim assignment
1953–1957	Congo	Parents served as missionary teachers
1957–1958	Hawthorne, New Jersey	Family furlough
1958–1960	Linga, Congo	Parents were missionary teachers
Jul 1960	Kampala, Uganda	Six-week evacuation from Congo

DATE	LOCATION	TITLE/ACTIVITY
1960–1961	Linga, Congo	Parents were missionary teachers
Mar 1961	Kijabe, Kenya	Six-month evacuation from Congo
1961–1962	Linga, Congo	Parents were missionary teachers
1962–1963	Glen Rock, New Jersey	Family furlough
1963–1964	Banjwadi, Congo	Parents were missionary teachers
Aug 1964	Kijabe, Kenya	Final evacuation from Congo
1964–1967	Kijabe, Kenya	Parents were missionary teachers
1967–1969	Ridgewood, New Jersey	Student, Ridgewood High School
1969–1974	New Brunswick, New Jersey	Student, Rutgers University BS, Mechanical Engineering
1974	Gatab, Kenya	Short-term humanitarian work
Aug 3, 1974	Ridgewood, New Jersey	Marriage to Judy DeYoung
1974–1975	Columbus, Mississippi	USAF undergraduate pilot training
1975–1976	San Antonio, Texas	T-38 instructor pilot (IP) training
1976–1978	Columbus, Mississippi	T-38 instructor pilot
1978	Columbus, Mississippi	Jonathan is born
1978–1980	Phoenix, Arizona	F-5 instructor pilot
1980	Chandler, Arizona	Jennifer is born
1980–1982	Nanyuki, Kenya	F-5 IP and weapons officer
1982–1983	Washington, DC	White House Fellow/NASA
1983	Tampa, Florida	F-16 pilot transition training
1983–1985	Las Vegas, Nevada	F-16 IP and Flight Commander
1984	Las Vegas, Nevada	David is born
1985–1988	Washington, DC	International Politico-Military Affairs Officer and part-time student at Georgetown University MA, National Security Studies
1987	Bethesda, MD	Katherine is born
1988	Norfolk, VA	Student at Armed Forces Staff College
1988–1990	Izmir, Turkey	Chief, Offensive Air Operations (NATO)
1990–1992	Ramstein, Germany	Operations officer and F-16 IP

DATE	LOCATION	TITLE/ACTIVITY
1992–1993	Washington, DC	Student, the National War College at National Defense University
1993–1995	Washington, DC	Executive officer to USAF Chief of Staff
1995–1996	Dhahran, Saudi Arabia	Operations Group commander, F-16 IP
1996–1998	Incirlik, Turkey	39th Wing commander and F-16 IP
1998	Panama City, Florida	F-15 pilot transition training
1998–2000	Anchorage, Alaska	3rd Wing commander and F-15 pilot
2000–2001	Washington, DC	Director of information operations (Joint Staff)
2001–2003	Washington, DC	Director of regional affairs (USAF Staff)
2003	Middle East	Commander, Task Force-West (CENTCOM)
2003–2004	Washington, DC	Assistant deputy under secretary international affairs (USAF Staff)
2004–2006	Stuttgart, Germany	Director of strategy, plans, and policy (EUCOM)
Oct 1, 2006	Stuttgart, Germany	Retired from US Air Force active duty
2006	South and East Africa	Traveled with Senator Obama
2006–2008	New York and New Jersey	Executive leader in two nonprofit organizations
2008–2009	Washington, DC	Member, Presidential Transition Team
2009	Washington, DC	Special assistant to the President
2009–2011	Washington, DC	US Special Envoy to Sudan
2011–2012	Nairobi, Kenya	US Ambassador to Kenya
2012–2015	Nairobi, Kenya	CEO, The Gration Group Limited
2015–Present	Mombasa, Kenya	Executive Chairman, Champion Afrik

1

Plunge to New Priorities

What we have done for ourselves alone dies with us; what we have done for others and the world remains and is immortal.

— Albert Pike

SINCE CHILDHOOD, my parents and religious teachers had pounded into my head that we were here on earth to glorify God and to serve mankind. I accepted this biblical teaching in theory, but in truth I was still pretty much "me focused" and oriented toward taking care of myself and my family. One day in 1979, my priorities dramatically flipped.

Wearing an anti-G suit and a parachute, and carrying my helmet and a small bag packed with civilian clothes, I walked briskly to my F-5 aircraft at Williams Air Force Base in Phoenix. Several rows of perfectly parked single-seat fighters filled our squadron ramp, each painted with one of several camouflage schemes. Today I would be flying a dark camouflaged fighter, affectionately referred to as the "green lizard." It was best suited for low-level missions over green foliage. My friend would be piloting an F-5 painted mottled grey. His aircraft's color was optimized for air-combat missions at higher altitudes where clouds, haze, and lighter shades of blue were the predominant background.

The two of us thundered off toward the east at 3 o'clock in the afternoon—I was flying in a loose chase formation, serving as the flight's safety observer. The pilot in the lead aircraft had his eyes glued inside the cockpit

Scott prepares to fly the F-5 Tiger II.

as he practiced for his upcoming instrument evaluation, so I was responsible for making sure our flight path was clear.

Our peaceful cruise at 35,000 feet across New Mexico's beautiful landscapes did not portend the life-changing event that awaited me in the next thirty minutes. The sun was beginning to set as we approached Texas en route to San Antonio. In the distance, puffy thunderstorm clouds dominated the horizon.

As the sun dipped toward the horizon, these clouds began to light up with flashes of lightning. Soon it felt as if we were flying in a pinball machine—we were the steel ball and the towering thunderstorms surrounding us were like the brightly flashing targets.

During our descent from cruising altitude, we entered the dark murky soup. There was so much water in the clouds that I could barely see the outline of the flight leader's aircraft. While our wingtips were separated by less than a yard, the rain streaking on my canopy made it very difficult to see the references I needed to fly formation off of the leader's gray-camouflaged F-5. His aircraft was a now just a fuzzy shape and a few lights.

Lead's voice cracked over my intercom, "Rotating beacon is giving me vertigo. I have to turn it off."

"Roger," I replied.

While I knew the beacon's flashing in the clouds could cause disorientation, this beacon had been a reference to help me stay in tight formation.

I would now have to rely on the three remaining small lights to stay in position.

Continuing our descent, we dipped below the glow of the sun's fading rays. It was now almost pitch black in the rain-filled clouds. Approaching 4,000 feet above the ground, it was so dark that I could barely see the ghostly outline of the solid metal object only a couple of feet away from me as we descended at 300 miles per hour toward the ground.

A few feet closer and we would have a mid-air collision; a few more feet apart and I would lose the visual cues I needed to stay in position. My heart was pounding. I used every ounce of concentration and flying skill to remain glued in tight formation. Recalling my pre-mission planning, I knew that we would be turning left at 3,000 feet above the ground to intercept a curved ground track that would take us to Randolph Air Force Base, just north of San Antonio.

Then the leader's aircraft vanished. It was there a second ago. Now I was staring at rain streaks and darkness.

"Tiger 2-2's breaking out, lost sight," I announced on the flight's intercom.

Quickly transitioning back to flying off my cockpit instruments, I could not believe what I saw on the attitude indicator. My jet was on its back in about 120 degrees of bank; I was pointed nose down in a steep dive.

My brain was confused. I had expected to be right side up and just about level—not plummeting toward the ground. The altimeter was unwinding and my airspeed was increasing. Yes, I was definitely hurling toward the earth.

Instinctively, I rolled level using my cockpit attitude indicator and yanked the throttles back to idle power. With only seconds until impact, I pulled hard on the stick until I felt a light tickle on the airframe—that learned feeling that experienced pilots use for an optimum recovery.

Blurry but discernible shapes of trees whizzed beneath my jet as I bottomed out just a few hundred feet above the ground. I had just been spared death by fireball.

Climbing back into the clouds again, I leveled at 3,000 feet on the altimeter.

"San Antonio Approach, Tiger 2-2, eleven miles southeast of Randolph, heading 210, request ILS, Runway 32 left," I said on the radio, sounding very calm. An instrument landing system (ILS) enables aircraft to land if the pilots are unable to establish visual contact with the runway.

"Roger, Tiger 2-2, San Antonio Approach, turn left heading 180, vectors ILS Final, Runway 32 Left," the controller replied.

While my voice was that of a confident fighter pilot requesting permission to land at Randolph Air Force Base, my head was spinning. Flying in the clouds while sitting in my small F-5 cockpit was like being locked in a dark closet—I had my cockpit instruments but no outside references. To make matters worse, my body's sensors were giving me seat-of-the-pants information that was totally out of sync with indications on the cockpit flight instruments. I had a severe case of vertigo; I was spatially disoriented as I struggled to control my single-seat fighter in the dark clouds over central Texas.

I repeatedly mouthed to myself that I was straight and level at 300 knots. Desperately, I tried forcing my brain, my entire physical being, to agree with those infallible cockpit instruments that stared at me so mockingly. After a few terrifying minutes, my breathing slowed and the dark closet was replaced by the warm cocoon of my comfortable cockpit. My brain was now orienting correctly. My sensory spatial awareness matched the information emanating from the large attitude indicator and backlit cockpit instruments that spilled their glow onto my lap, over my gloved hands, and onto my chest.

But it still took all my concentration to stay focused on flying the aircraft as my mind wanted to replay the last few minutes.

I had almost been killed.

After what seemed like an eternity, the runway lights of Randolph Air Force Base filled my forward view. The mission was finally over.

My flying partner was relieved to see me after I landed. Apologetically, he explained that he had become quite disoriented during the descent. While it had helped him to turn off the rotating beacon, my friend admitted that he had overbanked into a right turn as we passed 3,000 feet—instead of turning left. Realizing his error, he had quickly rolled back to the left. That is when I lost sight of his aircraft and broke out of formation.

I had been looking intently out the left side of the canopy as I flew formation off the leader's aircraft and had not been able to monitor my aircraft's attitude indicator during this critical phase of flight. Believing I was established in a 30-degree left turn when I lost sight, I started to roll out of this turn and away from the leader's last known position when I broke out of formation and transitioned to instrument flying. The flight leader's mistaken turn to the right, coupled with my instinctive reaction to roll right away from his aircraft and toward my perceived level flight, combined in just a few seconds to put my aircraft in its death dive to eternity.

My flight did not seem to end even after I shut down the engines, climbed out of my jet, and debriefed with my fellow pilot. As I walked to the base's lodging facility, I kept reliving the events of the last hour.

A miracle had just happened. Lying in bed later, trying to sleep, I could still see the F-5's altimeter whirling counterclockwise. I could see the lights of northern San Antonio rushing up to grab me. I could clearly see the airspeed increasing as I tried to save my airplane and myself. Yes, a miracle happened that night. I believe there was another hand on mine as I fought to escape certain death. It was the hand of God.

As I struggled to fall asleep, I realized how short life can be. I had achieved so much in my relatively short time in the military. Reflecting upon my awards, trophies, and plaques, it was clear I had been blessed with a wonderful life. But what did all this acclaim really mean?

Yes, I had a loving wife, a wonderful family, and close friends. But my career and daily activities were largely focused on Captain Scott Gration. If my life on this earth had ended that night, I would have left behind nice plaques and some professional accomplishments. However, not much more of significance would be associated with my name. This was a sobering thought. I had to change my priorities.

During that night in San Antonio, I decided that I would need to give my life more import than a room full of plaques and trophies. But my concern for mankind took root years before this life-changing incident. My parents had modeled selfless service long before this pivotal day in 1979. My close brush with death would change my attitude and make me sensitive to opportunities outside of myself to serve my community and humanity. Even though I continued to work hard to excel as a fighter pilot, I would also work to become a warrior dedicated to service.

2

African Roots

The most important things in life aren't things.

— Anthony D'Angelo

On a cold, windy afternoon in New York City on December 7, 1952, my mother and father joined ten other passengers on a cargo freighter bound for Africa.[1] The ship, called the "African Lightning," steamed for seven weeks across the Atlantic Ocean and around the Cape of Good Hope, passing near a hurricane on its way from Mozambique to the Kenyan coast. High winds and rough seas forced seasick passengers to spend most of their day leaning over the deck's railing while others worried they would end up treading water like passengers from the Dutch ocean liner, *Klipfontein* that had sunk off the coast of Mozambique January 8, 1953, only a week before.[2]

Somehow I remained peaceful through the turbulence, tied securely into a bassinet hanging from hooks between the two circular port holes.[3] It proved the old adage: If you can smile or sleep when everyone around you is upset and losing their composure, you have absolutely no idea what's really happening.

Our arrival in Kenya kicked off a strong connection with Africa that would feature prominently in my life for the next six decades. After our cream-colored 1952 Chevrolet station wagon was unloaded from the freighter, my parents packed it with personal belongings that had been collecting mildew in the ship's hold for almost two months. They were

Eastern Africa (top left), Kenya (lower left), and Democratic Republic of the Congo (lower right).

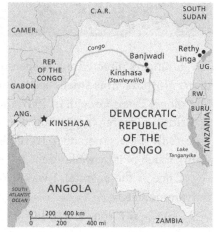

set to begin the thousand-mile road trip from Mombasa in Kenya to the Democratic Republic of Congo, known then as Belgian Congo.

Moving to Africa was not easy, but doing it with a sick baby made the experience even more difficult for my family. I may have sailed through the transatlantic voyage without apparent problems, but during the journey I had developed bacillary dysentery—a potentially dangerous bacterial infection of the colon. We had already travelled the 300 miles from the port of Mombasa to Kenya's capital city. Driving into the unfamiliar streets of Nairobi as it was getting dark, my worried parents scurried around town trying to find medical treatment as my mother wiped my forehead with a damp cloth to ease the suffering caused by a high fever, chills, and abdominal pain.

*The Gration family's 1952
Chevrolet station wagon.*

Strangers directed my desperate parents to Gertrude's Garden Children's Hospital. This small, beautifully landscaped infirmary was founded by Colonel Ewart Grogan in 1947 and was named after his wife, Gertrude. A British explorer, politician, and entrepreneur, Colonel Grogan was reportedly the first person to travel the length of Africa from Cape Town to Cairo, much of it by walking.[4]

Once at the hospital, I was swooped into the care of the medics on duty immediately.

"That's my son screaming back there!" pleaded my mother, as a large-bodied British nurse in a white uniform stood firmly in the doorway behind the nurses' station. "Please let me be with him!"

The woman's arms were folded menacingly; I am told that she looked a lot like a New York nightclub bouncer. "You can't see him until he's well," the nurse replied in a thick cockney accent. "If we let you in, everyone will want to be with their children. You'll just have to trust us to tend to him."

My parents came back every day for nine days trying to get in to see me, but the staff at Gertrude's remained adamant. It was not until my discharge that my mother noticed I had seven new teeth. However uncomfortable I was with dysentery or however homesick I was for my parents, I was probably also experiencing a lot of teething pain during that hospital stay!

Upon my release from Gertrude's Garden, my parents bundled me up in my bassinet secured to the back seat and trekked on to Belgian Congo, where they settled at Rethy, a small mission station in the northeastern corner of this country. While home to only a few foreigners, this area might have been prime real estate if it had been located in a less remote location.

The lush green vegetation that spilled over the gently rolling hills merged with the azure-blue sky at the horizon with haze-free definition. Clusters of grass-roofed mud huts, surrounded by small garden plots, dotted the hillsides. Thin ribbons of red clay paths snaked across the landscape to connect villages and provide a passable trail for livestock, pedestrians, and bicycle riders. Situated on the equator at an elevation of seven thousand feet above sea level, the climate was comfortable throughout the year—short-sleeved shirts were adequate during the day and a sweater or a crackling fire in the evening kept one comfortable.

Our first home was a two-bedroom house built with sun-dried bricks and covered with a thatched grass roof. The kitchen was outside, and it and the outhouse were on opposite sides of the fenced backyard. This was a drastic change from the New Jersey lifestyle my parents had left behind a few months before, but they were committed to making a difference and immediately immersed themselves into developing the region's nascent educational system, beginning with primary schools.

My parents moved to Linga, near Lake Albert (the northernmost lake on Congo's eastern border) where they helped build the local church by educating and training Congolese men and women—a work that my father often referred to as a calling and not just a profession. Their efforts were

John and Dorothy Gration with Scott at Rethy, Congo.

sorely needed. At the time of independence in 1960, Congo had roughly thirty university graduates.[5]

Home Away From Home

I stood with tears rolling down my cheeks. I was seven years old and was saying goodbye to my parents. They had just gotten me settled into boarding school at Rethy Academy in northern Congo and introduced me to my dorm parents.

As was customary, an older student took me for a walk around the cluster of red-brick school buildings so I wouldn't see my parents drive away. I felt alone and very frightened.

After the evening meal, I walked down the hill from the dining hall to the small room I would share with two second-grade boys. Entering my new quarters from the hallway, I saw three narrow beds jutting from the left wall. The orange glow of the setting sun was still visible through the two pieces of faded cloth that partially covered the window in the opposite wall.

"Hi, first grader," said one of the boys. His name was Harold McDowell.

My other roommate, George Veljun, pointed to a metal frame with a thin foam mattress next to the far wall. "That's where you sleep."

Soon after our room light went off, my roommates began flicking wooden matches off their matchboxes. I heard a soft swooshing sound as these projectiles shot into the air, igniting in flight. Peeking out from under my green woolen blanket, I trembled as the yellowish glow of lit matchsticks streaked across our dark room toward my bed. Petrified, I truly believed I was going to burn to death on my first night away from home.

Huddled under my covers, I realized all too soon that I would have to rely upon myself to survive. The security of my parents' home was gone; I was all alone. My success and survival now depended solely on my own attitude, skills, and ingenuity. This was the new reality.

Rethy Academy was a missionary boarding school where about sixty children were enrolled in first through ninth grades. Dorm parents served as my surrogate mother and father for each three-month term of school. I would soon learn that three times a year, my fellow students and I would be allowed to spend thirty wonderful days with our parents—during the months of April, August, and December. Still, our breaks always ended, and I always had to return to school.

I understand now that it was equally hard on Mom and Dad to leave me, helpless as they were to assist my adjustment to the separation. I was heartbroken every time I had to say goodbye, as were all of my school-age friends. But we soon learned to hide our "home sickness" tears and to survive without our real parents by bargaining, negotiating, and trading.

Rethy Academy had some very strict rules. For instance, we had to eat and drink everything that was put before us before we could be dismissed from the communal dining table. Every day, my dorm parents made me down a glass of milk at breakfast. I couldn't stomach the "white stuff" and generally refused to drink it. Monitored by a surrogate parent, I would have to remain seated at the long wooden table until I finally complied. When the school bell sounded and my grace period had come to an end, I would usually hold my nose, gulp down the milk, and shudder at that lingering taste as I ran to class.

There were many days, however, when my visceral dislike of milk and my inborn stubbornness combined to make me miss the first session of school—I would still be sitting on the long wooden bench in the empty dining room staring at my glass of milk when my friends were dismissed for recess at 10:15 a.m.

One evening, after the other students had been dismissed from supper, I saw Sandra McFall across the dining room. Chin in her hands, my blond-haired schoolmate was staring disgustingly down at a plate of fried liver between her elbows. Sliding onto the bench next to her, I made a proposal.

"Sandi, would you drink my milk in the morning if I ate your weekly meal of liver?" I quietly asked.

Sandi agreed and I quickly devoured her fried liver and onions. From then on, she would come by the dining room on the way to school and secretly drink my milk, while I ate those meat dishes that made her queasy. Reflecting on the situation, I am sure our dorm parents figured out that I had made this practical deal, but they allowed the win-win arrangement to continue.

This early experience was the foundation for the negotiating skills I would use as a senior military officer and diplomat. In addition, it appears I developed a strong belief in fairness and justice while at boarding school—I was deeply concerned about those who were being mistreated and would not hesitate to get involved.

Once, Mr. Raymond Stauffacher, a dorm supervisor, walked into the game room to find me, a second grader, straddling an older boy who was squirming on the floor pleading for mercy. When he heard me sternly warning this boy not to pick on my friends again, Mr. Stauffacher quickly turned around and walked out without disciplining me for fighting.

With a grin, Mr. Stauffacher later relayed to my mom and dad, "That big bully had it coming to him. I was happy to see Scott defending his classmates."[6]

Despite these minor deviations, I generally tried to follow the rules to stay out of trouble. Sometimes I tried too hard. On the last day of school, my surrogate parents assembled all the dormitory kids in the recreation room to prepare us for our upcoming one-month vacation. We sat in a circle on the floor, staring up at Mr. Stauffacher who was seated in an over-stuffed chair, looking like a grand king perched on a royal throne.

"Now pack all of your clothes because your parents will be coming tomorrow to take you home for vacation," he instructed. "Pick up your suit-cases from the storage room right after you're dismissed."

When I did not show up for breakfast the next morning, Mr. Stauffacher came to find me. Opening the door to my room, he found me sitting on my closed suitcase—stark naked.

"Where are your clothes, Scott?"

I looked up sheepishly and replied, "I packed them—you told me to pack all of my clothes."[7]

School was never easy for me. I really struggled with reading and had a hard time paying attention in class. Vacations were what I lived for. After three months of boarding school, these one-month respites with my parents at Linga, our mission station, were special times of exploring the forests around our house, playing with my African friends, and enjoying my mother's cooking.

In third grade, it became a fad in the dormitory to read Hardy Boys books or *Popular Mechanics* magazines by using flashlights after the "lights out" bell. Stealthily patrolling the hallways, our dorm parents would search for the telltale glow under a door that signaled a misbehaving dorm kid. Bursting into the room, the supervisor would often spot a reader under the covers struggling to turn off his light before being caught.

To solve this ambush problem, I installed metal contacts on my door-frame and the door, and routed wires along the wall to connect the door contacts to my flashlight switch. I could now break the rule in peace. When my dorm parent opened the door, my flashlight would turn off automatical-ly and instantaneously. I could appear to be sound asleep. This contraption worked brilliantly until the night my dorm parent walked all the way into my dark room.

"Scott, did you have your flashlight on?"

Before I could answer, the door shut behind him and the room lit up as the mated contacts turned my flashlight back on. My ingenious secret had been discovered.

I learned at an early age to think through all the possible outcomes of a situation because, as Murphy's Law says, if anything can go wrong, it will. I had a lot of opportunity to practice this, as I spent my free time taking things apart and putting them back together with my "improvements." This "fix it, improve it" predilection must be part of my DNA, for this bent has characterized my personal life and professional career. I have always tried to make things better—to make a positive difference. I recognize that this at times has been frustrating for those around me, but I hope that in the end the results were worth the hard work and innovative changes.

Despite my creativity and artistic ability, my school grades were consistently poor. One day, as I was working on a broken lawnmower, a staff member I respected and admired asked me, "Scott, what are you good for?"

I thought for a moment, and then said, "I can fix things; I'm a good shot with my bow; I help my friends."

He interrupted my list as he turned to face me. "I'll tell you what you're good for . . . good for nothing." With a stern voice, he continued, "Scott, if you don't start working harder in school, you'll never amount to anything. You'll end up being a ditch digger."

I dropped my tools and ran deep into the thick forest that bordered the school property. Tears blurred my vision as I stumbled to my favorite wooded spot. On the ground with my back against a large black wattle tree, I sobbed. I was devastated.

After the sun went down, I slipped back to my room without speaking to anyone. For the rest of the term, I avoided this man. Looking back now, I realize he was probably frustrated with my classroom performance and was trying to motivate me. But his approach was anything but motivating, and the emotional pain his words caused me lasted for years. I am sure he would be surprised to read my resume today. Yes, I have dug a few ditches, but I have also done a few other things in my career.

The lesson I took away from that experience was to be careful with my words—they are powerful, dangerous, and sharper than my sharpest knife. I have learned from experience that it is very easy to say things that leave the wrong message or hurt others, even the people we love. While I certainly do not heed this advice enough and have said many things I regret, I learned long ago that we should chew our words to see how they taste before spewing them out.

Congo Independence Brings Insecurity

I was only nine years old when Belgian Congo received its independence on June 30, 1960. Even so, I have vivid memories of the event and of what followed.

I can remember walking with my father to the local church at the bottom of the hill. We had a front-row seat to observe the ceremonial handover of political power in our district. As Belgian administrators traded their office chairs for a seat on the next flight to Europe, the government bureaucracy quickly faltered and chaos became the norm.

A few months after independence, Congo erupted with waves of political unrest. The Congolese Army mutinied and we had to escape with our missionary friends to Uganda for six weeks. When the situation stabilized, my parents returned to Linga and reopened their school.

Unfortunately, a few months later the security environment deteriorated again, after République du Congo's first leader, President Patrice Lumumba, was assassinated on January 17, 1961.[8] The military forces rebelled again and the Katanga region of the country seceded under self-rule.

A month later, the United Nations advised all foreigners to leave Congo. Our lives were in danger. We drove the twenty-three miles to Rethy, joined a forty-seven-car convoy of other missionaries and settlers from the surrounding area, and departed for the safety of Uganda under United Nations protection. After two weeks in Uganda, we were able to proceed to Kenya without a problem. We stayed in Kenya for the next seven months, and then returned home to Linga in October 1961.

Nearly three years went by quietly. But by August 1964, the security situation was much worse than it had been in the period just after independence. Rebel fighters, known as *Simbas*, believed they possessed mystical powers that would turn bullets fired at their forces into butter or water. They attacked villages and overran towns without fear and quickly overwhelmed the government defenses in their way.[9] These Simba rebels, under the leadership of Pierre Mulele and Christophe Gbenye, methodically gained control of northeast Congo and captured their near-term strategic objective, control of Stanleyville, on August 5.[10]

During that period of instability, my parents were teaching at a seminary at Banjwadi, about an hour's drive north of Stanleyville. When the Simba rebels threatened this area, my parents made the grueling two-day trip to Rethy to pick up my sisters and me from boarding school before moving back to our old house at Linga.

I remember seeing my parents and the other missionaries huddled around our large Zenith radio in the living room. Every evening, they would strain to decipher the Voice of America and BBC news bulletins through the loud static that was an integral part of the shortwave broadcast. It soon became obvious that we had no choice but to evacuate from Congo for the third time.[11]

"You can take only two things—you decide," my mother said as she walked through the house picking up mementos and pictures she would add to her suitcase. I thought of my dog, which had been a birthday present.

"Don't worry about Kuno. We've paid the staff to take care of your puppy," she said.

Now we had to leave him behind, along with almost everything else we owned. I wanted to cry, but I was thirteen and wouldn't let myself.

It was 4:00 a.m. when we departed our house. Left behind, our house help and African friends stood quietly in the moonlight. We watched their waving silhouettes disappear into the darkness behind us as we drove slowly down the hill. We did not have to say it; we knew their future was uncertain and clearly dangerous.

My two younger sisters, Barbara and Judy, and I huddled in the back seat with our few valued possessions packed around us as we drove in darkness to Rethy. No one talked. As the car's headlights illuminated the bumpy dirt road, we saw just enough of the roadside vegetation and its dark shadows to make our young imaginations race with fear.

My father positioned our car at the end of the growing line of vehicles that would form the convoy of departing missionary families. Each car was filled with the possessions that these families deemed to be most needed or most cherished. Adults gathered nervously in small groups and spoke in hushed tones; I could tell the situation was very tense. Heavily armed United Nations troops from Nigeria and Ethiopia walked anxiously around their large white and blue trucks. They would lead our way to the Congo border and cover the convoy's rear.

This trip normally took about three hours, but today's trip was not going to be normal. The procession of tightly linked vehicles crept steadily toward the border. Each car was connected to the one ahead of it by a swirl of red dust. After traveling for awhile, suddenly brake lights illuminated down the line like a stadium wave and the column of cars came to a stop. Congolese soldiers had blocked the main road and were diverting our convoy into their army encampment.

We all prayed and waited nervously near our cars. After six hours of interrogations and negotiations in the headquarters building, my father and several other missionary leaders returned.

"Army officers are going to search our cars," Dad said tersely as he opened the door. His face looked grim. "The soldiers will take the items they believe belong to Congo. Just stand quietly over there by the fence until they're finished."

I watched as Congolese soldiers, armed with Soviet automatic weapons, methodically searched each vehicle, confiscating belongings they deemed *mali ya Congo*, the wealth of Congo. The country's new caretakers took most of our possessions, including many of my parents' most-valued treasures.

I remember a Congolese soldier shooting at a crow with his AK-47. The sudden popping noise was terrifying. These loud gunshots were like a giant megaphone announcement foretelling our potential fate. *Would we be the shooter's next target?*

It was late afternoon by the time our convoy was finally granted permission to leave the army camp. Arriving at the Congo border crossing at nightfall, we learned that the immigration and customs officers had just closed their office and would not be back until the next morning. While disappointed about the delay, we were all relieved to be out of the army camp with our cars, our clothes, and our lives. After sharing food, we all found places in a nearby village to sleep—in our cars or wherever we could find a relatively smooth place to stretch out safely.

At 11:30 a.m. the next morning, customs officials informed us that we could leave, but only with the clothes we were wearing. Apart from our vehicles, they were taking every single item we had with us. The few things that survived the army's foray still had to remain behind. I did not let anyone notice that I was not sad about giving up my trumpet, which meant one less hour of practice every day. But I could see that the loss was obviously more difficult for my parents, whose wedding pictures and family heirlooms were confiscated, as well as a multitude of things they believed were essential enough to pack in their suitcases two nights ago.

Engines again roared to life down the long line of cars and trucks, and our convoy began to make its way across the lonely no-man's land that separated Congo from the West Nile District of northwestern Uganda. As darkness neared, we breathed a sigh of relief as we escaped from Congo with our lives. I understood at this point that family—and life itself—were special gifts to be guarded and preserved. The material things we left behind were insignificant when measured against these human treasures.

We had survived the harrowing twenty-seven hours that it took to get across the border. Now we were homeless refugees. This new status paled in significance, though, when we received news that the Simba rebels had overrun Banjwadi and several other mission stations in the Stanleyville area, killing nineteen missionaries and children. The sketchy stories of terror became very real to me when I heard rebel soldiers had shot my parents' co-workers at point-blank range on the banks of the Lindi River. The death of our friends and their young children was a heartbreaking and chilling reminder of the savage brutality often displayed by Simba soldiers. We were truly grateful to be alive and together as a family.

After living in guesthouses and a British-run boarding school for six months as refugees, we moved to Kijabe, a large mission station thirty-five miles from Nairobi, where my parents continued working as educators for the next three years. Established almost seventy years earlier by missionaries commissioned by Africa Inland Mission, an American missionary society, Kijabe was now known for its hospital, printing press, and boarding school—Rift Valley Academy.[12]

Our family lived off the generosity of others until we were able to get back on our feet. Now a thirteen-year-old, I learned firsthand about caring for others who were in need and about serving those who were less fortunate than we were as friends gave us towels, sheets, dishes, and other items we needed to establish our new home. But little did I know what this new home would be like. We had been chased across the continent; at least we had each other.

3

Out of Africa

There are only two lasting bequests
we can hope to give our children.
One of these is roots, the other, wings.

— Henry Ward Beecher

TWO YEARS LATER, at fifteen, I became close friends with a Masai warrior who was attending the Bible school at Kijabe where my parents were now teachers. Moses Ikayo and I hunted together and he worked with me on odd jobs during his free time. As our friendship grew stronger, he invited me to his village to meet his family. We traveled together to his *manyatta*. It was a temporary Masai settlement consisting of dung-covered houses and thick thorn bushes surrounding a central enclosure, designed to protect the inhabitants' cows and sheep at night from lions, leopards, and unfriendly neighboring tribes.

It was a great surprise when the village leaders announced that they planned to make me an honorary Masai tribesman. On my induction day, our procession followed a narrow dusty footpath into the thick woods. The chief had his place near the front of the line. I walked behind an entourage of spear-carrying, red-adorned Masai warriors who took turns carrying a large live goat. We had to transport the breathing animal because a Masai warrior is forbidden by tradition to eat butchered meat that has been seen by a married woman.

Arriving at a secluded clearing, I stood next to the chief while several young *morani* tribesmen—the warriors of the tribe—built a roaring fire. After suffocating the goat by holding its nose and mouth, the warriors then took turns drinking warm blood as it flowed from the goat's severed jugular vein into a small pouch made by pulling the skin away from the neck muscle.

I was rescued from drinking the goat's blood because the initial stream of red had dwindled to just a very slight trickle by the time it was my turn at the trough. That was a relief. But, I was now first in line to down the ceremonial mixture of cow's blood and soured milk. This concoction was made earlier from blood obtained by precisely nicking the jugular artery of a cow with an arrow. After collecting sufficient blood, the wound in the cow's neck was closed with a wad of mud and dung. The blood and milk combination was then curdled using cow urine. It was prepared just in time for our celebration.

I had disliked cow's milk since I was a child; trying to avoid drinking it had been a boarding school ritual. So although I dreaded what was coming, this time I had to participate. I was becoming a Masai morani. Slowly raising the colorfully beaded but dirty calabash gourd to my lips with both hands, I let the lumpy mixture fill my mouth. My stomach heaved with an involuntary jerk as the putrid odor wafted to my nostrils. Overcoming a most powerful urge to wretch in front of the chief and my fellow warriors, I forced the disgusting concoction of prized protein down my throat.

Fortunately, the shared meal of roasted goat delicacies was delicious. No, I was not thirsty the rest of the day—no more curdled milk and blood for me.

After our meal, the old Masai chief, whose earlobes dangled with traditional stretched holes, draped a red cloth over my shoulders and gave me special gifts so I would look like a Masai morani. First, he handed me a long thin spear used to kill charging lions and a colorful cowhide shield to protect me from the first attack of the big cat. He then presented me with a beautifully carved *rungu*. This wooden club, about eighteen inches long, was hand-rubbed with fat from a sheep's tail to give it a deep dark sheen. My last warrior gifts were a *simi*, a beaded belt, and wrist ornaments. The simi, a two-edged sword sheathed in a red leather scabbard, would be a useful tool and sharp weapon as I walked at night or through the woods near my home.

In return I gave the chief gifts of salt, sugar, and blankets. Then he bestowed the Masai name, *Katima*, on me with a ritual blessing. He explained the name meant "rich and brave." I was proud of my new name and of my identity with the Masai tribe.

As I departed from the ceremony, the chief told me, "The only thing that can separate true friends is death."

Hands-On and Results Driven

Kijabe is perched two-thirds of the way up the steep slopes that form the eastern side of the Great Rift Valley. Our house overlooked the beautiful Rift Valley plains and two extinct volcanoes—Suswa and Longonot. Shadows cast by popcorn-shaped clouds painted ever-changing patterns on the expansive valley floor. Our panoramic view of the Rift Valley remained the same, but the picture was always different. We never tired of living in Kijabe because of its magnificent location, spectacular scenery, and lush vegetation.

This mission station was and is well-known for its excellent hospital and its boarding school, Rift Valley Academy, better known as RVA. I began attending Rift Valley Academy in eighth grade. I am sure my teachers did their best to motivate me toward academic excellence. Unfortunately, their efforts were largely unsuccessful. I soon developed other hobbies and interests that held a higher priority for me than doing homework.

I learned to drive at age fourteen. Working at the local garage after school, I overhauled engines and replaced clutches and brakes. I also cut hair as the school barber, worked as an apprentice in a carpentry shop, and

View of Mount Longonot from Kijabe.
(© Mark Kinzer)

Scott provided meat for the dinner table.

took up woodcarving. A missionary electrician taught me his trade, and I became a sign painter and a butcher of wild meat.

One normally had to be sixteen years old to have a hunting license in Kenya. A month after my fifteenth birthday, I convinced my father to take me to Nairobi to see the individual in charge of issuing hunting permits. As we entered his office, a well-weathered man of British stock walked from behind his desk, exposing baggy khaki shorts and matching knee-high socks worn as the traditional uniform of the game department. Trembling inside, I boldly requested a Kenya hunting license while my father stood in support by my side.

Looking me over, the chief game warden said, "You look big enough to handle a large-bore rifle."

I took the required game identification test and was issued my hunting license in August 1966. On that day, I became the youngest person in Kenya to have a license to hunt wild game, and I used it to keep other missionaries and my family supplied with steaks, filets, and hamburger meat. We later learned that the head of the Kenya Game Department had been in a road accident near Kijabe station and had received excellent care at the mission hospital. I was the fortunate recipient of his gratitude.

That period in Kenya was pivotal to my personal development. Not only did I gain practical skills, but I came to realize that "everything is easy if you know how to do it." I developed a positive mental attitude toward taking on big jobs, learning to do them well, and helping others to do the same by breaking down daunting challenges into manageable tasks.

I enjoyed getting involved in activities and hobbies in which I could see clear results for my efforts. Whether I was carving a beautiful shape out of a nondescript piece of wood, making a dead engine roar back to life, or installing a certified lighting system in a dark building, I received great satisfaction from result-oriented jobs that produced measurable and sustainable outcomes, especially when these were service projects.

Kijabe is also where I became better acquainted with a young lady named Judy DeYoung. While I did not show it openly, I was infatuated with her. I did my best to sit next to Judy whenever our families had meals together and I enjoyed hiking with her when our two families had picnics on the floor of the Rift Valley below Kijabe. During those outings, we would spend time together sneaking up on zebra and chasing giraffe while we waited for the hamburgers to cook. This was great fun, but a bit frustrating—Judy treated me more like a brother than a boyfriend.

Judy's parents had attended graduate school in Boston, Massachusetts, together with my mom and dad in the late 1940s. A year after she was born

Scott (left) and Judy (right) were young friends.

in Nairobi, the DeYoung family traveled from Kenya to visit us in Belgian Congo. Our parents recorded in their letters that Judy and I enjoyed playing together. One passage described Judy in a pretty blue dress laughing and throwing toys out of her playpen. As a three-year-old toddler, I would retrieve the playthings and throw them back in.[1] I am very sure it was love at first sight.

We have been told that Judy had just celebrated her fifth birthday and her sister, Jocelyn, was only three years old when their mother drove them to the Monkey Park in Nairobi. At an appropriate moment, she took the girls aside, cuddling them in her arms.

Quietly she explained, "Your daddy is very sick. He's in the hospital." Edward DeYoung had been stricken with Landry's Palsy, a virus that attacked his nervous system and caused a paralysis of his major organs.

Judy remembers going to bed that night with her arms tightly wrapped around a photo of her daddy and praying that God would heal him because she loved him so much.[2] God did not. Despite getting superb medical care in Nairobi, Judy's thirty-six-year-old father died on July 8, 1958, after being sick for only two weeks.[3]

Ed DeYoung had been serving as an instructor at the Kijabe Teacher Training College in Kenya. Edythe DeYoung remained in East Africa where she raised her two daughters as a single mother and taught a variety of subjects at Rift Valley Academy.

When Judy and I were playing together in 1954, it is unlikely that anyone imagined we would get married twenty years later on August 3, 1974, at Grace Church in Ridgewood, New Jersey.

Wake-Up Calls

My adventurous, albeit admittedly nonacademic life at Rift Valley Academy ended in 1967 when my father accepted a job in Brooklyn, New York. I was sixteen. Moving back to the United States was a frightening, difficult adjustment for me. Adolescence is hard enough as it is, but here I was entering the eleventh grade, American by citizenship but Africa-raised and clueless as to how American teenagers were expected to behave.

Ridgewood High School in New Jersey was very big and so different from Rift Valley Academy. During my first day in woodshop, I had to cut a piece of paper. Pulling my Swiss Army knife from my pants pocket, I began to open the little pair of scissors. Immediately, my teacher rushed over and snatched the knife out of my hand with the quickness of a cobra strike.

"Come with me," he ordered, walking toward the door with the end of my little red knife protruding slightly from his tightly curled fingers.

I waited outside the principal's office and watched several school administrators enter his closed door. *Why,* I wondered, *were they so excited? What was wrong with having a useful Swiss Army knife?* I had always carried a knife; in fact, just a month before this I had been carrying around a high-power rifle! The principal telephoned my father, who carefully described my unique upbringing.

"We've just returned from living in Africa for the past fifteen years. Scott grew up carrying knives and hunting wild game," my father said, calmly. "I'll make sure he leaves his knife at home from now on."

Dad must have convinced the school officials I was not a troublemaker, but I was not sure I was going make it in America. While I physically looked like most people at Ridgewood High, I didn't know anything about television shows, movie actors, or American sports. Most of my survival skills and practical knowledge were useless in New Jersey.

By the spring of the next year I had made some progress, but then things took a dramatic downturn. My years of academic disinterest, coupled with my poor reading skills, were catching up with me.

In March 1968, our junior class took a series of aptitude tests designed to help guidance counselors point us toward college, trade school, or the military. I remember thinking as I walked home from school that I had not done very well on the tests. One machine had evaluated my reading skills as being slower than 360 words per minute with minimal comprehension—"360" was the lowest setting on that testing device.

The next day I was shown into the guidance counselor's office. A burly man with dark-rimmed glasses and graying hair was standing behind his large desk. His muscular arms made me think that he must have been a good athlete in his youth.

"Have a seat, Scott," he said with a warm smile.

Mr. Rebholz started by explaining the purpose of the aptitude test and then pulled out several papers from a manila folder. I don't remember his exact words as he revealed my test results, but they ended with something like, "Scott, you're best suited to be a shepherd."

A shepherd? Now I was scared. My motivation finally kicked into gear.

I enrolled in an Evelyn Woods speed-reading course, boosting my reading rate to 4,000 words per minute. Unfortunately, my comprehension dropped to nearly zero. I took Algebra II and Chemistry in my senior year, and worked extremely hard to raise my scholastic aptitude test scores enough to get into college. I also took up wrestling to get into better physical shape and became the president of the flying club and the trap-and-skeet shooting team to round out my college application.

I have had to compensate for my reading difficulties by developing strong memorization skills. My parents have told me that I demonstrated keen memory and association skills at an early age. Perhaps my ability to recall the details of a document long after reading it began even before I went to boarding school.

My mother tells of an incident that occurred when I was about two and a half years old. I had thrown my panda bear out of the car window as we were traveling to another mission station. My dad was not happy, but he went back to retrieve my stuffed animal. Seven months later, my parents and I were traveling on that same dirt road. As we passed by the exact spot where I had ejected my bear, I shouted out, "That's where you found Panda!"[4]

Fast forward to 1969. My extra efforts had paid off and I was accepted by several colleges. I decided to attend Rutgers, the State University of New Jersey. To avoid classes requiring large amounts of reading, I planned to study mechanical and aerospace engineering to prepare for a career in aviation or the aerospace industry.

This was a time when Americans were reeling at the assassinations of Bobby Kennedy and Martin Luther King, Jr. But we also cheered as our country made significant advances in space exploration. There were three lunar missions that year and Neil Armstrong put his footprints in the lunar dust as the first human to walk on the moon's surface. These space activities inspired and motivated me; I wanted to help explore the "last frontier."

With that decision made, I took Trigonometry and Introduction to Calculus in summer school and started the fall semester at the College of Engineering with the full load of required engineering classes. I studied exceedingly hard and did well in my freshman year.

My sophomore year was not so good. I erroneously concluded that I might actually be intelligent after doing quite well in my first year. I started playing rugby, joined the rifle team, and began dating. Academic activities were no longer my first priority in college. By Christmas break, I was failing thermodynamics and was barely squeaking by in my statics and statistics courses.

Locking myself inside my dorm room during the vacation, I crammed enough to salvage all my grades, except thermodynamics. Unfortunately, this failure caused me to fall behind because thermodynamics was a pre-requisite for classes that I needed to take in the upcoming spring semester. This "wake-up" call forced me to sort out my priorities.

Yet another event that occurred while at Rutgers forced me to focus even more. I was studying in my room one evening when someone banged on my door and said I had a caller on the dormitory payphone. I ran to the little booth at the end of the hallway and picked up the wall telephone's dangling receiver. It was my father.

"Scott, I have some bad news," my father said. "Judy's mother was killed in a car accident yesterday." I was dating Judy DeYoung and our relationship was becoming more serious.

"No," I gasped. Poor Judy. She was attending nurses training in Chicago. Now she was an orphan. "How did it happen?" I wondered out loud.

"She was driving back from a Rift Valley Academy choir concert in Nairobi, when she crashed into the back of a large truck that was stopped in the middle of the road," Dad said solemnly.

The truck, overloaded with bags of locally made charcoal, had apparently broken down without being able to pull to the side. Its lights were off and there was no advance warning of an immobile vehicle ahead. As Edythe DeYoung rounded the dark corner on this curvy escarpment road,

Edythe DeYoung in 1970 with Judy (left) and Jocelyn (right).

she probably saw the large truck looming in her headlights, but did not have any space available to dodge the truck and avoid a collision.

Judy's mother died on June 8, 1972, while being transported to the Kijabe Hospital. Her body was laid to rest next to her husband's grave in the Kijabe cemetery. She was in the prime of her life—just fifty-two years old. I will always remember her as a strong and courageous woman of God. It was incredibly brave of her to head out to Africa in the early 1950s. It was even braver for her to stay on as a single mother and to raise her daughters in Kenya.

Judy and I both missed being able to share our deepening relationship with her mother, but my parents did their best to "adopt" Judy while, at the same time, serving as her legal guardians. The loss of Edythe DeYoung was a painful one indeed.

Less than two years later in January 1974, I graduated from Rutgers with great memories of college, better study habits, wonderful friends, and a much clearer direction in life.

The stories of growing up in Africa, going to boarding school, becoming a refugee, moving to America with an African mindset, and struggling with academics might give one the impression that I had a difficult childhood. I did not. Yes, it was sometimes challenging, but my careers as a warrior, diplomat, and entrepreneur trace their solid beginning to these formative years. I would not trade the first twenty years of my life for anything.

Now I was poised and ready to really take off.

4

Wearing Green to Work

*Things turn out best for the people who
make the best of the way things turn out.*

— John Wooden

BEFORE GOING TO BED, I shined my boots to a high gloss and made
sure my green flight suit was perfect. I would start Air Force pilot training
tomorrow. I was impatient to get started—and a little nervous.

The sun was just peeking over the horizon as I walked into the T-37
squadron building to start my first real job after college. The doors to the
flight room were closed when I arrived at 6:00 a.m., so I quietly walked in
and looked for an empty chair.

"Come with me, lieutenant!" I turned around and saw a short, angry
captain motioning me to the door.

I followed him into an office just down the hallway from the flight
briefing room. "Sit here!" he said, pointing to a military-grey metal chair.
The captain turned on his heel and stomped out, leaving me in the empty
office to reflect on what had just happened.

Great start to my military career, I thought. *What have I done wrong?*

The agitated captain reappeared after forty minutes. I recognized the
name on his flight suit. LeBlanc. This officer had sent me a very nice note a
month earlier. The welcoming words in his letter had conjured up a mental
image of a tall, rugged fighter pilot who would teach me how to fly fast
jets. I now had a new image to associate with the name, Captain Jerry A.
LeBlanc, Flight Commander.

It was clear Captain LeBlanc was not happy about my walking into the briefing after the doors were closed. I soon learned just how unhappy he was. He thrust his face within inches of mine, from where, to make matters even worse, he could see the tan lines on my cheeks and chin making it obvious that I had shaved my beard just a few nights before entering USAF active duty. With two first lieutenants standing behind him like sentries, Captain LeBlanc gave me clear benchmarks for success in his flight room.

"Lieutenant Gration, *if* you're in your seat five minutes before I walk into the room; *if* you stand at attention any time I'm six feet from you; *if* you keep your hair cut short and your boots shined so I can see the spaces between my teeth from twelve inches away; *if* you keep your flight suit zipper all the way up and your sleeves rolled all the way down; *if* you are completely prepared for every flight and academic class; *if* you answer all my questions with 'Yes, sir!'—*then* we'll get along just fine."

My new boss's strong Cajun accent, coupled with his stern expression, seared these eight demands deep into my brain.

The only thing I could think to say in a confident voice was, "Yes, sir."

Captain LeBlanc responded with, "Now, get out of here."[1]

I walked to the flight room again and found my T-37 flight instructor, 1st Lt Glenn Mercer, and my tablemates, 2nd Lt Tom Kane and 2nd Lt Rod Bishop. My flight training class had fifty-seven Air Force Academy graduates. While I did not know who to salute or when to wear my flight cap, these classmates knew everything, having just completed four years at "the Zoo" in Colorado Springs.

While it turned out that my new friends would help me learn the ropes, at this point, I was not sure I would even survive my first week of pilot training. I didn't know it at the time, but only one in a thousand second lieutenants is ever promoted to general officer rank, a category in the uniformed services that in the Air Force includes brigadier general and above. It is interesting to note that Rod Bishop, Tom Kane, and I each achieved that distinction in our respective military careers.[2] Without realizing it, I was in very good company.

How I Got Here

My military career began while I was a student at Rutgers University. After receiving a mid-range number in the annual military service lottery held in 1970,[3] I decided to pursue an Air Force Reserve Officer Training Corps

commission and become a military pilot. Because this commissioning program on the Rutgers campus fell victim to anti-war sentiments and was
essentially closed down, I did not learn very much about military procedures or Air Force protocol while in college.

Graduating from Rutgers University in January 1974 and scheduled
to begin Air Force pilot training that September, I had nine months to
kill. I decided to return to the Northern Frontier District of Kenya for
four months to serve with missionary friends at a place called Gatab, atop
Mount Kulal near Lake Turkana. I loved every minute at this remote site—
riding motorcycles, building an orphanage, making roads, and helping to
install a water system.

We also traveled to an oasis called Kalacha in the Chalbi desert where
we built a small dispensary and an airstrip. I finished my time in Kenya by
putting a corrugated-tin roof on the new church at a mission station near
Marsabit. This period of hard physical work and relaxing recreation was a
perfect way for me to serve Kenyans in this harsh region and to make the
transition from college life to military service.

"I like your beard," my fiancée remarked when I returned from my
Kenya sojourn in June 1974. "You should keep it." Sporting my facial hair
until it was time to report for Air Force duty, I am probably one of only a
few general officers since Ulysses S. Grant to get married groomed with a
full beard.[4]

Because my parents had become Judy's guardians when her mom died
in Kenya, our wedding had some unique aspects, one of them being the
feeling that I was becoming my own brother-in-law.

I remember standing in the front of the sanctuary with my best man
and groomsman, anxiously looking down the aisle. My sister Judy, whose
name my fiancée would soon also bear, is a brilliant musician. When
she filled the church with the first notes of Jeremiah Clarke's "Trumpet
Voluntary,"[5] the congregation stood and swiveled toward the back, seeing
what I saw: my beautiful bride on the red carpet, guided by my father's arm.
It was a heart-stopping moment.

Smiles and tears (the audience's and, yes, mine) greeted the pair as
they slowly walked down the aisle in step with the majestic music my sister piped through the church's magnificent organ. I couldn't stop smiling
throughout the service, especially when a little green inchworm emerged
from the pastor's white boutonniere and made its way across the minister's
suit during the sermon. Nothing like a little comic relief.

*Judy and Scott were
married August 3, 1974.*

After a short honeymoon, we drove to Columbus Air Force Base in northern Mississippi for a year of undergraduate pilot training. I was excited to fly jets and start my career of military service. While somewhat traumatic, my initial meeting with Captain LeBlanc did not snuff out my eager anticipation of a career in aviation.

From Student Pilot to Flight Evaluator

Pilot training was very demanding—the academic classes were rigorous and the flight training was challenging. I did not like the T-37 "Tweet" primary jet trainer very much, but did very well in the T-38 supersonic aircraft and was selected to return to Columbus Air Force Base as a T-38 flight instructor. The T-38 Talon, with its sleek design and tandem cockpits, can soar above 40,000 feet and at supersonic speeds one and a half times that of sound.[6] I felt so fortunate to be selected as an instructor in this "white rocket" right out of pilot training.

Hard work paid off and I became a flight evaluator in the T-38 a few months after putting on my silver first lieutenant bars. In that role, I was

Northrop T-38 Talon. (Courtesy of the   *Northrop F-5E Tiger II.* (Courtesy of
United States Air Force)   the United States Air Force)

responsible for ensuring that student pilots could perform flight operations safely and with the required proficiency to graduate.

The Mississippi assignment was a wonderful time for Judy and me. We bought our first house, had our first son, and began our career in the Air Force together. Professionally, I accumulated lots of flying time and enjoyed the special responsibility of teaching new students how to think fast and fly safely.

In June 1978, my telephone rang. It was a call from the 425th Tactical Fighter Training Squadron at Williams Air Force Base in Arizona. This call ended my tour in the T-38 and put me on the fast track to becoming an Air Force fighter pilot.

Two Demanding Jobs: Fighter Pilot and Father

"We're looking for an officer to teach fundamental fighter-pilot skills to foreign pilots. You want the job?" the training squadron commander asked.

His unit was the F-5 flight training school that taught air combat skills to fighter pilots from our allies and partner countries. Since I would be the youngest pilot in the squadron by at least three years, I had a suspicion that they needed someone young like me to keep the squadron refrigerator filled with cold drinks!

"Yes, sir," I responded, trying not to sound too excited. "When do you want me to report?"

"Right away," he said.

In just over a month, Judy and I sold our house in Mississippi, packed our belongings, and drove to Phoenix, Arizona. I was eager to fly the F-5— my first aircraft with a gun.[7] Staying in the temporary living quarters at Williams Air Force Base, Judy sewed squadron patches on my uniform and I organized my paperwork in preparation for my first day of duty.

As the Air Force's newest fighter pilot, I walked with a dash of swagger into the F-5 squadron building. Lieutenant Colonel Bob Stewart, the newly assigned operations officer, met me as I approached the operations desk, the central hub for all flying activities at the squadron. I put out my hand and introduced myself.

"First lieutenant? We don't have any lieutenants in this squadron. Come back when you're a captain."

I thought Lt Col Stewart was joking, but he wasn't.

"Get this lieutenant a squadron scarf and a set of F-5 flight manuals," he instructed his assistant.

Turning to me, he said, "Now, get lost." He was serious.

I had just sold our home in Mississippi and rushed to Arizona. Now I was being told to go away?

Judy and I found a house we liked in Mesa and made it our home. I studied as much as I could while waiting for my promotion date. July 24, 1978, finally arrived and I again proudly walked into the flying squadron—this time wearing silver captain's bars on my shoulders.

I loved flying the F-5, as would anyone who ever dreamed of being a fighter pilot. Soon I was certified as an instructor pilot and functional test pilot. On test flights, I would zoom to 41,000 feet while checking the cabin pressure and other checklist items. If the aircraft was operating normally, I would do the high-altitude afterburner checks followed by a supersonic run.

Not all these flights were uneventful. I remember one week when I had four engine failures on five functional test flights. Fortunately, most restarted at low altitude. During weeks like this, I was thankful that the F-5 had two General Electric J85 engines and that each one was individually powerful enough to bring the aircraft home safely.

I enjoyed squadron life even if I was "volunteered" for everything. Being the youngest pilot in the squadron brought great expectations, responsibilities, and opportunities. My greatest challenge was learning to balance my career and passion for flying with my family and church commitments. I didn't always succeed.

By now Judy and I had a daughter, Jennifer, in addition to our young son, Jonathan. Because we depended upon my work for our resources, it was easy for me to let my priorities get insidiously out of balance. While I had to study hard and fly often to excel, I was also needed at home a lot. I wanted to be a good father and husband. Judy and I struggled to find the

The Gration family in Phoenix, Arizona.

right family-time balance not only during this assignment, but throughout my military career. This was not an easy task, and sometimes was a point of tension in our marriage.

For Judy, relationships with her family and friends were a priority. But after becoming a new mother, she found her daily schedule restricted and meaningful adult conversations infrequent. Judy craved quality time with me and her friends, but I was seemingly married to my flying career. To make things worse, I was developing friendships with squadron pilots so my professional activities exacerbated her feelings of loneliness and isolation within our home.

Following some heart-to-heart discussions, I finally realized that I was not being the husband I pledged to be on our wedding day. I made some changes, and worked hard to be home for evening meals and to help Judy put the children to bed. We also established a dedicated time when the house was quiet and we could share our deepest thoughts with each other.

Judy and I became volunteer leaders with our church youth group and we participated in family activities on the military base. We decided to make vacations a priority and we used my annual leave time to explore America's beauty. Of course, these initiatives were just a start . . . we had to work hard at making our marriage solid and our family strong.

My Turn to Serve

One month after I almost lost my life over San Antonio, I heard a news report about Idi Amin and the plight of Ugandan people under his dictatorship. This ruthless despot was now on the run and Uganda was in severe turmoil.

The Ugandan people had already experienced so much pain and hardship during the last five years of Amin's rule. Up to 500,000 people had been killed by his regime; many more were tormented and tortured.[8] Now things were getting worse. Fighting had broken out between tribal and political factions, food was scarce, and supplies were almost exhausted. One aspirin tablet cost almost five dollars. Water was hard to find and very expensive.

Judy and I discussed the unfolding crisis in East Africa. We decided that I should use the sixty days of military leave I had accrued to go to Uganda to assist in any way I could. I could not pass up this opportunity to serve. I had another reason for wanting to help the Ugandan people. My parents, sisters and I had fled to Kampala three times in the early 1960s as we sought refuge from rebellions in Congo. The Ugandan people had taken us in each time, generously assisting us when we had nothing; now it was my turn to serve them.

Communication would not be a problem for I had learned to speak Kingwana, a local language very similar to Kiswahili, before I could even speak fluent English.[9] My mother tells of the day she was preparing a meal on our wood-burning stove. As it was approaching time for lunch, she told me, a two-year-old toddler, in English to go out and find my father.

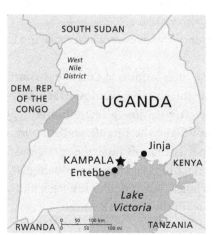

Map of Uganda.

"Baba yangu yuko wapi?" my mother overheard me say to an African worker. She was shocked. I could barely complete a sentence in English, yet I used fluent Kingwana to ask "Where is my father?"[10]

Fifteen years after departing Uganda as a refugee in 1964, I was excited to be on my way back to Kampala again.

During my two-day layover in Nairobi, Kenya, I walked all over town and stood in long lines to get my requisite travel permits for Uganda. With no regularly scheduled flights, I called friends and travel agencies until I found a small charter company with occasional flights from Wilson Airport to Entebbe, the international airport serving Kampala. Walking to the airplane, I recognized it as a high-wing, twin-engine, DeHavilland Twin Otter. The paint was faded and the exterior was very dirty—I could only pray that someone in the company was keeping up with the required engine inspections and airframe maintenance.

Strapped into an uncomfortable seat near the back of the cabin, I craned over other passengers to watch the pilot. I was not pleased when he pulled out a pair of pliers to turn one of the cockpit knobs. I wanted to get out of the aircraft, but it was too late—we were already taxiing for takeoff. I realized it would not help my state of mind whatsoever to watch our flight's captain, so I slumped in my seat and said a sincere prayer.

Instead of the expected intercom announcement from the cockpit after reaching cruising altitude, our pilot turned in his seat and passed back a ripped-off piece of envelope inscribed with the following handwritten note.

"Ldg 5:20. Cruising 12,000 feet. Speed 120 mph. Weather OK, except slight turbulence around Kisumu and Kericho."

This message gave me slight confidence that we were at least flying in the right direction.

As we taxied to the end of the runway after landing at Entebbe Airport, I looked out of the small scratched and distorted cabin window to see many green military tents and large anti-aircraft guns just a few hundred feet away. I had been too focused on the bumpy flight, the aircraft, and our pilot's competence to anticipate the serious perils that awaited me in Uganda. We parked facing the airport terminal, next to a deteriorating Boeing 707 airliner. Pockmarks from rusting bullet holes decorated its fuselage, and a detached engine rested on the ramp beneath the aircraft's wing.

Handwritten note from the aircraft pilot.

Most of the terminal windows were broken and the airport facilities were in utter disrepair. Much of this damage occurred during the 1976 Israeli raid on Entebbe to rescue one hundred three hostages held by Idi Amin's soldiers.[11] Fighting between the Tanzanian People's Defence Forces and Ugandan troops in the Tanzania-Uganda War between October 9, 1978, and June 3, 1979, had further damaged these buildings.

Standing at the rear of the aircraft, I watched as our bags were ejected from the open access door. Luggage soon stopped tumbling to the pavement; apparently everything was out. *Where was my box of tools?* I wondered. Peering into the empty luggage compartment, I confirmed there was no sign of the tools I had brought to repair hospital equipment—they were gone. Carrying only my small bag of clothes and a backpack, I hitched a ride to Uganda's capital city, Kampala.

"Show me your papers," the gate guard barked at our driver.

This was the first of nineteen roadblocks we encountered during the ninety-minute ride to Kampala. While some barriers were just a wooden pole suspended across the roadway, other roadblocks were fortified barriers manned by soldiers. The most worrisome blockades were those guarded by a collection of unruly militiamen dressed in mismatched camouflaged uniforms and wearing large sunglasses. Some of these guards had been drinking the locally brewed beer; all were armed with AK-47s, machetes, or clubs.

It was dark as we pulled into the Mengo Hospital compound.[12] The man greeting me was gracious.

"Good evening, I'm Dr. Musaba. Welcome to Mengo. Let me show you around and to your room."

I've Taken My Blessings for Granted

I knew who he was. Dr. Musaba had trained in Germany and had been a member of a successful medical practice before returning to Uganda to run Mengo Hospital as its only doctor.

His dim kerosene lantern illuminated the dirt path down the hill that went past the kitchen and laundry areas to my room next to the tuberculosis ward. Rifle fire cracked not far from the building, followed by the mournful echoes of dogs barking and people wailing. Here I was in war-torn Kampala, one of only a handful of white expatriates in the city. As I walked quietly behind the shadowy figure of my host, I questioned the wisdom of my decision to make this trip.

Dr. Musaba unlocked the door and handed me the key.

"We'll talk in the morning," he said as he bid me good night.

I stood alone in my room, my bag and backpack at my feet. Welcoming me was a steel-frame bed, a wooden table, and a straight-back chair. The increasing sound of gunfire stirred my numbed survival instincts back into high gear and I began thinking about "bullet billiards." If a bullet entered through my window, I figured the safest place for me to take cover would probably be under the window's casement. I moved my bed to that side of the room, hung a blanket over the windowpanes to shield me from shattering glass, and fell asleep.

The next morning, I passed two cute little children as I walked up the hill to meet Dr. Musaba. These youngsters had probably never tasted flour, sugar, salt, and possibly even milk because grocery stores had been looted or destroyed. Water was also very scarce. The hospital did not have a water

Our daily meal of matoke bananas.

source, so it traded medical services and surgeries for containers of water instead of accepting the inflated and nearly worthless Ugandan currency from its patients.

Despite these shortages, the hospital staff shared their food with me. We ate mashed *matoke* bananas with occasional groundnut sauce for every meal. I walked to the kitchen area one day to say "thank you" to the staff. A large aluminum container, perched over a bed of hot coals on three large stones, was full of our next meal—green matoke bananas wrapped tightly in large banana leaves that helped contain the moisture during the slow cooking process.

Every day I sat at a small table in a reception area next to the hospital's office for my meals. The kitchen staff delivered each meal on a metal tray with half a glass of water and a pretty leaf or flower placed in an empty penicillin vial that served as a little makeshift vase. That daily flower made me smile with gratitude for the kindness of the hospital staff and life's little blessings that I had often taken for granted before coming to Uganda.

I was served a cup of tea for breakfast and had mashed matoke for lunch and dinner. Served warm, the plate looked good, but the taste was starchy and bland. After eating this mush for over a month, I continued to thank God for the nourishment and the generous people that had provided it—but not for the flavor.

Using My Skills and Innovation

This missionary hospital had one hundred fifty-eight beds and a maternity ward that delivered an average of thirty-five babies a day. The electricity would often go out at night, sometimes during a caesarian delivery. Learning that the mother and her baby were likely to die due to the darkness, I decided to make the installation of emergency lights in the critical areas of the hospital my first priority.

First, since my bag of tools had suspiciously disappeared in the flight from Nairobi, I had to make some. Working with the hospital's handyman, George Katende, we fashioned a hammer from part of a bicycle pedal and a very large bolt. We made screwdrivers out of large nails and an electrical continuity tester out of a light bulb and some wire. A hotplate and a nail became my soldering iron, and I harvested solder from inoperative circuit boards. The gummy sap we collected from black wattle trees became insulating material and also served as makeshift glue.

The electricity generator on a wheelchair frame.

While exploring a storeroom with George, we found a small electric generator. This was an amazing find indeed. After repairing the motor, we mounted the now-working generator onto an old wheelchair chassis. Now, when commercial lights failed, hospital staff could wheel up the portable generator to provide electricity and an emergency lighting source.

But there was one major problem—it took too long to hook up the portable generator in the dark. Waiting for light, a patient could be without critical medical care for more than fifteen minutes. After much negotiation, we were able to get a hundred feet of wire brought in from Kenya. George and I then rewired the permanent lights in the maternity ward and operating theater to work with either the commercial power grid or the portable generator. This generator and modified lighting system saved many lives as the electricity changeover could now be accomplished in just a few minutes.

Dr. Musaba and the nurses also needed a way to sterilize the bottles used for intravenous (IV) fluid. We were able to repair the hospital's autoclave, fill it daily using a bucket and a small funnel, and sterilize IV-fluid bottles and surgical instruments every day.

Washing hospital clothing and sheets by hand was difficult and wasted lots of water. We found an old washing machine, but a rat had built its home in the electronic control compartment, eating away much of the plastic insulation from the wires. Using tree sap and other makeshift substitutes, we coerced that old machine to work again. Then George and I built a water

*Scott building the new
washing-machine system.*

recycling system, using a small tower and three 55-gallon drums, to reuse
and conserve our precious water supply.

"Soldiers are coming. Hide." I looked up from my laundry-room project and saw an out-of-breath nurse with a panicked expression on her face.
She repeated her urgent message.

I did not need the second warning; this had happened before.
Whenever gun-toting soldiers invaded the hospital and rampaged through
the pharmacy and wards looking for medicines, friends, and enemies, it
was time to scurry for cover. Dr. Musaba, some senior staff, and I usually
found temporary safety in the corn garden behind the hospital.

"Dr. Musaba," I whispered through a row of corn stalks. "Why are you
serving here at Mengo where there's a great risk of getting killed? Why
didn't you stay in Germany?"

He answered as I expected, "If I didn't come back, who would take care
of all these people?" I was deeply impressed with his servant attitude.

We remained hidden in the garden until dark. Then we cautiously
made our way back to the main clinic where hospital staff members were
already cleaning up the mess and calming the patients.

Although we had accomplished a lot, I was still desperate for my tools.
I found a chance to return to Entebbe Airport to see if they might have
arrived on a subsequent flight. Searching through cargo buildings, George
and I came across a warehouse filled with medical supplies and mattresses
donated by non-governmental organizations in Europe. Stacked in this

dark, rat-infested storeroom, these goods were not helping anyone in any way, and I decided that we should just take some of the supplies. I rented a large truck from the Catholic Church in Kampala, stealthily loaded it up, and took off early the next morning with two helpers toward eastern Uganda to distribute this aid to hospitals and clinics.

When it became too dark to travel safely, we pulled into a compound near Jinja where the Bishop of Busoga lived with his family. Right Reverend Cyprian Bamwoze graciously invited us to spend the night in his modest home. While sitting around his simple dining room table eating the thin soup and fruit he shared with us, the bishop described the acute suffering of his parishioners. Just that afternoon, he had buried a man and his ten-year-old son—killed because the attackers wanted the man's portable radio. Saddened and frustrated, my new friend explained that this kind of tragedy had become an all-too-common occurrence in Uganda, especially in the urban areas.

Christians were especially targeted by Amin's ruthless regime. His security forces would show up without notice at a residence to arrest a citizen—often without charges and never with a legal warrant. Family members would eventually learn that their loved one had "been disappeared" by government security forces.

An elderly woman wept as she told me about a church in her community that was burned down with worshippers still inside. Screams of the dying still echoed in her head, often bringing tears to her eyes. Others shared accounts about political and religious prisoners being thrown into the basement of the State Research Bureau, located in the former French Embassy on Nakasero Road. One individual told me the unventilated room was so hot from bodies crammed closely together that rice could have cooked in the heat and sweat. I visited a place on the Nile River where crocodiles had feasted on the bodies of those killed by Idi Amin's henchmen. Human bones still lay scattered on the bank as a chilling testament to this recent despicable period of Uganda's history.

Changed by Uganda

The past few years had been a sad time for most Ugandans. There was so much suffering, so much pain, and so much loss. On Sunday mornings, I would make my way up to the castle-like Saint Paul's Cathedral at the top of Namirembe Hill. Sitting in the wooden pew before the service, my engineering mind thought about the challenges of constructing this beautiful sanctuary in 1915. The massive columns and buttresses stand as true works of art; the stones had been hand-hewn in local quarries and transported up the hill. The enormous wooden arches and high vaulted ceiling had to be put up using a complex network of wooden or bamboo scaffolds. When dedicated over a century ago, this magnificent cathedral was both a grand tribute to dedicated architects, engineers, and laborers who constructed it and a quiet haven to help future generations worship our Maker, Provider, and Comforter.

Services followed a central theme—God's ways are perfect, forget the horrors of the past, and make a new future. The bishops and pastors would talk about forgiveness, looking at the brighter side, and being thankful for today's blessings. They spoke about valuing life itself as a special gift from God to be nurtured and cherished.

The Ugandan people taught me a great deal about priorities and the important things in life. My trip to Kampala was a life-changing experience. I left people behind who subsisted on matoke bananas and maybe half a glass of water a day. I left people behind who lived with gunshots shattering the quietness of night, followed by the sound of ricocheting bullets, barking dogs, and wailing people.

Prices of food and clothes were exorbitant. My new friends survived on so little, yet shared what they had. Their positive attitude in the face of nearly impossible struggles made me ashamed of my sometimes ungrateful attitude.

I realized anew that we have so much for which to be thankful and so many blessings to share. The optimistic outlook of my Ugandan friends challenged me to have a positive attitude regardless of my surroundings, to cherish life and nurture relationships, and to share my blessings with others, even if those were just a green leaf or a colorful flower in a used penicillin vial.

Arrogantly, I had gone to Kampala thinking I would change Uganda in some small way. I humbly came back from Uganda changed in a big way—I was almost a different person.

Physically, I had lost about twenty pounds in thirty-five days, had gone for a month without taking a shower or washing my clothes, and had lived on the verge of dehydration for most of the time I was in Kampala. Yet I did this for only five weeks while the Ugandan people endured these conditions for years. We have so many daily blessings—so much to use carefully, wisely, and generously. I rededicated myself to live the motto "service before self" and to embody the concept of servant leadership in all that I would do.

While my trip to Uganda had been a life-changing parenthesis in my duties as an Air Force flight instructor at Williams Air Force Base, I couldn't wait to climb back into the F-5's familiar cockpit. The trip to Kampala and my unusual experiences at Mengo Hospital were valuable and unforgettable, but that comforting seatbelt click as I strapped into my ejection seat brought a wide grin to my face.

I thought I was going home to a stable and secure job as a fighter pilot. Little did I know how soon we would be back in Africa.

I slept and dreamt that life was joy.
I awoke and saw that life was service.
I acted and behold, service was joy.

— Rabindranath Tagore

5

Back to Our Roots

What you get by achieving your goals
is not as important as what you become
by achieving your goals.

— Zig Ziglar

"Judy, we're going back to Kenya!"

I shared the exciting news with my wife by phone just after receiving it from my assignment officer at Randolph Air Force Base in Texas. Both of us were ecstatic. "Can you believe it?"

The US Air Force had just assigned me to Laikipia Air Base on the slopes of Mount Kenya. As the F-5 instructor pilot and weapons officer, I would train Kenyan fighter pilots and help the Kenya Air Force integrate this new weapon system into their aircraft inventory.

Back in 1976, my wife and I had hosted a group of Kenyan pilots who had come to Columbus Air Force Base in Mississippi for military pilot training. Major Felix Njuguna and Captain Joseph Owaga were the first Kenyan officers to spend time in our home, followed by another group of second lieutenants who joined them the next year. I would be going back to Kenya to continue training these pilots in the F-5 Tiger Squadron at Nanyuki.

No question about it. Returning to the land of our youth was a dream come true for both of us! We eagerly started to get ready for the move.

Kenya Air Force F-5E Tiger II.
(Courtesy of the United States
Air Force)

We received another surprise as we were painting our home in Mesa, Arizona, in preparation for putting it up for rent. Judy answered the doorbell and signed for a telegram.

"Scott, this is for you from the US Jaycees," she said, flipping the envelope in my direction.

I opened the envelope and began to read it aloud. "Congratulations, you have been selected as one of the Ten Outstanding Young Men (TOYM) of America for 1981."[1]

With white specks of paint all over my face and dressed in a pair of throwaway pants and an old tee shirt, I hardly fit my own image of a TOYM nominee, never mind a selectee. I knew the Air Force had nominated me, but I never expected to be selected for this prestigious award.

Judy and I sat for a while on the plastic-covered floor of our empty living room, sorting through emotions that swung from disbelief to elation. Together with the coveted assignment to Kenya, we felt doubly blessed and amazed that we were living such a charmed life.

A few weeks later, I departed for Kenya—I would be living alone at Nanyuki for the first two months. Judy and our two children planned to join me in January 1981, after we all attended the Jaycees national convention and Ten Outstanding Young Men award ceremony in Tulsa, Oklahoma.

Flying the F-5 fighter in Kenya provided me with another type of expansive view, one that required a blend of flying expertise and technical knowledge. It also required effective cross-cultural communication skills. While I put my functional check-pilot skills to good use as the Kenya Air Force technicians were still learning to maintain their fleet of brand-new aircraft, I really enjoyed working with the Tiger Squadron pilots. My daily schedule for two years included teaching these young aviators to fully employ the F-5's capabilities and weapons, upgrading them to two-ship and four-ship flight leader status, and training most to fly at night and in marginal weather conditions.

My favorite missions were low-level "*safaris.*" Skimming across the plains at nearly 500 miles per hour in tactical formation, my wingman and I honed our low-altitude flying skills while viewing Kenya's wild animals grazing just 500 feet below our jets.

I also enjoyed putting on air shows at the various national-day celebrations and agricultural fairs where Kenya's President Daniel arap Moi was speaking. The thundering roar of four F-5s streaking across gathered masses in tight formation without warning would definitely attract the audience's attention. We would time our arrival to cross the assembly area at exactly the right time to help the president make his points on law enforcement and simultaneously tame tribal tensions.

The view from our kitchen window in Nanyuki took in the magnificent Mount Kenya. Sometimes the peak was covered with clouds, but it was always majestic and inviting. Rising out of the surrounding plains as a solitary, snow-capped peak, Mount Kenya is the second highest elevation in Africa at over 17,000 feet and a regal landmark, guiding for centuries those who have traversed this region. The Kikuyu tribe calls it *Kirinyaga*, or God's resting place.

Mountains have always fascinated me. I am one who enjoys the challenge of climbing mountains, of going higher—even if the experience is difficult and painful. I like the feeling of accomplishment, the success of conquering a challenge, of reaching the summit.

The majestic Mount Kenya. (© Susan Hall)

The magnetism and charm of Mount Kenya beckoned Judy and me each day to climb its steep slopes. We finally gave in one weekend. The ice cap, the rugged rocks on the peak, the expansive view of Kenya's highlands—all were magnificent. Climbing Kirinyaga with Judy was an exhilarating experience and is still a cherished memory.

What Is a White House Fellow?

During this wonderful assignment in Kenya, I saw an advertisement in *Time* magazine about a White House Fellowship. Researching it, I learned that President Lyndon Johnson had established the White House Fellows (WHF) program in 1964. Its objective was "to give the Fellows first-hand, high-level experience with the workings of the federal government and to increase their sense of participation in national affairs."

White House Fellows typically spent the year working as full-time special assistants to senior White House staff, the vice president, Cabinet secretaries, or other top-ranking government officials. President Johnson expected the Fellows to "repay that privilege" when they left Washington by "continuing to work as private citizens on their public agendas." He also hoped that Fellows would contribute to the nation as future public leaders.

The selection process was very competitive. Approximately one hundred fifty of the most qualified applicants were interviewed by panels at the regional level, from which about thirty candidates were selected as national finalists. The President's Commission on White House Fellowships would then interview these candidates and recommend between eleven to nineteen individuals to the president for a one-year appointment as Fellows.[2]

I was intrigued. Having the opportunity to participate in roundtable discussions with renowned leaders from the private and public sectors, to travel both domestically and internationally, and to study US policy in action was something I definitely wanted to do. Undaunted by the stiff competition and rigorous application process I had heard about, I sent for a WHF application.

Of course, back in 1981 in rural Kenya, we did not have an electric typewriter. My desk was our dining room table. Illumination came from the single bulb suspended from the ceiling on a three-foot wire. A host of Kenya's flying insects and moths kept me company, incessantly circling the light and occasionally crashing into the large manual typewriter we had borrowed. Judy kindly kept our two children away from my makeshift office as I painstakingly located and struck the key for each letter I needed to finish the form. I wanted to ensure the application projected my attention to detail and high standards of excellence.

Whether or not that made any difference, I was excited to find myself in late February 1982 in cold Chicago participating in a two-day interview as a regional finalist. My competitors were very impressive—all were highly educated and recognized leaders in their respective fields. Being the only military officer in the group of fourteen regional finalists, I had worn my Class-A uniform, with its shiny pilot wings and colorful rows of ribbons, to stand out visually from the rest of the group. It must have worked because I was selected as a national finalist.

In May, I traveled back to Washington, DC, for the national finals weekend. Because I wore a green flight suit to work every day in Kenya, I didn't have a closet full of business suits. A friend helped me purchase new clothes that were in line with the dress code of the Reagan Administration. I was confident my new navy-blue blazer, khaki pants with cuffs, and burgundy Bass Weejuns shoes would help me project a "ready to go to work" image during the upcoming interviews.

Despite my new attire, I felt woefully out of place. I had been living in Nanyuki for the past eighteen months; now I was jet-lagged and staying at the Homestead Resort in Virginia with thirty-two other national finalists and thirty-three members of the President's Commission on White House Fellowships. I had no idea what my chances of being selected were.

Walking into the large dining room for the first dinner, I found my designated seat. I was seated next to Mr. Fred Fielding, the White House Counsel and President Reagan's lawyer. He was so kind and understanding of my awkward and somewhat disadvantaged position. I explained my recent arrival from Kenya where I did not have a television but listened to the local radio station for news. Sensing my information deficit, Mr. Fielding shared details about the key WHF leaders and commissioners around the room. He made me feel at ease and much more comfortable in my new surroundings.

After four days of intensive interviews, Dr. Sammy Lee, a commissioner, gave me his business card as I was leaving the Homestead. He told me to call him before I departed for Kenya. The next day, while waiting for my flight at Dulles International Airport, I dialed Sammy Lee's number from a pay phone in the main concourse.

"Dr. Lee, this is Scott Gration. I was one of the finalists for the White House Fellows program at the Homestead."

"I know," he said. "You made it. Congratulations, Scott."

My heart started to pound. "Thank you so very much for letting me know, sir!" I stammered as I hung up the phone. I was on my way to the White House!

By late July 1982, Judy and I had packed up our belongings and moved with our two children to the Mount Kenya Safari Club for our final three days in Kenya. This marvelous resort is nestled on the lower slopes of Kirinyaga, surrounded by natural greenery and the mountain's wild animals.

The magical old ambiance of the historic club's golden years still pervaded the hotel. One could picture European settlers, American movie stars, and wealthy British tourists from the 1950s and 1960s dining and relaxing at the exclusive Mawingo Hotel that William Holden and his two partners remodeled into this prestigious club.[3] All accommodations had fireplaces, which were lit each evening to ward off the 7,000-foot elevation's chill. If only the elegant mahogany décor could talk and share the captivating stories of bygone days.

I was not just lounging around the resort, though. On Friday, July 31, I lit the afterburners for takeoff, knowing this would be my last F-5 flight in Kenya. And I would have an audience.

We circled in a holding pattern eight miles from the show center, waiting for the one-minute warning to fly our four-ship formation over the Nyeri Agricultural Show where President Moi was presiding. Again, we startled the crowd right on cue.

After landing, I took my time walking around the aircraft, doing my post-flight inspection. Not only was this my last flight in Kenya, this was probably my last flight in the F-5 Tiger II fighter. Driving back to the Mount Kenya Safari Club, I reflected on my two years with the Kenya Air Force and mentally prepared my speech for the farewell party in my honor at the Officers' Mess on Laikipia Air Base.

The celebration was perfect: delicious food, happy mood, and warm conversations. Most of the Kenyan F-5 pilots were there, in addition to many other Kenyan friends. I left with a great feeling of closure and satisfaction that I had made a difference in the combat capability of the squadron and its safety record. We had become a strong team as well as good friends. We did not know this was a calm repose before a major storm.

One Last Leadership Challenge

On Saturday morning, one day before the family and I were scheduled to leave Kenya, I went back to the air base to pick up my anti-G suit that I had left hanging in the life support room after my last flight. It wasn't where I had left it. I asked the life support technicians to help, but they couldn't find it either. *How strange,* I thought. *Who would steal my anti-G suit, and why?*

The next morning at 6:45 a.m., Judy and I were awakened in our room by the telephone ringing. I sleepily wondered if it was a wrong number. *Who would be calling?*

The voice on the other end said, "We've taken control of the government."

Thinking the caller was from the F-5 squadron and was referring to the national exercise the Kenya military had been conducting during the past week, I mumbled, "Great. Have you completed the exercise?"

"No!" came the reply. "We've overthrown Moi's government!" The line went dead.[4]

Grabbing a shirt and pulling on a pair of pants as Judy checked on our children, I tried to call my contacts on the air base and in the American Embassy. No answer at any number. Running to the Club office, I hunted down the manager. Rumors were already flying about who started the suspected uprising. Stories were circulating about roadblocks manned by Kenya Air Force and Kenya Army personnel throughout Nanyuki town. A few hours later, we heard that the Army soldiers, now loyal to the Moi government, were killing Air Force "traitors."

The events, unfortunately, did not surprise me. About six months before, I had informed the US ambassador that I was hearing consistent rumblings of serious discontent with the Moi regime. He told me US Embassy staff were monitoring the situation and had all the information they needed to assess the potential for unrest in Kenya.

Only fourteen days before the coup, I had sent a message to the US Embassy stating that I strongly believed that plans were underway for some Kenyan military personnel to overthrow the government in the next few weeks. A very senior State Department official told me that the American Embassy had everything under control and they were on top of the situation.

Now, hurrying to the Mount Kenya Safari Club dining room to join my family for breakfast, I got cornered by anxious tourists. As stories of the coup d'état spread throughout the hotel, people were beginning to panic. Some had heard the radio broadcast on the Voice of Kenya by a Kenya Air Force senior private stating he was in control of the Kenya government in Nairobi. One terrified American bluntly said, "I'll give you $10,000 right now to get me and my family out of this country."

I did my best to reassure guests and staff that they were safe. As a senior military officer, people were turning to me for answers. It was obvious that I would have to take a greater leadership role to keep people from panicking. First, I had to conceal my distinctive KAF vehicle—it was a giant beacon for anyone looking for me. I hid it behind an old building at the rear of the property that had formerly been part of a movie studio used by William Holden and Stefanie Powers. Then I organized a meeting with the Club's managerial staff and asked them to help me keep the guests calm and away from the exterior windows.

With the hotel situation stabilized, I now needed a quiet place to make calls without having to go through the Club's telephone switchboard that was currently unmanned. I remembered that the sauna-massage room was equipped with an outside line. Located in a wooden structure a couple hundred feet from the main facility, Judy and I had often visited the sauna during the past two years. This would be my temporary command post.

I began to call contacts throughout Kenya to piece together the actual security and political situation. A friend in Eldoret said President Moi was alive on his farm, despite the rampant rumors of his death. Because the mutineers or government officials had shut down most communications within Nairobi, I spent much of the day relaying information between the US Embassy and the British High Commission, the equivalent of an embassy, to coordinate actions within the diplomatic community. At the same time, I continued to reach out to friends to get updates and to visit the hotel regularly to keep the guests informed of developments.

After three tense days, Nairobi's Jomo Kenyatta International Airport reopened and it appeared as if the Kenya police, Kenya Army units, and the paramilitary General Service Unit were beginning to restore stability throughout the country. On August 6, three days after the date we had been scheduled to fly to the United States, Judy and I drove to Nairobi. We stopped by the US Embassy, located across from the historic railway station on Haile Selassie Avenue, and visited that same senior embassy official who had reassured me things were under control just two weeks before.

Now, meeting with his aides in his nicely decorated corner office, the man asked, "How did you know there would be a coup?"

"Because I speak Kiswahili and I overheard some people discussing their plans," I explained.

I confess I sounded a bit frustrated. The whole coup experience made a vivid impression on me. It taught me to be aware of unintentional institutional arrogance and insidious isolation when dealing with security.

As our family departed Nairobi's international airport later that night, we were looking forward to the White House Fellowship. At the same time, we were very concerned about the Kenya Air Force friends we had left behind.

Because of the coup, President Moi disbanded the Kenya Air Force and jailed most of the pilots until all the coup plotters could be found and punished. I learned later that the group of Kenya Air Force enlisted personnel who initiated the coup made the final plans and solidified the schedule for carrying out the rebellion on the Friday of my going-away party.

I also learned later that certain Kenya Air Force pilots had been forced to fly two missions at gunpoint to drop bombs on key government targets. It appears that the rebel sergeant who flew in the back of a two-seat F-5F on one of these bombing missions had "borrowed" my anti-G suit for the flight. The disappearance of my anti-G suit now made sense.

After eight years of aviation-related duties, I would now be "flying a desk" as a White House Fellow. While still in the US Air Force, I would essentially become a civilian for twelve months—no more wearing green to work.

6

View from the Top

Don't cry because it's over.
Smile because it happened.

— Dr. Seuss

Our first week in Washington, DC, was very hectic. Besides renting a house in northern Virginia, buying a car, and registering our son, Jonathan, in a local preschool program, I found myself being summoned by a lineup of intelligence agencies that wanted me to detail my experiences in Kenya and give my perspective about the "Coup of '82." We quickly realized the next year would be lived at a break-neck pace.

A brick townhouse near the White House served as Headquarters for the President's Commission on White House Fellowships. Walking in on my first visit, I greeted friends I had made during that high-pressure interview week at The Homestead Resort. We had a great class, composed of Cathy Anderson, Mike Campbell, Paula Cholmondeley, Clayton Christenson, Paul Hasse, Frank Klotz, Doug Kmiec, Kathy Mendoza, Dan Oliver, Sharon Richie, Bill Roper, Adis Villa, Diane Vines, and me.[1]

After interviewing at several offices, departments, and agencies during the White House Fellows placement week, I decided to work at the National Aeronautics and Space Administration (NASA). The deputy administrator, Dr. Hans Mark, had been the Secretary of the Air Force a few years earlier; he called me his "young captain." We started from day one with a positive relationship that would continue to grow over the years. James Beggs, the

NASA Administrator and former Executive Vice President and Director of General Dynamics Corporation in St. Louis, was just as warm.

The Space Shuttle was transitioning out of the experimental phase. It was ready to be used to put satellites into orbit, conduct space-based experiments in zero gravity, and build the International Space Station—our permanent presence in space. I wanted to be in on the planning.

Seated in the beautifully manicured Rose Garden on a warm September morning, my wife and parents beamed with pride as President Reagan welcomed the 1982–83 White House Fellows to Washington. The swearing-in ceremony at the White House formally kicked off our WHF year. I had admired Mr. Reagan for years from afar. The significance of this special event hit home when he shook my hand, presented me with my certificate, and warmly welcomed me to the White House Fellows program.

That evening we had a reception at Blair House, across the street from the White House. Built in 1824, this historic and beautifully decorated building has been used by presidents as a guest house since 1942. Attending an event like this was a big change from our former lifestyle in

President Reagan presents the WHF certificate to Scott.

To Scott Gration
With appreciation and best wishes,
Ronald Reagan

Kenya, where we lived in a small African house without electrical appliances or a television.

"Good evening," my wife said as she reached out her hand to greet an older gentleman. "I'm Judy Gration."

"Hi, I'm Warren Burger. Are you a new White House Fellow?"

"No, my husband is the White House Fellow. We've just arrived from Kenya. We're really looking forward to this year," Judy responded. "And what do you do?"

"I'm the Chief Justice of the Supreme Court," Justice Burger said with a smile.

Judy and her new friend had a great conversation about Kenya and Washington, but it was probably the first time in a long time that someone had not recognized the Chief Justice.

In addition to my work at NASA, we had lunches and dinners with former presidents, cabinet secretaries, visiting dignitaries, and individuals who had interesting accomplishments and backgrounds. We discussed Herman Wouk's best sellers with him, great films with Charlton Heston, and life in the White House during the 1960s with Lady Bird Johnson. We attended concerts, had orientation visits to most of the departments and agencies in the Executive Branch, met with the Supreme Court justices, and had discussions with members of Congress. We sat in on cabinet meetings, joined news conferences, and participated in Rose Garden events as our schedule permitted.

We were not confined to Washington, either. The Department of Defense hosted our WHF class on overnight trips to experience Navy aircraft carrier operations, an Air Force firepower demonstration, an Army night assault, and Marine Corps riverine maneuvers. We also traveled around the United States to study social and economic issues facing our nation.

In addition, we went to Asia in advance of President Reagan's planned visit to the region. Our class spent two days in Japan where we visited the National Diet (Japan's bicameral legislature), toured a fully automated steel plant, and rode the bullet train to Kyoto.

One specific event deserves mention here. Jogging in Kyoto early on Saturday, I heard some yelling behind me. I turned around to see a Japanese jogger waving me back as I started to cross the street. He pointed to the traffic light. Yes, I was crossing against a red signal, but I had looked both ways.

There weren't any cars in sight when I stepped into the street. Respectfully complying with his rigid instruction, I jogged in place next to him until the light turned green. Speaking only a few words, we ran together for about a mile through the tidy neighborhoods.

As I was about to turn back toward the hotel, my Japanese running partner turned and said, "You come to my house for breakfast."

I was a little surprised. "I'm very sorry, but I have to get back to the hotel to prepare for my morning meetings," I apologized.

"Please come; meet my family first," he insisted.

"Okay," I agreed. "But I can't stay long."

I followed him through a maze of beautifully manicured gardens and potted plants to his door. As we prepared to enter, I wondered if I would invite a foreign stranger into my house to have breakfast and to meet my family. I kept asking myself if there was something wrong with this situation. Would I be safe?

Removing our shoes, we walked inside. While simple in design, the house was tastefully decorated and everything was neatly in its place. My host introduced me to his two young children. I could not believe it. These preschoolers were getting ready to spend the day with tutors while mine would be rolling out of bed to watch cartoons. All because it was important for them to get into one of the best elementary schools in Kyoto.

After sharing a traditional Japanese breakfast, I departed with a better insight into this culture and society. While I don't recall his name, I will never forget this man's kindness and generosity. His spontaneous hospitality made a great impression on me.

The same trip took us to Hong Kong and on to the Shenzhen Economic Zone, the first of its kind in China, which was just a year beyond groundbreaking. Only a few buildings stood on this barren ground—a restaurant, a newly opened paint store, and the political offices. It was clear from the number of bulldozers and road graders, however, that this area would become a booming manufacturing zone in just a few years. It did.[2]

After another day in Hong Kong, we flew to Bangkok, Thailand; Jakarta, Indonesia; and Manila in the Philippines. In all those stops, we met with key political and economic leaders and had tours of cultural, technological, and academic facilities. We visited military bases, research laboratories, factories, schools, and orphanages. Our class was able to write a comprehensive report that President Reagan's staff used to adjust his itinerary and produce useful "prep books" for his upcoming trip to East Asia.

I opted to extend my trip in the region for a week and return to China for a longer visit. China was not yet a popular destination for tourists, so I was able to get a five-day tour for only $725, including airfare. Of course, I expected the package deal would mean sleeping in youth hostels and eating basic meals wherever I could find them.

Walking out through the glass doors of the Beijing airport terminal as the sun was setting, I looked for a taxi to take me to the YMCA. I was surprised when I spotted a young well-dressed man holding a sign that read GRATION.

"Good evening," he said in perfect English as I walked toward him. "Are you Mr. Gration?"

Wondering how this man knew my name, I affirmed that he had the right person and that I was looking for a ride to the YMCA Hotel in the Dongcheng District, near the Forbidden City.

"I'm Li Ke Ming. I'll be your guide for the next five days," he said, matter-of-factly. "Follow me."

Li motioned for me to get into a relatively modern dark-green car parked near the terminal. I hesitated for a moment and then opened the car door and slid into the back seat. I figured there was no reason for the Chinese government to involve me in any nefarious plan, and besides, my government knew where I was. For now, I'd take the ride and see what developed. Our chauffeur sat motionless in the driver seat, eyes ahead.

Li Ke Ming got in beside me from the opposite door. We drove to the four-story Quang Mien Hotel—one of the tallest buildings in the city. The driver carried my suitcase inside as Li walked confidently to the reception desk. I followed cautiously, still wondering what was happening and how much I was going to have to pay for Li's personalized service and this upscale hotel.

After a short exchange in Chinese with the clerk on duty, Li motioned for me to follow him upstairs to a clean but spartan room on the second floor. There was no lock on the door and I would share a communal bathroom down the hallway.

As Li departed, he instructed, "Don't leave the hotel. I'll meet you tomorrow at 8:30 in the lobby."

"Thank you, but are you sure I'm supposed to be in this hotel? I made reservations at the YMCA and I didn't pay for a tour guide and driver," I queried again.

Li Ke Ming just nodded, smiling, and walked away.

I slept well despite my somewhat insecure accommodations. The next morning I used the hotel phone to call the defense attaché at the US Embassy. I quickly described Li and explained what had happened the night before.

"Enjoy your visit," he advised. "They likely just want to keep an eye on you."

His comment made me recall my visit to the Chinese Embassy in Washington when I was applying for visas for the WHF trip and for my personal trip to China. Now it seemed clear that the Chinese consular officers had noticed that a White House Fellow would be traveling all over China by himself. So they fixed the problem.

Li Ke Ming showed up on time the next morning, and we set out to see some of China's magnificent historical sites. Over the next few days, he drove me to the Summer Palace, the Forbidden City, Tiananmen Square, Valley of the Kings, and the Great Wall. We saw pandas, watched the Shanghai acrobatic show, and shopped at the Friendship Store using foreign exchange certificates—the special currency used by foreigners in China. We had a great meal of Peking duck at the Quan Je De restaurant, in the same ornate room where Communist Party leaders were celebrating their new political appointments.

Dressed impeccably each day, Li always carried his large camera and took pictures of me often as we toured sites in the Beijing area. In some places, all traffic was restricted to one side of the paved road because the other side was being used to dry grain. Most of the trucks looked as if they had been manufactured in the 1950s. I was surprised to learn they were actually brand-new trucks—the body styles had not changed much in the past three decades. Citizens primarily rode bicycles to get around, and most men and women wore outfits that look more like pajamas. Buildings were less than five stories tall and most stores had prominent signs pointing to the "bomb shelter" in the basement.

I have been back to Beijing several times since this extraordinary visit in 1983. On my most recent trip, I stayed on the 26th floor of the Sheraton Hotel overlooking the smog-filled highways and a long skyline of tall buildings. We relaxed at the Hard Rock Café and shopped at modern malls. The Chinese people wore stylish clothes with the latest fashion designs. These phenomenal changes—not all positive—have occurred in just over thirty years.

A Strained Family

The White House Fellowship year gave me a unique snapshot of domestic and international issues, and I had experiences that few would ever get in a lifetime. But the hurried pace was difficult for all of us. On average, we had four White House Fellows activities per week and the remaining time in our already packed schedule was filled with optional events, such as concerts on the National Mall or at the Kennedy Center, where we could reserve the president's box when it was available.

On one such optional occasion I rang Judy's telephone, excited to invite her to the Rose Garden event celebrating the bipartisan Reagan-O'Neill agreement on the future of Social Security. This landmark deal was significant in many ways and the invitation list was very select.

I detected some lack of enthusiasm when I told her about the evening. "Do I have to come?" Judy asked in a tired voice.

"Yes, I think you should," I answered. "This is historic and very special."

"Scott, we go to special events almost every day. I have two children to rear and a home to manage."

I realized she was right. I was cherishing every minute of the fellowship year and stretching to absorb valuable lessons in leadership and information I could use in the future. My wife was not as enthused. Through our marriage, I had learned to listen for the subtle indicators in Judy's words and tone that the family needed more time from me. Even though I wanted to adjust, balancing high priorities and competing schedules to get the most out of my career while maintaining the overall quality of life continued to be a personal struggle.

Astronaut or Fighter Pilot?

Working for Dr. Hans Mark and James Beggs at the NASA Headquarters during my White House Fellowship year was a deeply fulfilling experience.

Among my tasks was that of working on a transportation canister for the Boeing 747 shuttle transporter to ferry larger satellites and the Hubble Space Telescope.[3] I also participated in the filament-wound solid rocket booster project required to launch the Space Shuttle into polar orbit from Vandenberg Air Force Base.[4] NASA's challenge was to "man rate" these large cylinders and to figure out how to test the new cylinders without permanently damaging the epoxy fibers. I came away with tremendous respect for the engineering expertise and dedication to excellence of NASA's team of professionals as they determined how to certify these non-metallic solid rocket boosters that would carry humans into space.

Dr. Mark and Mr. Beggs were superb mentors. Dr. Mark's assistant and later NASA's chief engineer, Dr. Milt Silveira, was another generous fount of knowledge. He had worked on the Apollo program and was a design engineer on the space shuttle. I learned so much about leadership and management by listening to these three leaders ask probing questions and suggest innovative solutions. Exploring our solar system, developing leading-edge technology, and transitioning the Space Shuttle from an experimental vehicle to an operational transportation system were happening every day at NASA—and I had a front-row seat.

During my year at NASA, I accompanied Mr. Beggs and Dr. Mark to the countdown meetings prior to the space shuttle launches at Kennedy Space Center in Florida. After the launch, we would travel to Houston to monitor flight operations from NASA's Mission Control Center.

In my free time, I flew the shuttle flight simulator and took flights on the zero-G simulator aircraft, affectionately called the "Weightless Wonder." This specially modified Boeing KC-135 could create a weightless environment on earth by flying a series of "roller-coaster" parabolic maneuvers, achieving zero-G flight with the push "over the hump."[5]

For a couple of hours, NASA's KC-135 aircraft would perform thirty to forty cycles of microgravity during which astronauts could practice donning their space suits and repairing satellite components with special space tools. While many folks became nauseous during the zero-G flight in the

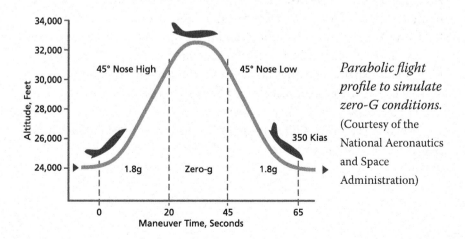

Parabolic flight profile to simulate zero-G conditions. (Courtesy of the National Aeronautics and Space Administration)

General Dynamics F-16 Fighting Falcon. (Courtesy of the United States Air Force)

"Vomit Comet," I enjoyed pushing off the back wall and floating to the front of the well-padded cabin while weightless.

While working at NASA, I met many astronauts and technicians who encouraged me to apply for the Space Shuttle program. When I met with the director of the Flight Crew Operations Directorate, Mr. George Abbey, he explained the selection process and the current flight schedule. Then he told me something that made me pause. "If you're selected, your first opportunity to fly into space as an astronaut will be in about three years."

The idea of training for three years to fly once or twice into space was a tough hurdle to face. Still, I seriously considered this career path. Space exploration had a very strong pull on my heart and mind.

However, a month later, the US Air Force offered me the opportunity to fly its state-of-the-art fighter—the new F-16 Fighting Falcon—at Nellis Air Force Base in Las Vegas, Nevada.[6] Known as Fighter Country, Nellis was home to the Air Force Air Demonstration Squadron (the Thunderbirds), the USAF Fighter Weapons School, and three operational F-16 squadrons.

As an F-16 pilot at Nellis, I would fly on the Air Force's best tactical ranges and experience some of the most challenging training scenarios. This would be the perfect place to get back into flying after my year off in Washington. Space would have to wait.

My one year as a White House Fellow had been amazing, but now a new adventure was beckoning.

7

Office in the Air

Find something that you love to do and you'll
never have to work a day in your life!

— Harvey Mackay

THE GATE GUARD SALUTED SHARPLY under a blazing September sun as we drove past a huge sign reading *Nellis Air Force Base, Home of the Fighter Pilot.* I was happy to be back in my element and to be flying the Air Force's newest fighter in the 429th Tactical Fighter Squadron, the Black Falcons. Our squadron had a wartime nuclear commitment and we trained hard to be able to deploy on a moment's notice to an airbase in England to fulfill our nuclear-alert duties.

The F-16, also known as the Fighting Falcon, is a superb aircraft with so many switches and so much capability. This frontline fighter has one seat, one very powerful engine, and a fly-by-wire flight control system. At the time, only the F-16 and the Space Shuttle used electronic controls, instead of the traditional pulleys and cables attached to the cockpit's control "stick," to move the flight surfaces. This feature, along with the bubble canopy's unrestricted visibility and the nine-G turning capability, made the F-16 one of the world's most formidable aerial fighting machines, if not the best.

Flying the F-16 also has inherent risks, as our Black Falcon squadron was tragically reminded on one fall day in 1984. Upon returning from an air-combat mission one afternoon, I saw a group of senior pilots with concerned looks on their faces huddled around the squadron operations desk.

A friend whispered to me, "Glenn's down. Wingman didn't see a chute."

Major Glenn Hessel, a seasoned instructor pilot and my friend, had been teaching basic fighter maneuvers to the newest member of our squadron. He was a superb aviator who was dedicated to excellence, and a trusted friend to all of his squadron mates. It would be hard to believe he was gone. I prayed silently that Glenn had somehow survived.

The operations officer was still trying to contact Glenn's young wingman by radio when I left the operations desk. We were all concerned about this young second lieutenant who had just witnessed his flight leader's aircraft crash and burn.

As I began to debrief the four-ship mission we had just flown, I heard an announcement crack over the squadron's loudspeaker system.

"One of our aircraft crashed this afternoon in the Caliente training area. The condition of the pilot is still unknown. Do not make any telephone calls home or to anyone else outside of this squadron until we have more facts about the situation. If you have any questions, see your flight commander or squadron commander. Tomorrow's flying schedule is cancelled."

The briefing room door opened. Lt Col Carl Parlatore, the officer in charge of squadron operations, motioned for me to join him in the hallway. As the flight debriefing was almost over I dismissed the other members of my four ship and followed my boss to the flight commanders' office.[1]

"Scott, I just heard Glenn didn't get out of the jet. I want you to take over as the A flight commander. You need to take care of your new team; they've just lost the leader they respected and admired. I'll also need you to coordinate the funeral arrangements with Maxine."

As he departed, Lt Col Parlatore paused and turned slightly. "Rick is now your wingman. Make sure you take care of him; the next month will be difficult," he said, referring to Glenn's young wingman who had just landed.

It would be a tough few days. Our flight worked with the chaplain's office, the funeral home, and Maxine Hessel, Glenn's wife of only a few months, to ensure a fitting farewell. I could not stop to mourn his death.

We would hold the memorial service in the Nellis airbase chapel—an unpretentious building with a high apex roof near the flight line that had unfortunately witnessed many similar rituals over the years. As the focal point for the service, we set up a memorial table in the center of the chapel platform—a large picture of Glenn on one side and a beautiful bouquet of flowers on the other. In the middle, we covered a cardboard box with several Black Falcon scarves and placed a squadron helmet on top with its dark visor down and the oxygen mask folded in place. It was a simple display but striking and meaningful.

Participating in Glenn's memorial service was the hardest part of the week for me. As the primary escort officer, I met each car of distinguished visitors and family members. When the Hessel vehicle drove up, I greeted the family and escorted them to their seats in the front row. I quietly took my place behind them.

As I tried to listen to the chaplain's homily honoring the life, faith, and memory of Major Glenn Hessel, I reflected on the week. Investigators believed that Major Hessel had blacked out in a high-G defensive turn. Each fighter pilot in that chapel was probably thinking the same thing: *If it could happen to Glenn, it could happen to me.*

We likely all committed, as I did, to make our anti-G suits a little tighter and to respect the amazing turning capability of the Fighting Falcon a little more. G-forces are integral to fighter-pilot maneuvering. When sitting in a chair, the force of gravity on an individual is one G. That force of gravity pulls things toward the center of the earth and gives us our weight. As a fighter pilot pulls back on the flight-control stick to maneuver the aircraft, the force of gravity increases proportionately to the tightness of the turning circle. An F-16 can generate nine Gs, or nine times the force of gravity, in a tight turn. Therefore, if a pilot weighs 200 pounds on the ground, this individual would weigh 1,800 pounds at nine Gs.

The F-16 was the first aircraft that could black out a pilot without his first passing through ocular tunnel vision—our physiological warning of impending unconsciousness. Because water makes up 60 percent of our bodies, a secondary side effect of high G-forces is the drainage of blood from the head to the legs. Fighter pilots wear an anti-G suit that inflates rapidly during the onset of G-forces to restrict the flow of blood around the midsection and to the legs. In addition, we also do weight-training work-outs and practice special breathing techniques to prepare for the strenuous dogfights that drain blood and oxygen from our brains.[2]

My morbid but practical thoughts were interrupted when we all stood up to listen to a recording of Lee Greenwood singing "God Bless the USA." Released only a few months earlier, the song's lyrics were new to many of us. We all tried to hide our emotions as the words echoed through the Air Force chapel sanctuary. Glenn and all of us had volunteered to defend America, its freedoms, and its values with our lives, even if the ultimate sacrifice was required.

F-16s perform the missing-man formation. (Courtesy of the United States Air Force)

I escorted the Hessel family to the closed parking lot next to the base chapel. After most of the congregation had joined us, a flight of four Black Falcon F-16s streaked toward the chapel from Sunrise Mountain. As our fighters approached, the number three aircraft pulled sharply into a loop-type maneuver, leaving an empty space in the "missing-man formation" in honor of our friend and squadron member, Major Glenn Hessel.[3] It was a tribute we were much too familiar with.

The next few weeks were difficult. Glenn's beer mug was turned upside down at our bar and the squadron started flight operations again. While normalcy returned to our flying activities, it did not return to our thoughts. I missed Glenn a lot. My mind often drifted to his wife, mother, and dad. There was no question that my family and friends were a priority in my life, but did I somehow take their lives for granted at times? Unfortunately, the honest answer was, "Yes."

Was I ready to die tomorrow? I continued to wonder. *Was my spiritual life in order? Was Judy prepared to carry on without me?* These deeply personal questions were probably on the minds of all Glenn's friends. While we all planned to live a full life, we had to live as if it was our last day. As the new commander of A flight, it was my responsibility to help my men deal with this difficult time as fighter pilots do . . . without visible emotion.

To Become a Thunderbird?

The precision flying that honored Glenn Hessel was something I admired greatly. I enjoyed the fighter pilot's challenge of always being in perfect formation position. In early 1984, I learned that the Air Force's Air

Demonstration Squadron—the Thunderbirds—was taking applications for the 1985 team. I decided to do whatever it took to be chosen. I wanted to be part of the stunning aerial demonstration team that built morale, aided recruitment, and conveyed to the public the Air Force's skills and commitment to excellence.

Even though I trained very hard and worked long hours at Nellis Air Force Base, Judy and I were having a great time in Las Vegas. We bought a beautiful house and I purchased a blue 1979 MGB that was fun to fix and drive. Our firstborn, Jonathan, started first grade and our daughter Jennifer was learning to swim.

Meanwhile, I poured my heart into honing my formation-flying skills, and I passed the first interview on the way to becoming a Thunderbird. Then I proceeded to the very thorough flight physical.

I was buttoning my shirt after a chest x-ray when a young Air Force medical technician stepped into the room and asked me to return to the eye clinic for a follow-up meeting. I sat down across from the seasoned doctor—his military-gray desk between us. The writing area was cluttered with medical charts and records, two coffee cups, and an array of colored pens and highlighters. Several certificates of ophthalmology training hung in simple black frames on the back wall.

Looking over his reading glasses, the doctor said, "You have a basal-cell carcinoma on your right eyelid. It must be removed as soon as possible."

I was stunned, but not as stunned as I was at what he said next.

"This surgery will eliminate you from flying with the Thunderbirds in the next season."

I was speechless. I just sat there in unbelief. The doctor scheduled me for surgery the next day, and I was back on flying status in a month. My eyelid healed perfectly and I was free from the cancerous growth. But my head and heart were neither healed nor free. I was devastated.

There wasn't anything I could do now but return to my squadron and pretend everything was fine. Looking back, I realize that up to this point, I had been quite successful in accomplishing all of my personal goals. I had fulfilled my dreams through hard work, determination, perseverance, and right priorities. But this time I had failed. My dream of joining the Thunderbird team was dashed—and that was all I could think about.

This major disappointment tested my faith—in myself, in the Air Force, and in God. Though I firmly believed that God was in control, this was a time in my life when I struggled with my faith. Eventually, my mind convinced my heart and I emerged with a stronger assurance of God's faithfulness in all situations.

A few weeks later, we learned that Judy was pregnant. The timing was not lost on me. I knew the Thunderbird team was mostly away from home during the February-to-November show season. As a squadron fighter pilot at Nellis, I would have more time to spend with Judy and our family during her pregnancy and to assist as the "coach" during David's birth in May 1984. Yes, things did work out for the best.

Deployments to England

Even though tensions associated with almost four decades of Cold War were lessening, America kept its land, sea, and air defensive nuclear-capability forces on constant alert. We were ready to defend our country with very little notice. When conducting nuclear operations, there is only one passing score: 100 percent. Close is never good enough.

Our F-16 squadron's academic knowledge was tested frequently and we practiced our combat procedures until they became routine and instinctive. We deployed periodically to our squadron's wartime location in England to become familiar with the flying environment in the United Kingdom, and to get comfortable in our temporary operations and maintenance facilities. All of these NATO-standard structures were hardened against bomb blasts and could withstand a chemical attack.

The preparation for deployment was a mammoth undertaking. Squadron personnel would pack up all the maintenance tools, testers, and spare parts we would need to conduct simulated wartime operations. Maintenance crews configured each of the twelve primary F-16s and two spare aircraft with two 360-gallon tanks, an electronic jamming pod, a baggage pod, and inert training missiles on the wingtips.

A few days before the transoceanic crossing, each deploying pilot flew his fighter to a KC-135 tanker aircraft to receive 4,000 pounds of gas. We needed to ensure the air-refueling system would transfer fuel into our aircraft properly and we had to confirm that our two 300-gallon external tanks were feeding gas into the internal fuel system without a problem.

After landing, we went home to pack personal items for the deployment and to transition into a daytime sleep cycle—we would be taking off for England at night and we needed our mandatory eight hours of rest before the launch.

The deployment day was extremely busy, but orchestrated to the last detail. About two hours before takeoff, I walked into the large briefing room and took the seat corresponding with my flight number. My final review of the flight data cards was interrupted by, "Room, a-ten-hut!"

We leaped to attention as the wing commander, squadron commander, and mission commander walked briskly to their seats reserved on the front row. After synchronizing our watches, the mission commander highlighted our expected weather conditions, reviewed emergency procedures, and briefed the plan for tanker refueling and lost communications.

"Any questions?" he asked. After a brief pause, the wing commander stood up and wished us a safe flight. We snapped to attention again as our senior leaders departed.

There wasn't much talking as we made our last-minute preparations and quickly changed into our specialized flight clothing. Donning the flight gear designed to protect us should we have to eject from the warm F-16 cockpit into the cold Atlantic Ocean was not easy—not even for an experienced fighter pilot.

The first garment to put on was the one-piece thermal liner. The next layer was the rubberized full-body "poopy suit." This individually fitted waterproof suit came with glued-on booties and tight bands around the wrist and neck to keep the salt water out, and it had a crosswise waterproof zipper just below the waist. Worn over these was the third layer of clothing—an oversized fire-retardant flight suit, G-suit, flight boots, gloves, and jacket.

These three layers were bulky, hot, and uncomfortable. In addition, the orientation of the zippers was problematic. Using the "piddle pack" to urinate in flight was a real chore: our outer flight suit zipper went up and down, the poopy suit zipper was aligned left to right, and the zipper on the front of our thermal liner was vertical. While completing this tic-tac-toe-like unzipping process, we still had to fly our single-seat F-16 in formation with three other fighters and the tanker aircraft at 29,000 feet.

One of the greatest feats of an ocean crossing was to empty your bladder into a small plastic bag that contained a dehydrated yellow sponge without spilling a drop.

Judy and my seven-year-old son, Jonathan, joined other families on the lower control tower deck to watch us take off at about 2:00 a.m. It was an impressive sight. Our families beamed with pride as their young warriors took flight, an event not seen or even thought about by the majority

F-16 taking off at night with full afterburner.
(Courtesy of the United States Air Force)

of Americans. Every twenty seconds an afterburner would light, shooting a 30-foot flame out the back end of another fully loaded F-16. As an aircraft accelerated down the runway, the ground shook and the engine noise was deafening.

After a couple of hours of night flying, our group of fourteen fighters approached the eastern coast of the United States and joined up with our three tanker aircraft. Every F-16 took on some gas to ensure every part of the air-refueling system was still working properly before going "feet wet" over the Atlantic Ocean.

Fueling may sound simple, as if F-16s just pull into an airborne gas station when the needle approaches "E." But fuel management is a constant and challenging priority while flying a single-seat fighter. We must always have enough fuel to reach our desired or at least suitable destination. Unfortunately, we can't just coast to a smooth stop on the side of the jet route when our engine flames out from fuel starvation. In addition, a fighter pilot must manage his throttle from takeoff to landing so that the jet engine burns about the same amount of gas as the other flight members. It is never good to terminate a mission early because one pilot in the formation did not manage his fuel properly.

Following a well-scripted refueling plan, the flight leader uses his aircraft radar and on-board navigational aids to locate the flight's assigned refueler and completes the rendezvous with this tanker aircraft.[4] He and his wingman generally rejoin to the left side of the tanker while the second element, the third and fourth F-16s, takes its position on the opposite side. Then each fighter aircraft rotates down in turn to receive gas from the tanker's boom in a predetermined refueling order.

Once the fighter aircraft is connected to the refueling boom, the pilot maintains position with the aid of two sets of indicator lights on the tanker's belly as his reference. The left-hand director lights provide up and down information, and the right side gives fore and aft guidance. The fighter pilot makes smooth power and control-stick inputs to remain in the

F-16s refueling from a KC-135 tanker aircraft.
(Courtesy of the United States Air Force)

small imaginary box defined by the movement limits of the boom while compensating for weather-related turbulence, air disturbances generated by the tanker's engines, and bumpiness resulting from the tanker's turns.

Pilots' hearts always beat just a little faster when refueling at night or in low-visibility conditions. It is easy to become spatially disoriented when taking on gas in these marginal flying conditions. But we have to do it and we do.

In keeping with our professional fighter pilots' image, I never heard anyone admit that he was frightened when dealing with vertigo while refueling at night. I didn't admit it either, but I remember a few white-knuckle moments connected to the refueling boom in the dark. My eyes were glued on the director lights. Yes, they were "green," but my brain was telling me we were diving steeply toward the ground. On these missions, waiting for the tanker to fill the F-16's internal fuel tanks, in addition to the two 370-gallon external wing tanks, seemed to take forever although we were usually latched onto the boom for less than five minutes.

When each of the twelve primary pilots confirmed he had a fully operational jet, the two spare F-16s peeled off and returned back to Nellis Air Force Base.

Because we had to keep enough fuel in our tanks to be able to reach an airport in the event of a fuel-transfer problem, we had to refuel ten to twelve times during the ten-hour ocean crossing. Obviously, we were all quite tired by the time we reached Europe. It seemed as if the weather over England was always poor and we would have to complete our long day by flying into the unfamiliar airfield at dusk and in the clouds. This is where the years of realistic training, sound flying habits, and personal discipline were drawn from to overcome fatigue and fear.

Crime or Mistake?

While deploying to our wartime location was not easy, we all enjoyed the change of scenery and the professional challenge. I always looked forward to flying with our allies in Europe, navigating on Dutch and German low-level routes, and training against non-American fighter aircraft.

One evening in 1985, on the way home from a mission in Central Europe, my wingman's aircraft developed engine vibrations and a significant hydraulic problem. About the same time, I noticed cockpit indications of a minor electrical problem in my F-16. After declaring an in-flight emergency, I put my wingman in the formation leader position because we would have to go through clouds during our approach for landing. I wanted him to be focused on flying his jet, not flying in formation.

As I talked him through the various emergency checklists to resolve or at least moderate the engine problem, we orbited in a short holding pattern on the final-approach course to be near the runway, should our aircraft malfunctions worsen.

With his landing gear finally locked in the down position and the engine stabilized, we began our descent in formation. As my wingman flew the instrument approach, I took sufficient spacing to land behind his aircraft.

As we rolled down the runway after touchdown, I could see all the red, white, and yellow flashing lights from the numerous fire trucks, ambulances, and safety officer vehicles that were positioned to meet us. From a distance, the broad array of brightly colored lights made it look as if we were joining a festive Christmas celebration. Upon pulling off the runway, a crew chief pinned the landing gear of my wingman's aircraft and the maintenance team towed his broken F-16 back to a hangar for repairs.

Typical NATO hardened aircraft shelter in England.
(© Bernie Gourley)

As I taxied into my aircraft's parking area, I saw the wing commander's car parked off to the side of the taxiway. My landing light then illuminated the colonel in blue uniform; he was standing beside the large clamshell door of the open hardened aircraft shelter awaiting my arrival. I tried to think why the big boss would be here and finally concluded that he must have come to congratulate me for bringing two broken single-seat fighters safely back to the base in formation, in bad weather, and at night.

I completed my post-flight checklist procedures and climbed out of the small cockpit that had been my airborne office for the last three hours. I walked up to the wing commander and saluted sharply.

Saluting back, he asked sternly, "Did you read the NOTAMs this morning?"

I thought this must be a trick question. We all read the Notices to Airmen, commonly known as NOTAMs, when we are at the base operations center to get our weather briefing.

"Yes, sir, I did," I said, feeling a bit confused.

"Then I assume you saw the purple dot over Snape today," he continued.

The purple dot informed aircrew that the royal family would be near the dot and we should plan to avoid that area. At this point, I decided confidently that he was not here to congratulate me for saving two malfunctioning aircraft.

"The Queen of England was in Snape today to attend a concert sponsored by the Aldeburgh Festival of Music," he scolded.[5]

This concert had been recorded with special high-fidelity equipment so that it could be released as a "live" event. Unfortunately, the sound of F-16 fighters orbiting above the concert was now clearly part of this special soundtrack. At least two high-level British officials had called the command post to complain.

"Major Gration, you're grounded for the next three days. I know you were dealing with multiple aircraft emergencies, but you should have handled them somewhere else other than Snape. I want you to write letters of apology to Buckingham Palace, the mayor of Snape, the recording company, and the ministry of defense."

I had learned a long time before that my response was to be, "Yes, sir," and I obligingly said it. But it appeared to me that this wing commander was more worried about his personal reputation than about the safe completion of our flying mission. What would have been his response if I had tried to resolve the engine and gear problems farther away from the airfield, if the emergency situation had deteriorated quickly, and if we did not make the runway? I believed I knew the answer.

This experience reinforced my commitment to do what I believed was right, even if I was humiliated and punished for my actions. I would put integrity first and trust my gut, even if it was not politically expedient. When faced with a tough decision, I resolved to collect as much data and as many perspectives as appropriate, determine the relevant facts, decide whether a "mistake" or "crime" had been committed, and settle on a suitable punishment.

My passion for fairness would guide my future decisions as a supervisor and commander. A "crime" usually required swift and just punishment. A person committing a crime generally knew what was right, yet did what was wrong for personal gain or comfort. The Air Force could not trust this individual to do the right thing when no one was looking. On the other hand, if someone made a "mistake" while trying to do the right thing, that individual should be counseled, retrained, and retained because he or she could generally be depended upon to put the mission and the team before self.

I learned early in my career to understand the persons' motives and demonstrate firmness and fairness in punishment decisions. It is easy to lump reprimands for mistakes and for crimes together, but unit morale and cohesion depends on leaders taking the time to fully understand an individual's intent in cases such as these, as well as the outcome.

Humility: Asking for Help

After serving in two staff assignments—two years in the Pentagon and two years at NATO's Allied Tactical Air Force Headquarters in Turkey—the US

Air Force assigned me in 1990 to an operational billet at Ramstein Air Base in Germany, near Kaiserslautern.

Our family enjoyed a quaint German lifestyle during this two-year tour. Pretty flowers spilled over window boxes, where bustling worn cobblestone streets made our civilian neighborhood look as if it had leapt from the pages of a Hans Christian Andersen storybook. It was safe for our children to scamper down to the lively village center to chomp on bratwurst and chips, or share a drippy ice cream cone with the neighbor's dog.

Family trips to the Black Forest in the summer, Oktoberfests in the fall, and Kriskindelmarts in the winter still generate warm memories of German fun and food that we often reminisce about today. Life was idyllic except for one thing.

I was at a severe disadvantage when I arrived for flying duty at the 512th Fighter Squadron at Ramstein. Even though I was coming in as the operations officer—the second most senior leader in this squadron—I had not worked in a fighter squadron over the last four years and I had never flown in this part of Europe. Now I was responsible for our fighter operations, including eighteen F-16 aircraft and fifty-six pilots.

Soon after finding my new office in a cubby hole between the operations desk and the bathroom, I brought the four flight commanders into my office for a heart-to-heart talk. These officers were the senior pilots in the squadron and each was responsible for a group of younger aviators.

"I don't have enough knowledge or experience to make consistently correct judgments about squadron operations," I explained.

"I'll always do my best to be prepared. I'll learn as fast as I can. But I need your help to get me through the next few weeks."

These four experienced pilots knew exactly what I needed and agreed to shadow me when I was on duty at the operations desk. On my first day as the duty supervisor, I received a call on the squadron radio frequency.

"Ops, Viper 1-1. My flight controls won't pass the BIT check and Ramrod says there are no more spares. Request Viper 1-2 be cleared to TRA 207 for AHC."

"Viper 1-1, stand by," I said as I looked at the scheduling board.

Our maintenance supervisor, call sign of Ramrod, had briefed me earlier that there were no more spare aircraft on the ramp. I knew Viper 1-1, the pilot with the built-in test problem, was a strong flight leader. However, I did not know if his wingman could safely navigate to the TRA 207 training area to explore the F-16's aircraft handling characteristics. I looked up and saw a flight commander in the corner moving his head slowly from side to side.

I picked up the microphone with confidence and transmitted, "Negative, Viper 1-1. Have Viper 1-2 shut down and come back to the squadron."

My guardian angel shot me a thumbs-up and smiled.

It was an important lesson for me and for my flight commanders: one must never be too proud to ask for assistance. I trusted those I supervised to give me solid advice and feedback, because team members must carry each other.

An old African proverb says it best, "If you want to go fast, go alone; if you want to go far, go together."

Our squadron's F-16s were the first operational Fighting Falcons to be fitted with the AIM-120 Advanced Medium-Range Air-to-Air Missile, or AMRAAM. This supersonic, radar-guided missile was capable of all weather, day-and-night operations, and pilots could fire this weapon beyond visual range.[6]

As preparations for the 1991 Gulf War began, our squadron was ready to deploy to Italy with AMRAAMs to protect the cargo "air bridge" as transport aircraft from the United States and allied nations crossed the Mediterranean Sea en route to and from the Middle East.

We came to work every day waiting for our deployment orders to join the Gulf War build-up; every night we went home to watch the war on television and sleep in our beds. We had trained our whole careers to defend our country, its ideals, and its policies. Now we would sit out the first big conflict since Vietnam. Our wives and families were delighted to have us safely at home, but our hearts yearned to be in the middle of combat action.

A Safety Day to Remember

While we all worked hard to maintain our combat skills at the highest state of readiness, I was probably best known for the 1991 86th Wing Safety Day. To keep the ground and flying accident rates down, most bases would schedule periodic down-days to focus on safety concerns. Flying operations would be cancelled and we would listen to recitations of safety statistics, reviews of recent mishaps, and lectures on dreary topics such as overloaded wall sockets or driving with bald tires. I found this fill-the-square exercise to be extremely boring and unproductive.

When it was my turn to organize the Wing Safety Day, I asked the wing commander if we could do something different. The plan was to have the squadrons run their individual safety programs in the morning and then we all would meet at the base's football field at 1:00 p.m. for the combined 86th Wing portion. The theme would be *Live Safety, Live Safely*.

He agreed and our team went to work getting the props for the four corners of the football field. First, we enlisted an Army helicopter to transport an old F-86 aircraft and position it on one corner of the football field. Next, we went down to the local junkyard and borrowed two old cars—only one of them in running condition. Finally, we constructed a bar area on the corner adjacent to the F-86 fighter and a kitchen set on the opposite corner, complete with a refrigerator, stove, counters, and a sink inside the four-foot-high walls. The arena was now ready for our safety-day show.

When the crowd arrived, "Captain Valiant" was already strapped in the aircraft cockpit and his wife was in her kitchen, both fitted with wireless microphones. At 1:00 p.m., the wing commander kicked off the event with a word of welcome and then the narrator gave a brief background on our typical fighter pilot.

"Sabre 1-1 is aborting, engine fire, smoke in the cockpit," an anxious voice boomed over the loudspeakers, interrupting the narration.

Fire engines and ambulances raced toward the aircraft from behind the bleachers with lights flashing and sirens blaring as white vapors generated from dry ice billowed from the F-86's tail section. The narrator talked the audience through the crash recovery procedures as the rescue personnel removed our pilot from his burning aircraft. The crowd roared with laughter when Captain Valiant almost fell on his head after getting his foot stuck while being pulled from the cockpit.

On his simulated way home from the burning F-86 fighter, Captain Valiant drove his dilapidated car to our makeshift bar on the next corner of the football field to relax. As he drank several beers, the narrator summarized the Air Force's designated-driver policy and highlighted the merits of our base's volunteer driver program.

Now continuing to drive home while a little tipsy, Captain Valiant crashed his car into the other vehicle, parked along his path, which we had borrowed from the junkyard. Again, first responders sped toward the accident with screaming sirens and flashing lights. Rescue crews quickly extracted the inebriated pilot from his wrecked car using metal saws and the Jaws of Life. While being carried to an awaiting ambulance, Captain Valiant called his wife to explain his delayed arrival.

"Honey, I'll be a little late for dinner . . . I had a small aircraft accident this afternoon and a little fender-bender on the way home."

Distracted by her husband's news, the woman left her frying chicken unattended on the kitchen stove and it soon burst into a large grease fire. Once again, fire engines responded from behind the stadium bleachers to put out the large flames and rescue Captain Valiant's distraught spouse.

While these four action-packed events were taking place on the sports field, the narrator reinforced messages about incorporating safety into everyday routines so one can live safely without having to risk life. This fun-filled afternoon clearly conveyed our message: *Live Safety, Live Safely*, and it certainly was not boring.

Make No Small Plans

Mr. Beggs had been right. I remember sitting on the long white couch in the NASA administrator's corner office in Washington, DC, when I was a White House Fellow, listening to a discussion on a new probe to study Venus' atmosphere. After a lively debate over the size and cost of this contentious program, Mr. Beggs, who had been listening quietly, paraphrased Niccolo Machiavelli.[7]

"Make no small plans for they have no power to move men's minds," he said with authority.

I do not remember the outcome of the Venus-explorer debate, but I'll never forget that maxim which is now tattooed inside my brain. These words proved to be true as we planned the Ramstein Safety Day. We kept thinking big and the results were better than expected.

As Henry Ford once said, "If you always do what you've always done, you'll always get what you've always got."

While it is easy to safely repeat the same routine tasks that have produced success in the past, the world is changing, technology is transforming, and our processes must adjust to the new normal. Resisting the mediocre, stirring the soul, aiming high in hope, making big plans, and moving men's minds became foundational pieces of my leadership style in Mr. Beggs' office in 1983. This attitude, along with big plans for new initiatives, worked in my military and diplomatic roles and continues to characterize my approach as an entrepreneur.

Change is Hard

Nevertheless, change is hard for some individuals and for corporate structures as well. Bureaucracies gravitate toward the status quo and often resist those who "rock the boat" with new concepts or big plans. Throughout my career, I have been largely successful in making big plans and bringing about changes to make a positive difference, but sometimes it has come with significant personal and professional cost.

In looking back, I believe that I should have been more sensitive to the fears and concerns of those who were uncomfortable with change. I am sure I pushed some people too hard when I should have tried to win them over to my ideas with a slower and gentler manner. Unfortunately, some lessons are learned too late in life.

8

Combat Operations

*Life is ten percent what you make it and
ninety percent how you take it.*

— Irving Berlin

It was 11:30 p.m., Friday, April 5, 1991, when I received a call from the 86th Wing Operations Center to be in the Command Post by midnight for a high-priority briefing. I had gone to bed about forty-five minutes before and was still waking up as I quickly put on a flight suit and pulled on my boots.

What was going on? I wondered. *Had there been a tragedy on base or were we going to war?*

The conference room at Ramstein Air Base in Germany was buzzing by the time I arrived. Colonel Charles (Chuck) F. Wald, the operations group commander, motioned me to the empty chair beside him. A minute before midnight, the meeting started with a time hack.

". . . Three, two, one, hack. Twelve o'clock." We all set our watches to the second, based on the Naval Observatory's digital clock in Washington, DC.

The watch supervisor then read a secret message directing the 86th Wing to deploy twelve F-16s to Incirlik Air Base in Turkey and to have a combat air patrol over Iraq within the next thirty hours to enforce the new northern no-fly zone established to protect the Kurds. In addition, we were to escort cargo aircraft that would be airdropping water, food, and medical

Map of Turkey.

supplies to stranded Kurdish villagers, many of whom were trapped on barren and rocky hillsides.

The dreadful plight of 500,000 displaced people in the freezing remote mountains in northern Iraq had prompted President George H.W. Bush to order the United States Forces in Europe to provide immediate relief assistance. In addition, the United Nations Security Council passed Resolution 688, calling on Iraq to provide humanitarian access and to end the repression of its population.

As per the orders, Operation Provide Comfort would establish a no-fly zone north of the 36th parallel on April 6, and we, along with British and French aircraft, would enforce this UN mandate. Coalition cargo aircraft under our protection would begin to deliver humanitarian relief to the Kurds on April 7.[1]

Looking directly at me, Brigadier General Richard Swope, the wing commander, said, "The 512th is our lead squadron, but I expect the entire wing to provide any and all support required to have combat-ready F-16s over Iraq in less than thirty hours."

I recalled my stop at the Ramstein Officer's Club earlier in the evening to relax with my squadron mates before having dinner with my wife. Many of our squadron pilots already were well into their weekend partying mode by then—they certainly would not pass our twelve-hour "bottle-to-throttle" restriction.

The operations group commander interrupted my troubled thoughts. "Good luck, Scott. Call me anytime if you need anything."

I quickly called one of the flight commanders. We were able to find sixteen pilots who had not been drinking and we put a flight schedule together with twelve primary pilots and four backups. These pilots would have to be briefed quickly and put into their twelve-hour crew rest. While my flight commander was finishing that task, I initiated the telephone recall to get all the maintenance personnel and non-flyers into the squadron as soon as possible.

It was now 1:15 a.m. The flight to Incirlik was roughly four and a half hours, so we would need to launch the fighters no later than 2:45 p.m. We had thirteen and a half hours to get them all airborne. The first C-130 with the maintenance load could depart at 3:00 p.m., and the rest of the personnel would follow in the second C-130 at 4:00 p.m. Our most critical task was to configure fourteen aircraft for the deployment to Turkey, each loaded with two external fuel tanks, a full load of ammunition, a baggage pod, and a jamming pod which is a critical component of our electronic warfare capability.

That night I mirrored the deployment plan I had learned at Nellis eight years before. I was very grateful that I had paid attention as a young major when we packed up the Black Falcon squadron and prepared to fly to England.

General Swope and Colonel Wald came by at about 7:15 a.m. and I gave them an update on flight preparations. I reported that our squadron commander would lead the deployment and briefed them on our plan to air refuel en route to Turkey.

"We're planning to use tankers from Morón Air Base. If there's a problem, our fighters will land at Sigonella for gas," I said. Morón was in Spain, and Sigonella in Italy. "I've already coordinated for stand-by ramp space and gas."

I accompanied my two bosses to their blue Air Force staff car parked in the VIP space next to the squadron's front door.

"Is anything worrying you about this deployment?" the wing commander asked me as they prepared to depart.

Yes, several things were worrying me. We hadn't had time to check all the external tanks at altitude, and I did not like the possibility of not having the twelve jets working properly as the president requested.

"I have sixteen pilots in crew rest. If we can generate sixteen jets, I'd like to launch them all. I don't believe two spare aircraft will be enough."

He nodded with a smile and said, "Press ahead with sixteen. Well done."

Our pilots showed up at 1:15 p.m., attended the mass briefing, and were out the door in time to make the 2:45 p.m. takeoff. One aircraft aborted with a brake problem while taxiing to the runway. We needed all fifteen airborne F-16s to get twelve good fliers out of Germany and on their way to Incirlik Air Base.

The rest of the deployment went smoothly. Our team had fighters over Iraq on April 6, 1991, as the president directed.

I flew my first Combined Task Force Operation Provide Comfort combat mission on April 7. It was the first of 274 combat missions I would fly over Iraq during the next seven years—more combat missions over Iraq enforcing the no-fly zones than any other American fighter pilot. This was not because I flew more often than other pilots, I just spent more time assigned to units flying combat operations over Iraq. In all, I logged 1,065 hours of combat and combat support time.

Over the next few weeks, the US-led coalition ground force deployed into northern Iraq as part of Operation Provide Comfort to construct resettlement areas and establish demilitarized zones. US Special operations forces were also on the ground to help protect coalition forces and locate Kurdish villagers in need of food, water, and medical supplies.[2]

Did You Hear That Radio Transmission?

On April 22, 1991, I was leading a combat air patrol mission along the Great Zab River Valley in northern Iraq. Since it was my wife's birthday, I carried a small American flag on that sortie for her, stamped with the date *22 Apr 91*. As I approached the small town of Cukurca, I heard a faint radio transmission calling for help.

"Any radio, this is Tailpipe Alpha. Can you read me?"

I could barely distinguish the words, but I was sure it was not a radio call between aircraft on our working frequency.

"Beater 1-2," I asked my wingman on our discrete radio frequency. "Did you hear that radio transmission?"

"Beater 1-2, negative."

"Tailpipe Alpha, this is Beater 1-1, do you copy?" I broadcasted blindly—no answer.

I immediately descended and set up a search pattern of gradually widening circles while I continued to broadcast in the blind.

Then I heard this: "Beater 1-1, this is Tailpipe Alpha. Can you read me?"

My heart raced—there was someone on the ground calling me. Who could it be? Judging from the accent, I believed it must be an American.

"Tailpipe Alpha, Beater 1-1, say your position and nature of the problem."

"We're a Special Forces team located on the south bank of the Zab River. One wounded. Need medevac ASAP. Over."

"Roger, copy all. Beater 1-1 will relay to AWACS. I'll fly down the river. Let me know if you see or hear my aircraft."

I contacted the mission controller on the E-3 AWACS aircraft and relayed what I had heard. I directed my wingman to remain at 4,000 feet above the ground to relay messages to and from the AWACS controller and to be above the maximum range of small-arms fire as I descended to 500 feet above the ground.

Flying up and down the river, I tried to use the Special Forces team's radio transmissions to pinpoint its location. My wingman relayed that the AWACS had dispatched a combat search and rescue team from Turkey. I communicated this information to the team on the ground, but still could not find their location.

Already low on fuel because our flight had been in the area for almost two hours, I led our two-ship flight back to the KC-135 tanker, filled up our tanks, and returned rapidly to our last location. Again, my wingman stayed high and I went down to search the rocky banks of the muddy river.

After a few more radio calls, I spotted four figures huddled around someone on the ground—the special operations forces team. I relayed their exact GPS coordinates to the AWACS so the combat search and rescue helicopter could fly directly to our position. Then I asked for details about the injuries so the medevac crew would be ready and our clinic at Incirlik could begin preparing to receive this soldier.

I learned later that Sergeant 1st Class Todd Reed, a special operations soldier, had stepped on a land mine. The shrapnel wounds to his legs were very serious and he lay immobilized while his teammates administered "buddy care" first aid to minimize his bleeding and stave off shock.

Our flight continued to orbit the area looking for enemy troops until the HH-60G Pave Hawk arrived from Diyarbakir, Turkey. I then vectored the medevac helicopter to the exact location of the special operations forces team. Once at the scene, the HH-60 rescue pilots were reluctant to land because of all the landmines in the area. They decided to pick up Reed and his teammates while hovering just above the ground.

As we flew back to Incirlik, I reflected on our US armed forces team. Each member had the training and professional skills to do the right things, even when encountering new and difficult challenges. I was proud to be part of the US team that was carrying out the orders of our commander-in-chief while taking care of our own.

After our flight debriefing, I drove over to Incirlik's clinic to meet Sergeant Reed before he left on a medevac flight to Germany. Walking into a small recovery room, I saw Todd—a handsome, strong paratrooper lying in bed with a heavily bandaged leg. He had lost his right foot and he had many shrapnel wounds over his body. I introduced myself and expressed my condolences. Todd was very appreciative of our efforts to save his life. He told me that hearing my first answer to his team's numerous radio calls had really lifted his spirits—he was confident at that point that help would be on its way.

Then he said, "Sir, may I have your flight suit patches?" I smiled because I knew I would probably ask the same thing if I were in Todd's place. Such a souvenir would be a fitting reminder of this day.

I pulled the four Velcro'd patches off my upper arms and chest, and proudly handed them to Todd.[3] Then I was struck with another idea.

"Today is my wife's birthday," I said, pulling a small flag out of my pocket. "I took this on my mission today to let her know I was thinking about her. Todd, I'd like you to have it as a reminder of this day." My voice cracked as I handed him the flag.

This was an emotional meeting between two warriors who had been brought together by an Iraqi landmine. Todd Reed may not have lived if he had spent that night shivering and bleeding on that riverbank in northern Iraq. He is yet another patriot in a long line of heroes who have given more than their time—they have given life and limbs in dedicated service to the country we love and serve without reservation. I will never forget the incident, and am grateful to have been able to locate that faint distress signal and help save his life.[4]

Back to the Classroom

My transition to being a senior Air Force leader began at the prestigious National War College at Fort McNair, Washington, DC, in September 1992. My class consisted of about forty officers from the three military services, along with students from the Department of State and other federal departments and agencies. For a year, we listened to a cast of "movers and shakers," studied excellent core subjects, and learned from stimulating electives. Professors and their assistants used a combination of history and current events to reinforce lessons of analytical thinking and strategic planning.

As I was finishing my studies at the college, the Office of the Chief of Staff of the Air Force offered me a job as deputy director of his planning cell. Secretary of Defense Les Aspin signed a rare waiver exempting me from the congressionally mandated joint assignment following senior service school, and I started work a few days after graduation.[5]

One day General Merrill A. (Tony) McPeak, the Chief of Staff of the Air Force, asked me to diagram the command and control relationships of Operation Restore Hope, a United Nations-sanctioned multinational operation in Somalia from late 1992 to May 1993. He believed there were some detrimental factors in the mix, and asked me to analyze the effect of these relationships on daily operations and the outcome of US operations in Somalia. America had lost eighteen US soldiers on October 3, 1993, during the seventeen-hour operation beginning with the raid on the Olympic Hotel in Mogadishu searching for Somali leaders.

I had accompanied General McPeak to Mogadishu just before this incident. We had visited the various senior leaders, talked with the troops, and taken a helicopter tour of the Somali capital to see the operating environment. I had worked in Mogadishu in the mid-1980s and still had clear memories of the city from an on-site perspective.

After studying this military operation in detail, it was evident to me that General McPeak was correct—the organizational lines of authority were blurred and flawed. While many factors contributed to the operational failure, the multiple chains of command and the informal command relationships were the most problematic. Operational success in Somalia essentially depended on personalities of the senior leaders and on the extent to which these men decided to share information. Unfortunately, there was no single person in charge of all of the US military operations in Somalia and there were too many informal lines of authority.[6]

My study showed me the importance of having correct and streamlined command authorities in my future leadership positions. This lesson was invaluable as I fought organizational-chart battles when I was the wing commander in Turkey, Combined Joint Task Force-West commander, and again as the US Ambassador to Kenya.

In addition to the lesson on organization, I further refined my perspectives on security. My planning approach is basic.

First, I do not accept entering a high-risk situation in order to do things that are not critical to the mission. I have resolved to expose myself and/or my subordinates to high risks only when the mission is highly critical and justifies taking on an increased danger.

Second, I take every precaution possible when facing a security threat—and then take a few more. It is imperative to think about every possible point of vulnerability in the chain of security and fix each one of them immediately.

Lastly, I learned that there will be times when a leader cannot mitigate all the risks to personal security, yet he or she must still carry out the nation's mission. It is a tough call when a commander must send men and women into danger, but leaders must make those decisions, accept the responsibility on behalf of our country, and be prepared to live with the consequences.

I am extremely grateful to General McPeak for mentoring me on critically important aspects of organization, security, and leadership. Although I enjoyed my two-year assignment in the Chief of Staff's front office, swapping my blue staff uniform for a green flight suit was a trade I would make any day.

Leading Warriors into Combat

I pulled on my "green bag" for the first time in almost three years on April 18, 1995. I loved wearing a flight suit with its convenient front zipper, comfortable fit, and so many pockets. It brought back good flying memories. Donning this fire-retardant garment in the morning also meant I would soon be surrounded by fellow fighter pilots and ground technicians whose goal for that day was to do their best to make us all better and safer. I was proud to be a senior aviator in the Air Force.

My next assignment was in Dhahran,[7] on Saudi Arabia's eastern coast (across from Bahrain), where I would serve as the operations group commander in the 4404th Composite Wing (Provisional). Our wing supported Operation Southern Watch and its United Nations-mandated mission to enforce the no-fly zone over southern Iraq. First I had to refresh my skills on how to fly the F-16 at Luke Air Force Base in Phoenix, Arizona.

Some say it's like riding a bicycle—that you can never forget how to fly. That is somewhat correct. But there is one big difference between riding a bicycle and flying a fighter: you will definitely scrape more than a knee

*Map of the Kingdom of
Saudi Arabia.*

if you lose control. Motivated to be competent and safe, I used every free minute during my refresher course to study and prepare.

While I looked forward to leading American fighter pilots into combat again, I was sad to be leaving Judy and our now four children in Springfield, Virginia, for a year. US military personnel go into harm's way because they have volunteered to defend our national interests. We sometimes forget that their families are a significant part of that call of duty.

During my year in Dhahran, Judy would be one of those temporary single parents so common in the military community. My wife would have to bear the full load of household decisions and would independently shepherd our children through their schoolwork and everyday issues. Yes, our military families are a special group of people who deserve much more gratitude than they are given for the sacrifices they make.

As the operations group commander at King Abdul Aziz Air Base, I was responsible for aircraft operating from four bases in Saudi Arabia, three locations in Kuwait, and one each in Bahrain and Oman. I was in charge of a variety of aircraft, including F-16s, F-15s, A-10s, C-130s, U-2s, and search-and-rescue HH-60G helicopters. Our operations center had to integrate the various capabilities of these aircraft, along with naval air assets, into the daily air operations plan in order to accomplish our mission in Iraq effectively.

Arriving in Dhahran, I noticed that all the enlisted personnel and most of the officers working at Khobar Towers wore desert-camouflaged uniforms, known as DCUs. On the airfield, the pilots wore green flight suits, accessorized with tan desert combat boots, a tan nametag, and a DCU cap. I thought this mismatch of colors was silly. Aircrew had the greatest chances of having to avoid capture in the desert, yet we would be trying to evade an enemy wearing a green flight suit designed for the forests of Europe or the jungles of Vietnam.

Searching the Internet, I found a manufacturer in the United States willing to make tan flight suits for me. After six months of letter writing, telephone calls, and meetings with senior leaders, Air Force headquarters finally agreed with me and approved tan flight suits for pilots operating in desert environments. Within a year, the tan flight suit became a standard-issue item for Operation Southern Watch.[8]

Being in the middle of flight operations was like heaven for me. I usually flew one of the first missions of the day, so I could spend the rest of the day doing my non-flying duties. To cross the Kuwait-Iraq border at 7:30 a.m., flight members had to be at work at 4:15 a.m., which meant getting up at 3:30 a.m. Let me describe a typical flying day.

Upon arrival at the squadron, we would all do our respective jobs to prepare for the flight. The flight briefing would start precisely at 4:30 a.m. For the next hour, the flight leader would review the flight routing, communications plan, and response to emergency situations. Most of the briefing time, however, would be spent detailing the target area, describing the timing and tactics we would use to reach the target while dealing with potential enemy threats, and assigning individual bomb-impact points to each flight member. By then it was 5:30 a.m. The next step was to "sanitize" and don our anti-G suit and combat vests, and load our 9-millimeter pistols. A waiting cargo van would take us to the aircraft shelters.

After using a flashlight to inspect the F-16 airframe and all its armament thoroughly, we would each climb into our cockpit, strap into the ejection seat, load the communications encryption, and complete the prestart checklist. At the designated time, all four of us would start our engines and ensure our aircraft was combat ready. At 6:15 a.m., after radio check-in and taxi out to the end of the runway in perfect spacing, our crew chiefs would conduct a final inspection of the F-16 fighter and then armament crews would remove all the safety pins in our missiles and bombs to make them "live."

After takeoff at 6:30 a.m., we would fly about forty-five minutes to rendezvous with our designated air-refueling tanker. All four of us would

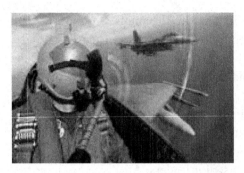

View of the wingman from an F-16 cockpit. (Courtesy of the United States Air Force)

get a full tank of gas and our flight would proceed in tactical formation to the "gate," ready for combat. After checking in with airspace controllers onboard the AWACS, we would depart into bad-guy territory right on time at 7:30 a.m. Depending on the mission, we would be back at Dhahran between 10:00 a.m. and 1:00 p.m. After filling out the post-flight paperwork, we would debrief the mission for an hour.

Based on this description, one might think that flying a combat mission was not hard work; after all, we were mostly just riding around seated in an ejection seat. I admit I was having fun and I loved flying, but many missions were mentally exhausting and very hard on the body. I often returned from a combat sortie with white salt stains on my flight suit caused by dried sweat.

When we trained, we flew our missions as if they were actual combat. When completing a training flight involving a high-G dogfight, the underneath portion of my forearms would be covered with "geasles." These little red spots were caused by small ruptured blood capillaries that could not survive the intense G forces on my body.

Am I complaining? Absolutely not! I would climb back into a fighter cockpit this very day if the Air Force would let me.

My year in the Saudi Arabian desert had passed surprisingly quickly. It would soon be time for me to leave Dhahran. I had been selected as the next commander of the 39th Wing at Incirlik Air Base in Turkey, and was looking forward to returning to a country I had enjoyed, and to flying duties I understood very well.

Ready for my final week at King Abdul Aziz Air Base, I planned to wake up by 4:00 a.m. the next morning to welcome my replacement. It was about 9:50 p.m. when I flipped off the light and walked toward my bed in the darkness. The dimly lit clock on my bedside table guided my steps.

9

Warrior Commander

Success is not final, failure is not fatal; it is the
courage to continue that counts.

— Winston Churchill

Without warning, a bright yellow-orange flash engulfed my room.[1] It was followed immediately by a thunderous, deafening boom. I dropped to the floor. I knew what had just happened and thought there might be another blast.

Pain raced through my side and leg. My ears were ringing. I smelled the strong pungent odor of explosives. Groping around for my flight suit and boots, I felt shards of glass all over the floor. As my eyes adjusted to the darkness, I pulled slivers from my side. At least the bleeding wasn't profuse; it hadn't punctured an artery. I grabbed three T-shirts and pulled them on to absorb the blood. Then I slipped into the flight suit. Not able to find any socks, I just pulled my flight boots onto my bare feet.

It was Tuesday, June 25, 1996. Someone had bombed Khobar Towers.

Before heading out the door with my handheld radio, I glanced at what was left of my three-bedroom suite. We had been expecting my replacement to arrive the next morning. Earlier in the day, I had changed sheets, swept a little, and put two bottles of drinking water out on the bedside table—my version of hospitality. I remember thinking that the walls were appropriately bare, since we were here not to feel at home but to engage in daily combat operations. Now his space, and mine, was a shambles.

I ran through the fifth floor pounding on doors, looking for wounded. Descending in darkness I did the same on the fourth and then the third, where I finally found an airman. He was unharmed and looking for a way to help.

"Go into every room in the building to make sure everyone has the medical care they need," I ordered.

Responding instinctively to the emergency situation I perceived, I raced out of the building toward my Jeep. There was an eerie silence—I heard no screaming or alarms. There was just enough light from the moon for me to see that the windshield and back window of my vehicle were gone and the side windows were broken. The roof of the maroon Cherokee was caved in about eight inches and glass fragments covered the seats and floor. But the tires were still inflated and the engine turned over, so I was in business. I brushed out what glass I could, and then sped toward the dim shape of the structure that had taken the brunt of the bomb attack: Building 131.

The voice of the US wing commander, Brigadier General Terry Schwalier, came over my handheld radio. "The support group commander is the on-scene commander. All other commanders report to the command post."

General Schwalier would also be departing within a week. I had been able to watch what he had done during his tenure to make our living areas in Khobar Towers more secure. He was very conscientious and worked diligently to mitigate the security threats we were facing. As a newly selected wing commander, I planned to adapt his example into my own leadership style.

But it was not time to ponder any future role; I needed to focus on the moment. The massive truck-bomb had gone off in a parking lot outside the perimeter of the Khobar Towers compound. Between that deadly spot and the eight-story Building 131, there had been an eight-foot-high fence topped with concertina wire, three rows of large cement barriers, and a road. But all those prudent security measures had not been sufficient to protect the Air Force personnel inside, primarily members from the 4404th Wing's (Provisional) combat search-and-rescue unit deployed from Patrick Air Force Base in Florida, as well as some members of an Eglin Air Force Base F-15 squadron from Florida who also lived in the housing facility.

We would learn later that the casualties could have been higher, if not for the quick thinking of Staff Sergeant Alfredo Guerrero, Senior Airman Corey Grice, and Airmen First Class Christopher Wager who were stationed on top of Building 131 as sentry guards. They had watched a large sewage truck enter the parking lot, drive along the perimeter wall, and then turn as if to exit. The truck then slammed into reverse and backed against the perimeter fence, and two men jumped from the cab and ran to a waiting car. With just seconds to spare, the rooftop security guards raced through the hallways, yelling for people to evacuate before the truck exploded.

Now I stood about twenty yards away, staring at the damage. The explosion had blown the entire front exterior wall off the eight-story building. The top three floors were now sagging perilously, no longer supported from below. My gut twisted with anger and frustration at the pain and death I saw in front of me. Suppressing these feelings, I instead tried to determine what immediate actions were needed.

The support group commander, Colonel Gary Boyle, and the logistics group commander, Colonel Pete Mooy, drove up and jumped out of their vehicles. Colonel Boyle would have to decide whether he should risk more lives by sending rescue teams into the extremely hazardous structure. After a quick exchange, they walked toward the front of the building and I headed back to the small parking lot where I had left my car. I needed to hurry back to the command post.

Just then, I saw people sprinting out of the dark building carrying wounded comrades. It was clear that some airmen had already made the decision to rescue their friends despite the danger to themselves. They were trying to put victims in a commandeered blue step van.

"Hey, give us a hand!" someone yelled to me from the dark.

The airmen and I loaded four bleeding men into the back of the van. Blood was everywhere. Their faces looked so young. We used pieces of clothing as compresses to slow the bleeding; some of the wounds looked very serious. The nearest clinic was on the ground floor of one of the housing towers. The driver sped off with me in my Jeep close behind, and slammed to a stop up on the sidewalk just outside the medical center. We raced to get stretchers and carry the wounded men inside.

The courtyard of the towers, in front of the clinic, was barely the size of a volleyball court. It was filling up fast. Several pararescue jumpers (known to us as PJs) and nurses were doing triage as doctors worked frantically to stop bleeding and begin medical care. Two airmen were already dead.

It was clear that our small medical staff would soon be overwhelmed as more wounded were arriving every minute. I grabbed a medical techni-cian whom I recognized. "Have someone call the Saudi hospitals to request more ambulances and doctor support," I ordered. I learned later that some Saudi doctors were already on their way to Khobar Towers, reacting to telephone calls between Lt Col Jim Traister's security force personnel and their Saudi police counterparts.

My boss had directed me to join him at the 4404th Wing command post. I sped off. I knew every bump and turn along the route. The command post was located next to my office in the coalition military compound on the Royal Saudi Air Force's King Abdulazziz Air Base. Enclosed with high fences and guarded by Saudi and US forces, this area was used to support Operation Southern Watch. Physically separated from Khobar Towers by about a mile, this secure area still had the lights, telephones, and other communication systems we needed to plan our response to the terrorist bombing.

General Schwalier was on the telephone with his boss at 9th Air Force headquarters in South Carolina when I walked into the communications room. Other senior leaders sat in the few available chairs or leaned on the edges of desks speaking quietly as we waited for our commander.

Hanging up, General Schwalier rattled out assignments to all of his senior officers.

"Gary is the on-site commander. Pete, you help the docs. Make sure they get what they need. Scott, we need an accountability check of our people. Tell the squadron commanders I want them to look into the eyes of every one of their airmen to make sure we have this right."

He barked out a few more directions and then we headed out into the darkness. We all knew what had to be done to stabilize the situation, to rebuild our organization, to find out who had done this, and to honor our dead.

We had to know how many people might still remain in Building 131. The Wing personnel office was located next to the bombed building. The computerized personnel databases were now buried under piles of stone, rubble, and dust. We would have to methodically search the entire housing complex, locate each assigned individual, and manually compile a list in each squadron of who was accounted for, who was injured, who was dead, and who was missing.

I set out for the dining facility to set up the accountability effort. First I stopped by the clinic to see if I could get stitches for my side and leg wounds. Doctors and ambulances from local Saudi hospitals had arrived soon after they were alerted, but still our staff was inundated with the seriously wounded, and the courtyard was now overflowing with bloodied bodies. We needed a larger area to care for the people who needed minor medical attention or just a place to lie down. I had an idea.

General Schwalier had told Colonel Mooy to work with the medical staff to get them everything they needed. I didn't see Pete around right then, so I went ahead and tracked down the head doctor, Lieutenant Colonel Douglas Robb.

"Doug, do you think we should set up a triage center in the Desert Rose dining facility?" I asked.

"Great idea. Here, these two PJs will help you," he said.

We set up a holding area for those in need of "buddy care" first-aid and another area for those needing minor medical procedures. We left the seriously wounded patients in the courtyard near the clinic as they would likely have to be transported to a larger hospital in Dhahran for treatment. I took advantage of a lull in the activities to have a medical technician stitch up some of the larger cuts on my side and leg.

Reconstructing the lists of deployed personnel was challenging and locating each person on the roster was difficult. Squadron commanders, first sergeants, unit supervisors, and volunteers worked together through the night to accomplish this task. By 4:30 a.m., almost seven hours after the bomb went off, we had accounted for all but thirty-four of the approximately 2000 people housed in Khobar Towers. We kept searching the compound for the missing people, trying to determine if they might have been in the blast area. The death toll kept rising; we now had eleven Americans confirmed dead.

In between tasks, I assisted in the triage area. We had stacked most of the dining tables against a far wall. Scrounging for blankets from nearby living quarters, we tried to make people as comfortable as we could—some on the floor and some on tables—as paramedics stopped the bleeding and stitched up wounds. A Saudi triage doctor rotated through the room prioritizing the wounded and identifying those who needed treatment for shock.[2] I can still remember seeing one pararescueman putting stitches in a patient while a friend held a compress on the PJ's forehead to stop his own bleeding. I was so proud of our team.

At about 5:00 a.m., Colonel Boyle called me on the mobile radio, asking me to come to Building 131. There I found General Schwalier standing with a group of white-robed Saudi officials, updating them on our initial response to the bombing. I knew most of these host-nation leaders from interactions during the past year. The responsibility fell on me to give them a walking tour through the rest of our heavily damaged facilities. They expressed their regrets and condolences both to me and to several of the wounded airmen they met. The delegation departed as the sun was beginning to define the horizon with its faint glow.

That was a Close Call

The bomb had gone off eight hours earlier and I still had not been able to tell Judy that I was alive. I learned CNN was broadcasting sketchy details about a bomb explosion in Khobar Towers. I tried to use several telephones, but it appeared that all communication lines in this housing area were still down.

I was tired; I needed to wash my face and clean up a bit. Returning to my room, I found a pair of socks and changed my bloodied undershirts and flight suit. Even though the medical technician had closed the larger gashes, there were still small bits of glass in my side and leg. I had stopped several times during the night to remove small fragments that were protruding far enough to irritate me when they rubbed on the inside of my T-shirt or flight suit.

The blast damage to my room was no longer hidden by darkness. I saw spikes of glass embedded in the concrete wall opposite my blown-out window—some pieces were sticking out of the wall like darts on a dartboard. If I had been a pace slower walking to my bed the night before, I would have taken the full load of the flying glass. Instead, relatively few small projectiles had caught my side and my left leg.

The aluminum frame of my window lay twisted on the floor—torn right out of the concrete. The air conditioner, housed in a metal frame built into the exterior wall, had been blown out of its casing and was lying on the floor below the now empty rectangular hole. My television was on its side; the screen was shattered.

I glanced into the bathroom. My plastic bottle of shampoo, perched precariously on the sill of the small window above the bathtub, was leaking—shot though both sides by flying glass. When the high-pressure shock wave from the blast hit the outer wall of our building, the structure flexed so much that pieces of tile from my shower landed on the opposite side of the bathroom.

Then I found a three-inch piece of the exploded truck in my room. That deformed melted steel had been hurled across a large playing field with such force that it ended up going through my fifth-floor window. It's a good thing my body didn't intercept its high-speed trajectory.

Grateful to be alive, I departed for the airfield. I still needed to meet the airplane from Germany and greet our replacements. A protocol team took the newcomers to temporary quarters. I hurried to get back to work at Khobar Towers.

Approaching the bombsite damage in bright sunlight, it was difficult to comprehend the magnitude of this blast. Investigators later determined that the sewage truck contained a mixture of gasoline and explosive powder equivalent to 20,000 to 30,000 pounds of TNT. The force of the blast was so powerful that it was felt as far as 20 miles away and a crater 85 feet wide and 35 feet deep now marked the spot where the truck had been.

The entire front of the fortress-like structure was gone. I could look right into all the bedrooms. I had a crazy thought. It reminded me of an old dollhouse my sister had when we were young. One side was open to give her access to the rooms, furniture, and dolls. Obviously, though, this was a real-life scene of great tragedy, not make-believe. I was almost ashamed of contemplating the comparison.

We continued organizing unit rosters and double-checking names until we had accounted for everyone. By 9:00 a.m., we confirmed that nineteen Americans had been killed by the blast. By mid-morning, the situation at Khobar Towers had stabilized enough that I could leave. I drove the fifteen minutes back to my office on the air base side.

I called Judy, even though I knew it was the middle of her night in Virginia. I was eager to hear her sweet voice. The sleepy "Hello" on the other end of the line made my emotions swell and I blurted out, "This is Scott, your husband, calling from Dhahran. I'm OK!"

"Scott! Oh Scott!" Judy cried out. "We were so worried. We've been watching the television. It looks terrible. Christiane Amanpour is on her

Building 131 after the terrorist attack. (Courtesy of the United States Air Force)

way. She was on television a little while ago talking about the bomb damage and injuries. Did you get hurt?" Judy shot a burst of words, as she finally was able to release her pent-up emotions.

Time had been a blur for me and I had forgotten that it had been over twelve hours since the bomb went off. For family and friends glued to the television and radio, this must have seemed like an eternity. I am sure in the back of her mind Judy was preparing herself for two Air Force officers wearing their blue Class A uniforms to ring the doorbell. She had lost her dad when she was five years old and her mom when she was eighteen. She was probably thinking her husband would be the next loved one to suffer a premature death. All those terrible thoughts vanished when she heard my voice.

"I'm doing fine, babe," I said, taking a deep breath. "We have to minimize personal calls because there's a lot going on over here. Please pass my love to Jonathan, Jennifer, David, and Katherine. Please let the rest of our family and friends know that I called. Tell them to pray for us. Our hardest hours are probably still ahead. I love you so very much."

"All right," she said. "Thanks for calling, Scott. We'll be praying for you and all the other Americans in Dhahran. We love you, too. Can't wait to see you."

I hung up the phone in my office and sat at my desk, staring straight ahead. What if I been in a different spot in my apartment and had lost an eye in the explosion, as one of my friends did? What if the bomb had detonated a few hours earlier when I was jogging on the road next to Building 131?

The shock was wearing off and the pain of the loss really started to sting. It was a reminder of how short life is and how close I came to losing mine. At the same time, I was keenly aware that my life had been spared for a reason. I thanked God for keeping me safe despite the blast and recommitted myself to being available for a greater purpose.

Still Flying, but Grieving and Honoring the Fallen

But life had to go on. The mission had to continue. I called in a couple of commanders from our fighter squadrons. We discussed the feasibility of flying a four-ship of US aircraft into Iraq the next day or two. Not only would it refocus some of our idle units back on the Southern Watch

Nineteen coffins of service members killed in Dhahran.
(Courtesy of the United States Air Force)

mission, but it would send a powerful message to our Wing that while we might be hurt, we could still fight. It would also send a clear message to the Iraqis and the rest of world that American forces would still enforce the United Nations-mandated no-fly zone.

After thinking through who was available to generate and arm the aircraft, and which pilots would be ready to fly this first mission, my supervisors agreed to press ahead with a plan to fly four F-16s with a 10:00 a.m. takeoff on Saturday, thirty-six hours after the devastating bombing. Our team flew the mission smoothly and safely, as if nothing had ever happened—a tribute to the strength and resiliency of America's warriors.

Colonel Boyle's casualty affairs team did a superb job identifying our dead while under great pressure to deliver numbers and names. Members of the protocol staff were brilliant as they greeted and cared for incoming distinguished visitors and host-nation dignitaries. Their actions enabled me and my senior colleagues to carry out General Schwalier's orders with minimal disruption.

In addition to giving media interviews, I participated in the plane-side ceremony for our deceased comrades before their remains were sent to Dover Air Force Base in Delaware. We watched in silence as the flight-line professionals loaded each flag-draped casket with precision, dignity, and respect as a final tribute to our departed airmen. In addition, I helped to farewell our severely wounded with words of thanks and best wishes as they were transported to Landstuhl Regional Medical Center near Ramstein, Germany, for further care.

We needed to have a memorial service, because many of us had not stopped to honor the fallen as we tried to put our own lives back together again. I called General Schwalier and volunteered to take charge of it.

Our team cleaned out a large warehouse, set up white plastic chairs in neat rows, and ordered nineteen large bouquets of colorful flowers to be put in front of the small stage we constructed for the podium. The massive storeroom now looked like a solemn sanctuary befitting the memorial service we would soon conduct.

Since eighteen of the nineteen airmen killed by the terrorist bomb worked in the operations group, General Schwalier asked me to give a eulogy. It was one of the hardest things I have ever had to do. I kept thinking about my evening jog on that Thursday when I had stopped to speak with the F-15 maintenance supervisor, Master Sergeant Kit Kitson. He and a friend were walking back to Building 131 after having dinner together at the Desert Rose dining facility. Just a few hours later, he was dead. These eighteen men were professional warriors serving under my command. Now they were gone.

It was hard to know what to include in my eulogy. I had been up for almost two straight days and felt a bit frazzled. Now I had to honor these men, comfort those who grieved, and put everything that had happened to us into some patriotic context and eternal perspective.

The room was packed when I arrived. Television cameras were positioned to the left of the stage; I could see Christiane Amanpour with her TV crew. I walked directly to my chair on the right side of the podium, making sure I did not get emotional before the service started. Lieutenant Colonel Thomas Shafer, the deployed commander of the 71st Rescue Squadron, was first to speak after the chaplain gave an introduction and opening prayer. Tom, himself wounded, gave a very moving talk about his roommate and other squadron personnel who were killed in the blast. Tom also relayed that he could not find his boots in the rubble after the bombing, so he put on Chris Adams' boots . . . he had been wearing his dead roommate's flight boots since he laced them up that night in the dark. Tom had worked without stopping until now to make sure his people were cared for and that family members of all who had died were notified quickly and properly.

The commander of the deployed F-15 squadron, Lieutenant Colonel Douglas Cochran, then told some personal stories about his airmen who had lost their lives. Twelve of the dead were from his unit and had been deployed from Eglin Air Force Base in Florida.

Now it was my turn to speak. General Binnie Peay, commander of the US Central Command, and a host of dignitaries were there, but I spoke directly to my friends and coworkers. I began by reading the names of the nineteen slowly.

"Captain Christopher Adams, Captain Leland Haun, Master Sergeant Michael Heiser, Master Sergeant Kendall Kitson. . . ."

I was moved by the response. A few shrieked in anguish, others just held their friends and cried. Most looked solemnly straight ahead fighting back tears, hiding their broken hearts. This was the first time that many of us had paused since the bombing to reflect on each airman we were honoring, to remember their names and faces, to feel the loss, and to express our grief.

I understood this was part of the grieving and healing process, but it was very hard to talk as I looked out over the audience and shared their pain. Many in front of me were close colleagues of those who had lost their lives just three days ago. We were bonded in a special way as a unit of Americans who understood in a new way that freedom is not free. Indeed, freedom is not free.

The week that followed the bombing revealed our many heroes—leaders who stepped up to the challenge, warriors who responded with calm and courage when attacked, and men and women who made me proud to be an American.[3] I saw it all night in the way people put themselves in harm's way to make sure others were safe. People supported each other, comforted each other, and practiced our core value of "service before self." It was very impressive to see our little band come together with such cohesion and unity of effort to get a job done.

Even though we are tough combat warriors, we are also very human. I still grieve for the friends and families of our fallen who will always carry the pain of June 25, 1996. Nineteen colleagues lost their lives while serving the United States—they are American heroes, each one of them.[4]

Change of Command

Exactly a month later, my wife and I descended the aircraft to a welcoming crowd of 39th Wing leaders and Turkish officers at Incirlik Air Base, Turkey. We had lived in Izmir on Turkey's west coast for two years in the late 1980s and had learned to speak some Turkish. I had also been deployed from Germany to Incirlik Air Base (near Adana—not far from Turkey's

Map of Eastern Turkey.

southeastern coast) in 1992 to fly Provide Comfort combat missions over Iraq. It was great to be back.

The next day was the change of command. Lieutenant General Richard Bethurem, my new boss, came from Italy to officiate. The change of command is a dignified ceremony steeped in military tradition that predates the Norman conquest of England. This formal transfer of responsibility, authority, and accountability takes place whenever a new commanding officer assumes command and control of a military unit.

The centerpiece of the ceremony is the symbolic passing of the guidon, the unit flag that identifies the organization. The guidon is transferred from the outgoing commander to the incoming one, ensuring the unit and its personnel are never without official leadership.

Whenever I participate in a change of command ceremony, I think of the quote from Victor Hugo that says, "Change your leaves; keep intact your roots."[5]

Compartmentalized Days

It was wonderful to be back together as a family after a year of separation while I was in Dhahran. My oldest son, Jonathan, had just started his freshman year at the US Air Force Academy, so we always felt as if someone was missing at mealtimes and during other family activities. Jennifer was a junior in high school, and David and Katherine were twelve and nine respectively. As she had always done on our Air Force moves, Judy was determined to restore normalcy to our home expeditiously and to make this new assignment as memorable as possible.

While returning to Incirlik Air Base was relatively easy, taking command of a wing fully engaged in combat operations was a challenge. Yes, flying combat missions in support of Operation Northern Watch was similar to my experiences in Dhahran; however in some ways, it wasn't the same at all. This was the first time I would fly combat missions while living at home. It was almost surreal to have breakfast with my family, kiss my wife good-bye, and then drive to the combat side of the base where I would brief up, suit up, and arm up before taking off with three other fighter pilots to enter a dangerous combat zone over Iraq.

On one of those days while in flight, bright symbols on the threat-warning receiver started flashing wildly just below the glare shield in my left peripheral vision. Simultaneously, the distinctive and dreaded aural tones in my helmet indicated one or more enemy missiles had been launched at our formation.

"Rumble 3, singer six, right, four o'clock!" a flight member shouted on our inter-flight frequency. I reacted by immediately rolling upside down, dispensing lots of aluminum chaff to confuse the missile's radar, and maneuvering hard with abrupt flight-path changes to force the surface-to-air missile to miss my aircraft. Two flight members reported seeing a missile smoke trail pass behind our formation.

Back at Incirlik, we discussed the details of this missile event with our intelligence section and finished the mission debriefing. Then I went to my office to do some paperwork before going home. As I walked through the front door to my house shortly before 6:00 p.m., my children rushed up to meet me. Hugging them, I heard Judy greet me from the kitchen.

"How was your day, honey?" she asked.

"It was fine, babe. What are we having for dinner?"

It was hard to believe I was having this compartmentalized conversation with my wife and getting ready to sit down with my family to discuss their day—school, drum lessons, homework, and all. Just six hours ago I was aggressively maneuvering my combat-configured F-16 to save my life while an Iraqi missile was trying to take it.

Another dangerous situation occurred about a month later when a very large hawk flew down my F-16's intake while I was flying far inside Iraqi territory. I immediately zoomed the aircraft to get as much altitude as I could, while turning northward and slowing to maximum-range airspeed. Assisted by the little thrust my severely damaged engine was still producing, I was able to land safely at Diyarbakir Air Base in Turkey. Again, I did not want to reveal some of these treacherous ordeals that would cause my family to worry about me, when my home life seemed so normal.

I enjoyed being the commander of the 39th Wing and the newly established 7440th Air and Space Expeditionary Wing as a colonel.[6] In essence, I was "mayor" of the base and had to ensure the 1,200 US personnel deployed to Incirlik had food, billeting, and places to work. I was ultimately responsible for making sure personnel were trained, aircraft were operable, and combat missions were flown in accordance with the air tasking order.

And of course, I was responsible for security. The Kurdistan Workers' Party, commonly known as PKK, and the Revolutionary People's Liberation Party/Front began to target Turkish government facilities and military installations in 1996.[7] The threat to our base and personnel increased significantly.

We installed barricades around our critical buildings and set up an alarm and loudspeaker system that could be heard around the air base. The Wing practiced drills to disperse our base population in the event of a chemical attack, and we conducted exercises to prepare our families and dependents for an evacuation of non-essential personnel. While one can never prepare for every eventuality, I believe we were ready for most attack scenarios.

From experience, I was convinced the best way to keep our people safe was to have a close relationship with my Turkish counterparts. The Turkish commander on the base and his personnel were responsible for perimeter security and for jointly manning the entry points with US security forces. I visited my counterpart's office every week, and Judy and I met with his family for a social event at least once a month. We worked hard to know what was happening on the Turkish side so that I could write timely letters of appreciation or condolence, recognize significant events, or reinforce positive activities.

I also wanted to build a strong team and therefore introduced several initiatives to reduce the perceived and real divisions between our officers and the enlisted force. We instituted an informal "Breakfast with the Boss" every week where I would meet with unit representatives to discuss issues and hear their complaints. We also instituted regularly scheduled meetings with groups of airmen, junior non-commissioned officers, and senior NCOs to round out my understanding of enlisted issues.

Another highly successful initiative was the "Airman Mentor" program. We would select a junior airman each month to spend thirty days in the Wing commander's office as my mentor. More accurately, we mentored each other. I wanted the opportunity to hear directly about issues from an enlisted person's perspective. This individual would attend all my meetings and accompany me on my professional activities. This airman would often ride in the air refueling tanker when I flew an F-16 combat mission to watch me fill up my aircraft's fuel tanks before going into Iraq. I also included my airman in my weekly base-wide radio show, called "Let's Talk Turkey." This program was so successful that I used it in subsequent assignments when practical and appropriate.

Leadership Lessons

My time at Incirlik reinforced several leadership lessons that became professional priorities. First, my experiences growing up in Africa, living through the Khobar Towers bombing, and protecting our personnel against terrorist attacks targeting Incirlik Air Base taught me to make security and safety part of my initial leadership plans. One must never be arrogant or complacent about personal and physical protection because we are most vulnerable when we least expect an attack. I have always "rocked the boat" when I believed I did not have enough protective forces or when the threat level was too high to safely and successfully perform our mission.

Another lesson was about teamwork, building relationships, and getting the job done. Whether conducting negotiations, cooperating with international counterparts, or striving to accomplish a challenging mission, each individual must feel that he or she is an integral part of the process and that his or her input matters. As the senior leader—and servant leader—it was my job to ensure all team members understood our vision, mission, and essential tasks. When leading an effective organization, there is no room for "good old boy networks." Everyone has to be an active team member and it was my job to make sure they knew their job, received the requisite training, and had access to the resources needed to be successful.

The enlisted cadre in Turkey gave me an honor I deeply treasure to this day. I was surprised and humbled to be inducted into the enlisted ranks as an honorary chief master sergeant.

Dressed in the Air Force formal mess attire, which is the military equivalent of a civilian tuxedo, I accompanied Judy into the large ballroom at the Incirlik All-Ranks Club. We strode under nine rows of crossed swords, each set held by members of the nine ranks from airman basic to chief master sergeant. Over three hundred enlisted personnel attended the gala dinner to witness this event. I closed the evening with a speech expressing my deepest gratitude for this priceless honor and pledged to live in accordance with the words and intent of the Chief's Creed.[8]

On the way home, I commented to Judy, "Making Chief means more to me than being promoted brigadier general, and the responsibilities are about the same."

I was both touched and blessed by this meaningful gesture of trust by those I had the honor to command. During the remainder of my Air Force career, I would continue to seek and include the enlisted perspective in my command decisions.

We had been at Incirlik for just under two years, but it was time to move again.

10

Making a Difference

There are two primary choices in life;
to accept conditions as they exist, or accept
responsibility for changing them.

— Dennis Waitley

ON JUNE 7, 1998, TWO WEEKS AFTER TAKING COMMAND of the 3rd Wing at Elmendorf Air Force Base in Alaska, I went to McChord Air Force Base in Washington to cheer on our 23-person C-130 team from the 517th Airlift Squadron that was representing our Wing at the 1998 Airlift Rodeo.[1] This biennial airlift contest brought sixty-three teams and two thousand people together from air mobility forces around the world.

Our C-130 aircrew flew on three consecutive days, performing a different type of airdrop mission each day. On all three drops, Elmendorf performed perfectly—hitting every turn point and gaining maximum points for safety, precise takeoffs, altitude control, and the avoidance of enemy threats. On landing, our aircrew put the C-130 down within a 400-foot landing zone at the proper airspeed. Elmendorf's maintenance team also played a key role as they performed flawlessly.

After five intense days of competition, the Elmendorf team proudly carried home six trophies, including the Rodeo's top honor, Best Air Mobility Wing. We also carried the pride that comes from knowing we had competed against the best units in the world and had won.[2]

In addition to being one of the largest operational Wings in the US Air Force, the 3rd Wing provided support to several tenant units operating on the base. The largest of these was the 11th Air Force under the command of Lieutenant General David McCloud, with whom I was developing a strong professional relationship. General McCloud had taken command of this organization seven months before I arrived. As avid an aviator as I was, he shared my long-range vision for the base and was open to my ideas. I was eager to tell him about our Wing's over-the-top success at the Airlift Rodeo.

Standing next to our C-130 being loaded for the trip back home, I dialed General McCloud's telephone number. Surely he would be up by 8:00 a.m. I couldn't call any later as we would be boarding the C-130 within five minutes. By adding instead of subtracting the one-hour time change, I unfortunately gave my commander a six o'clock wake-up call on a Saturday morning.

General McCloud was very kind, though, and was excited to learn about the Wing's stellar performance. "I'll be out there to welcome you back to Elmendorf," he said, and we ended the call. Sure enough, he was there when we arrived.

One month later, July 26, 1998, I was sitting in the base chapel with my family when I felt a tap on my left shoulder. A security police officer motioned me to follow him. Once outside the chapel door, he stopped and spoke to me with a hushed voice.

"We think General McCloud is down. He was flying over Fort Richardson. An eyewitness saw his airplane in a tailspin. The support group commander is at the command post. He asked you to join him."

My heart sank. Lieutenant General McCloud was a superb fighter pilot and a brilliant thinker. He was a model Air Force officer and a fighter pilot's fighter pilot. Judy and I had bonded with the McClouds during the six weeks we had been together at Elmendorf. I refused to believe he was hurt.

Slipping back inside the chapel, I gave our car keys to Judy and whispered that I had a meeting to attend and I would get a ride home later. On the way to the command post, the officer and I passed Anne McCloud jogging along the road, as she often did with her husband. I did not want her to see me now.

Colonel Joel Peterson, the support group commander, met me at the command post door and ushered me into a private room.

"We're pretty sure General McCloud's Yak-54 crashed. Three

individuals called the command post to report that a small red airplane doing acrobatics over by Fort Richardson had gone straight up and then fell to the earth while spinning. We have two crash-rescue teams en route," he said.

Within minutes, the first rescue team on the scene called back, reporting that they had found the aircraft nose down, caught in some trees in a wooded area near the paratroop drop zone. I knew I would have to be the one to inform Anne about the accident.

Dave McCloud had lots of experience in both military and civilian aircraft. Like me, he loved to fly and seized every opportunity to get airborne. Only four months earlier, he had purchased a new Russian-built Yakovlev-54,[3] a single-engine, acrobatic aircraft, after logging many hours on his previous Yak-52. I remember going with him to the large hanger where he kept it. Gently touching the bright red airframe as we talked about its capabilities, Dave beamed with pride.

Now he was gone. After telling Judy of the accident, I drove both of us to the 11th Air Force commander's house and we knocked on the back door. We found Anne in the kitchen with her daughter Robyn who was visiting from Chicago. Their faces looked worried—Dave had not returned for lunch.

I had to inform Anne that her husband and the love of her life had died that morning in an aircraft accident. Judy and I stayed to comfort her as long as possible. When I had to leave to prepare for the official notification that was standard protocol when the Air Force loses one of its members, Judy remained at the house with the McClouds.

Returning dressed in Class A dress blue uniforms, the base chaplain, the mortuary affairs officer, and I walked to the McClouds' front door. I rang the doorbell. Anne answered the door and invited us in. We stayed standing and formally faced Anne.

"Anne," I said, "I'm very sorry to have to inform you that your husband, Lieutenant General David McCloud, was killed this morning in an aircraft accident involving his Yak-54. We are deeply sorry for this loss and express the sincere condolences of our senior Air Force leadership and the Elmendorf family."

I went over and hugged Anne as she cried quietly on my shoulder. When she was ready, Anne sat down as the chaplain and mortuary affairs officer offered their assistance and the support of their offices. I again expressed my condolences and deep personal loss, and then we departed.

Judy and I made sure there was food and drinks at the McCloud residence for friends who stopped by to support Anne and her two children during this time of grief. When it was appropriate, I spent time with the family to hear their preferences for the memorial service.

Five days later, we gathered in a large aircraft maintenance hangar to celebrate Lieutenant General David McCloud's life and passion for flying. The ceremony concluded with a fifteen-cannon salute, which thundered though the hangar and shook the ground like an earthquake. As the thick, white smoke cleared, we moved outside to watch four F-15s fly overhead to perform the missing man formation in honor of our fallen friend and comrade-in-arms. This ceremony was more familiar than I ever wanted it to be.

Honoring a Distinguished Heritage

I had been promoted to brigadier general in 1997 during my assignment at Incirlik Air Base. Now, at Elmendorf Air Force Base, Alaska, I commanded one of the Air Force's largest installations. Located just outside Anchorage, the 3rd Wing included twenty-three squadrons, seventy-two aircraft, and a total population of 25,550 active-duty personnel, civilian employees, family members, and retirees. Our mission was to provide units ready to project air power around the world. The busy base was also a critical logistics hub for supplies and equipment en route to other locations in the Pacific theater.

While some aspects of Elmendorf were superb, my initial impression was that this installation needed an overall facelift and more visual indicators of unit pride. Tracing its history to the Army Surveillance Group activated on July 1, 1919, the 3rd Wing was the oldest continuously serving unit in the Air Force.[4] Unfortunately, this distinguished heritage and long legacy of outstanding service was not evident on the base or in our facilities.

Adding an aircraft static display to each main entrance was the first step in changing the airbase's bland first impression. Relocating the softball diamond in front of the Wing headquarters and replacing it with our Heritage Park was the next step. This new airpark displayed six aircraft that had been an integral part of our aviation history: the F-15, F-4, F-102, F-89, T-33, and C-130. Our base newspaper began running stories reflecting our illustrious history, and squadrons began adding more historical memorabilia to their unit decorations.

After ten months of intense preparation, we celebrated the 3rd Wing's 80th anniversary over the Independence Day weekend. It was a fun-filled

Scott (left) with son, Jonathan, in 1997.

two days as we commemorated the Wing's rich history with an emphasis on pride and professionalism. We brought back five previous Wing commanders and offered tours of all the squadrons and our aircraft.

In addition to hosting the 80th anniversary gala and award ceremony, we inaugurated our new Heritage Park, the Wall of Heroes, and the Prisoner of War/Missing in Action memorial. The base open house for the local community kicked off at noon with aerial demonstrations and tours of static displays. In the end, we had more than 50,000 people from the Anchorage vicinity on base for the open house and air show.

My proudest moment took place after the Air Force Academy glider flew a series of precise acrobatics over the runway followed by a flawless landing in the grassy area next to the runway. When my son, Jonathan, emerged from the sleek glider, I felt the inner elation that comes from being a proud father who is watching his son mature into a young adult. Jonathan had chosen to attend the US Air Force Academy to pursue his passion for aviation. He excelled in flight training and quickly became a glider instructor at the academy. Judy and I were proud to witness this early milestone on his way to becoming a top Air Force fighter pilot.

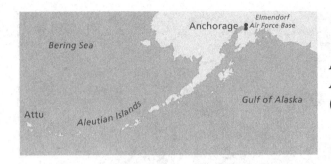

*Map of the
Aleutian chain
(Attu is at the left).*

There were many indications that the base family was becoming more united and prouder of our outstanding heritage of flight and of the significant role we played in our nation's defense. One development stands out for me.

Lt Gen McCloud had been working to retrieve a P-38 Lightning[5] that had crashed January 1, 1945, on the island of Attu in the Aleutians, the western-most point of Alaska. The P-38 Lightning was America's first turbocharged combat aircraft and was far ahead of its time when it first flew in 1939. It truly was a product of daring and brilliance.[4] In this incident, a pilot named Second Lieutenant Robert Nesmith was troubleshooting a left propeller problem when the aircraft hit a snow bank and bounced back up into the air. Lt Nesmith managed a smooth wheels-up landing on the drifted snow. The damaged P-38G, tail number 13400, had been resting untouched in Attu's Temnak Valley for more than five decades.[6]

I believed this P-38 would not only make a fitting memorial to the men of the 54th Fighter Squadron, who risked so much to take back the only American soil that was lost to the Japanese in World War II, but it also would symbolize the resilient spirit of General McCloud.

P-38 Lightning on Attu Island.
(Courtesy of the United States
Air Force)

Restored P-38 on display in Elmendorf AFB. (Courtesy of the United States Air Force)

After negotiating approval from the US Fish and Wildlife Service to recover the plane, I authorized Don Delk and Ed Lamm, civil-service maintenance officers, to retrieve the P-38G and restore it at Elmendorf. These two individuals had more than seventy years of aircraft-maintenance experience between them and were passionate about this assignment.

In June 1999, six of us set out to retrieve this only known G model in existence. Contrary to what we had expected to find in the harsh Aleutian environment, the aircraft was still in surprisingly good condition. Don Delk and I dug the nose gear out of the mud and then we all worked together to disassemble the major components of the P-38. We used a helicopter to sling each aircraft piece to the Coast Guard station on Attu. The parts were then loaded onto an Alaska Air National Guard C-130 for the trip back to Anchorage.

The "Lightning Save" team rebuilt the crashed P-38 piece by piece and the magnificently restored aircraft was mounted in its final resting place near Heritage Park. Unfortunately, Don Delk passed away a few days before the P-38's dedication, but his fingerprints remained all over this beautiful P-38G Lightning. This aircraft now provides a fitting memorial to our former commander of the Alaskan Command, Lieutenant General David J. McCloud, and to those members of the 54th Fighter Squadron who died in the Aleutian Campaign during the Second World War.

Practicing Principled Behavior with Fairness

I wished Lt Gen McCloud had been around to support me when I stood alone against what I believed was injustice. The incident took place before I arrived at Elmendorf, but after taking command I sensed that perceptions surrounding the case were dragging down unit morale.

On July 20, 1997, Captain Charles (Corky) Corcoran was ferrying an F-15 to the depot at Warner Robbins Air Force Base in Georgia for scheduled maintenance. After spending the night at Rickenbacker International Airport in Ohio, he started the engines with the help of two line-service technicians working on the ramp.

As Captain Corcoran began to taxi, one of the technicians signaled for him to stop. With the left engine shut down and the canopy raised, the ground technician told Capt Corcoran that something was lost or missing. But Corky saw no cockpit indications of a problem. He decided to press ahead with the mission and flew uneventfully to Robbins Air Force Base in Georgia.

The post-flight inspection at Robbins revealed damage to the compressor blades of the aircraft's left engine. Capt Corcoran annotated this issue in the aircraft maintenance forms and returned to Elmendorf on a commercial flight. When the engine was taken apart for repairs, further inspection revealed damage totaling $861,460. This was now a reportable mishap and would require a formal investigation. Depot maintenance personnel concluded that the engine had ingested a noise-protection headset.

The safety investigators concluded the mishap was caused when the "line-service technician disregarded pre-start instructions and entered the intake area *[the hazardous zone in front of the aircraft engine's air inlet]*." A month later, a Letter of Counseling was put in Capt Corcoran's records, documenting that he had demonstrated "poor judgment," and would be grounded for two weeks. The case was closed and Corky returned to flying status in the squadron.

He continued to perform superbly at Elmendorf and was selected for F-15C Fighter Weapons School in October, to be followed by an assignment to Eglin Air Force Base in Florida. The Corcorans packed up and moved in December 1997.

But things were not settled, after all. In January 1998, General Patrick Gamble, the commander of Pacific Air Forces in Hawaii, reopened the investigation based on new findings. A new safety report concluded that Capt Corcoran failed to brief the line-service technician adequately, which caused him to get too close to the engine. The report also stated that the pilot knowingly accepted a damaged aircraft for flight, causing even more damage to the jet engine.

Faced with this new information, my predecessor pulled Capt Corcoran out of Fighter Weapons School on March 20, 1998, cancelled his planned assignment to Eglin, reassigned him to Elmendorf in a non-flying job, and fined him $2,000 as part of the Article 15 punishment.

In June, Capt Corcoran submitted a formal appeal to the 11th Air Force commander, but the appeal was still in the coordination process when Lieutenant General McCloud died. The interim 11th Air Force commander sent a short letter to the 3rd Wing denying Capt Corcoran's appeal.

Since I was a newcomer to the situation and was not sure of all the pertinent details, I summoned Capt Corcoran to my office on July 10, to hear his side of the story. I then drove to the flight line and sat in an F-15 cockpit to recreate the scenario that Corky, as we all called him, had described to me. I concluded it would have been almost impossible to see a technician walking in front of the engine's intake while the aircraft canopy was closed.

Recounting Capt Corcoran's account in my mind, I believed he should have suspected something had gone down the intake, but I was convinced he did not know anything had actually been ingested. It was obvious to me that Corky had exhibited very poor judgment, but I concluded that he did not intentionally violate flying regulations.

I asked myself if Corky's mishap was a "tolerable mistake" or a "crime." Were his actions premeditated, were they a willful disregard of directives or regulations, were they a dereliction of duty, or did Capt Corcoran merely lack sound judgment?

In the end, I was convinced that although Capt Corcoran had demonstrated extremely poor judgment and had made a terrible mistake by deciding to fly his F-15 that morning, he had not done anything deserving the punishment he was given. I called the acting commander of 11th Air Force, but he informed me that he would not change his mind—the case was closed and Capt Corcoran was guilty as charged. I told him that I would elevate this appeal to the commander of the Pacific Air Forces.

Sitting in my empty office, I spent an hour going over the details to ensure I was not "falling on my sword" for a captain who was actually guilty. Convinced more than ever, I drafted a letter of resignation from the US Air Force in long hand. I penned that I had examined all the statements Capt Corcoran made, not from the luxury of hindsight, but from the perspective of what he knew on the day he gave testimony.

Satisfied with my decision, I picked up the phone and dialed the Pacific Air Forces commander. "I believe in a 'one-crime Air Force,'" I explained, "but I run a Wing that tolerates honest, even expensive, mistakes. There's no question that Corky made a serious mistake, but his poor judgment was not premeditated, nor does it constitute a crime, in my view. I want to give him another chance. I cannot in good conscience be part of a system of justice that does not seek to protect both the Air Force and the accused."

I paused to give my boss an opportunity to accept my veiled offer of resignation.

Having listened quietly to my monologue, General Gamble responded, "Scott, if you feel that strongly, do what you believe is best and I'll support you."

"Thank you, sir," I answered. "I appreciate it that you trust my judgment."

I scheduled a Wing aircrew meeting where Corky could tell his story, admit his mistakes, and reveal the lessons he learned. After he spoke, I would give my perspectives on honesty, integrity, character, and trust. As his peers arrived, there was very little small talk. Corky took the stage and recalled the events of the day, stressing the lessons he had learned through this painful process. He was very honest, insightful, and instructive in his comments.

I concluded my remarks by saying, "The events of July 1997 are behind us now. Captain Corcoran has been formally reprimanded and the incident has been documented in his records. I plan to let him start flying with the 19th Fighter Squadron soon."

With that, I embraced Corky and told the Wing to "get on to being the best Wing in the Air Force."

There was a thunderous standing ovation and shouts from his squadron mates of "Cor-ky! Cor-ky!" This was a significant turning point in the Wing's performance. It initiated the healing process that improved Wing morale and united us as "Team Elmendorf."

It has been a real pleasure to watch Capt Corcoran's stellar career. He completed the F-15C Fighter Weapons Instructor Course as the top graduate and went on to be one of the first pilots to fly and test the F-22 stealth fighter. He has been a superb squadron and operations group commander, and has served with the highest distinction in the Pentagon.

Colonel Charles Corcoran later went on to be the commander of the 3rd Wing at Elmendorf Air Force Base—the same position I held sixteen years before when I intervened in regard to his professional fate. Corky was definitely worth keeping—he has been a model and a mentor to many young fighter pilots. I would be the first to follow him into combat any day.

Fairness and justice are very important principles to me. I strongly believe it is important to end injustice and to make life fairer for everyone whenever possible.

Inspection Time

During my tenure as Wing commander at Elmendorf, we had thirteen inspections, and the 3rd Wing was rated "Excellent" on almost all of them. However, the one that made me the most proud of our team was the Initial Response Readiness Inspection (IRRI).[7]

We did not know exactly when the Pacific Air Forces Inspector General team (PACAF/IG) would arrive for the "no notice" inspection, but we knew the general time frame during which to expect its visit. This would be a five-day evaluation to assess the Wing's ability to deploy personnel and equipment to a combat location in support of the Pacific Command's contingency plans while under attack at our home base.

I was confident that we were ready for the inspection after we completed our last realistic exercise. Things ran so smoothly that I was really just a cheerleader, saying things like, "Excellence is our standard; outstanding is our objective" in response to our team's performance. At the next week's staff meeting, I volunteered a friendly challenge.

"I'll shave my head if the Wing receives an Outstanding rating on the IRRI."

Many thought my hair was free from threat because no Pacific Air Forces wing had ever received this top rating since the Air Force was formed in 1948. My outlook was different, though. I quietly planned on being bald in a few weeks.

Mrs. Joanne Frank, my secretary, burst into my office.

"Control tower just called. IG's on final approach. They'll be here in ten minutes," she exclaimed excitedly.

Together with other senior leaders, we rushed to the passenger terminal to meet and greet the team of Pacific Air Forces inspectors. Everyone was smiling as we all shook hands.

There is a "little white lie" often heard when a no-notice IG visit begins. They say, "We're here to help you," and we politely respond, "We're glad you're here."

At 9:00 a.m. the next morning, the inspection kicked off and we all quickly transitioned into our "game faces." The Wing demonstrated a sense of urgency as its squadrons prepared to deploy. Maintenance teams configured aircraft in accordance with the IG's tasking while other personnel loaded pallets with mobility gear. Pilots were briefed and put into crew rest for the next day's deployment flight. Our innovative tracking system for wing and squadron deployment enabled us to stay on top of anomalies and fix them as they occurred.

Our team was reacting so well to PACAF/IG exercise inputs that the inspectors put buildings off limits, shut down key transportation arteries, and diverted our security police to respond to simulated intruders. On the last day of the exercise, I was taken "out of action" so the IG team could evaluate how well the Wing would operate without its commander. (Everyone did great—I should be gone more often!)

As I watched the aircraft preparation, I knew we had met the criteria for an "Excellent." The Wing still had one broken F-15C that we would likely fix in time to deploy and we had an F-15E that was completely unserviceable with an inoperative heads-up display (HUD). I went to bed believing we would be able to generate seventy-one of our seventy-two aircraft for deployment in the morning.

When I checked on our operational status early the next morning, I was surprised to learn we had generated 100 percent of our aircraft, even the F-15E with the broken heads-up display.

Colonel Dan Falvey, the officer in charge of logistics, explained, "One of my airmen checked the HUD in our emergency procedures cockpit trainer. When the part numbers matched, he called the F-15E program office at Wright-Paterson Air Force Base last night and requested permission for a one-time-only flight using that part."

With the approval message in hand, the avionics specialist quickly transferred the heads-up display from the Wing training simulator to the waiting F-15E. It worked perfectly. We now met the criteria for an "Outstanding" in aircraft generation.

One day later, we all assembled in the base theater for the final PACAF/IG inspection briefing. I was happy to see many signs with our *Excellence is our Standard; Outstanding is our Objective* slogan. Little did I know that on the back side of these signs was a photoshopped picture of me with a shaved cranium. The room quieted down as the IG team walked in and took their seats on the front row.

Picture of Scott that was used to fire up the crowd.

The IG team leader walked to the podium on the elevated stage to narrate the IG's PowerPoint™ presentation. As he read off each inspection category and followed them by mostly Outstanding and a few Excellent ratings, the slides changed appropriately. With each successive Outstanding score, the applause grew louder. Finally the audience was on their feet cheering. Then came the final slide.

"The overall rating for the 3rd Wing is . . . Outstanding."

The place went wild. The cheering gradually morphed into words that I slowly began to decipher in my joy. "Shave it off! Shave it off! Shave it off!"

I knew what was next. The vice wing commander rolled out a barber chair from behind the curtains on the stage, and then my wife came up and shaved off my hair. Words were drowned out by thunderous clapping, mixed with ear-numbing shouting and cheering. The 3rd Wing had done what no other Wing had done for five decades nor has done since—it achieved an Outstanding rating on a Pacific Air Forces Initial Response Readiness Inspection!

That was more than worth losing a little hair over.

Making People a Priority

More than all the awards, I was most proud of the things our team did for people.

When Judy and I arrived at Elmendorf Air Force Base in June 1998, I recognized that the Wing needed a centralized place to meet, greet, process, and train its new arrivals. I had seen a boarded-up, two-story brick building not too far from the main gate that had once been an Airman dining hall, and thought, *this would be the perfect place for our new Arctic Warrior Orientation Center.*

In mid-January 1999, we cut the ribbon on our new one-stop welcome center that was complete with parking, heat, babysitting facilities, and snacks for military members and their families who were arriving at Elmendorf. We condensed the long and arduous orientation process into two well-organized weeks tailored to the individual's needs. The Arctic Warrior Orientation Center concept became the new standard and other military bases have constructed similar centers patterned after our model.

We also started a Warrior Care Program to serve our Wing's personnel. Noticing that all of the officer houses at Elmendorf had garage-door openers, while our enlisted personnel had to get out of their cars in Alaska's often freezing temperatures and manually lift the heavy garage doors open, I decided this needed to change. Two weeks later, we ordered six hundred thirty garage-door openers, and our civil engineering electricians installed the necessary electrical outlets in each garage. We used volunteer labor to install the openers with an efficient, assembly-line process and all of our enlisted personnel had garage-door openers by Christmas.

This self-help program proved so successful that we then put up fences around enlisted family housing areas in the summer and upgraded more than seven hundred bathrooms, tearing out the old sinks and replacing them with vanities, mirrors, and medicine cabinets.

In order to stimulate good ideas and better ways of doing business, we initiated the "Idea Fair" that was held once a quarter. Our inventors designed new tools, optimized procedures, and eliminated waste with streamlined processes. We reduced our aircraft overhaul timeline by 50 percent, repaired parts that the Air Force recommended we discard, and received authority to manufacture parts locally that were difficult to get through the standard procurement process.

However, the best thing that came out of the idea fair was an attitude toward finding innovative ways to do things "faster, cheaper, better." Gone was the old mindset of settling to do things the way they had always been done.

Getting Lost or Asking for Directions?

Not everything I did made people happy. For example, some locals will always remember me as "the Wing commander who couldn't find his way around so he changed the street signs." While it may be partly true that I could not find a house based on its street address, I changed the signs because the old system was not working as the base grew in size and expanded its facilities.[8]

When civil engineers laid out the base during the Second World War, they used an arc and radial system to number all the buildings. This numbering system was difficult for drivers and pedestrians because house numbers did not follow a sequence as one moved along a street.

We decided to switch to a standard grid system. This numbering scheme was easy to understand. The first two digits of a building number gave the location along the north-south scale and the next two digits described the position along the east-west scale—the intersection of these coordinates was the location of the looked-for facility. Fire trucks, ambulance drivers, command post controllers, and pizza delivery cars now only needed the four-digit street address number, and they would be able to easily locate any house or facility on base.

Knowing we would have to change everyone's house number, we figured we might as well change the street names also while we were at it. We decided to swap names such as Prune Street and Pansy Court for names that were significant to our Wing or to the state of Alaska.

After numerous town hall meetings, newspaper articles, and mail notices, a team of technicians from the 3rd Civil Engineering Squadron replaced more than five hundred street signs and nine hundred sixty building numbers—all on one Saturday morning.

After the new signs went up, a few people who did not like the change voiced their loud objection. The *Air Force Times* newspaper covered the story with an article asking the question, "What happens if you get lost driving around Elmendorf Air Force Base, Alaska?"

It continued, "If you're General Scott Gration, the new base commander, you have every street sign, building number, and residential address changed in favor of a system you hope will be more organized and understandable."

One unhappy individual wrote a letter to the editor saying, "Why can't we have women Wing Commanders? When women get lost, they just stop and ask for directions."

Freezing Final Flight

It was now time to leave Alaska. The Air Force had reassigned me to a very good job on the Joint Staff in the Pentagon, but I knew that my military flying days were probably over. Fortunate to fly jet fighters until reaching the rank of brigadier general, I would leave the cockpit with more than five thousand flight hours and more than two thousand hours flown as an instructor pilot.

I decided to make my last flight special by taking Timmothy Dickens, the Wing's top chief master sergeant, up in the back seat of a two-seat F-15 (yes, his name is spelled, "Timmothy"). It was mid-January and blistering cold. We briefed the flight early so we would have enough time to change into our polar-fleece undergarments and don the oversized flight suits.

The sun would not rise until 9:57 a.m., so it was still dark as we walked together to our waiting F-15D. We both were shivering—the temperature and wind-chill factor combined to make us feel as if it were 15 degrees Fahrenheit below zero. Before climbing into my front cockpit and closing the canopy, I made sure Chief Dickens was strapped securely into the back seat.

I used the intercom to explain everything I was doing so the chief would not be surprised when the engines rumbled to life or the stick moved as I did my flight-control checks. We taxied to the end of the runway and I switched my radio to the control tower's frequency.

"Tower, Warrior One, ready for takeoff. Request quick climb," I transmitted into the tight fitting oxygen mask attached to my grey helmet.

"Warrior One, Tower, wind 250 at 12 knots, cleared for takeoff. Quick climb approved," the tower controller replied.

I acknowledged the takeoff clearance and asked my passenger if he was ready for the ride of his life. "Yes, sir," Chief Dickens replied with a mix of apprehension and excitement in his voice.

"It's very cold today—this jet's gonna accelerate like a scalded jackrabbit. Hold on," I said as we taxied onto the freshly plowed runway.

I pushed the throttles up to military power, released brakes, and then slammed the throttles as far forward as they would go. The afterburners kicked in and the F-15 threw us back in our seat as it shot down the runway. In just 1,800 feet, we were airborne with the airspeed indicator accelerating past 150 miles per hour. By the end of the runway, we were going 400 miles per hour with speed still increasing. I pulled the nose straight up and we watched Elmendorf grow smaller behind the screaming Eagle as dawn began to chase away the darkness. Approaching 18,000 feet of altitude, I rolled the aircraft smoothly onto its back and pulled the F-15's nose to the horizon. We rolled out pointing toward Alaska's highest mountain peak.

As we cruised toward Mount McKinley, now known as Denali, the rising sun slowly began to illuminate the top of the snow-covered pinnacle—it looked like a special holiday candle just lit for my last flight. The yellow glow continued to wake the sleeping valley as we swooped down to find moose and caribou resting in the morning shadows. After an hour of frolicking near the snow-covered tundra, we zoomed toward the bluing sky and turned toward home.

Coming in over Cook Inlet for the last time was nostalgic and a bit difficult for me—I wanted to stay airborne as long as I possibly could.

Down came the landing gear and we banked again toward the runway, rolling out about a mile from the concrete ribbon. Looking toward the F-15 area on my right, I could see a large crowd of well-wishers standing near the maintenance hangar and a fire truck parked next to them. But I refused to land. I could not let their cold noses and frozen fingers shorten my final flight.

I looked at my fuel gauges—I had enough gas for another pattern. Pushing the throttles forward just seconds from touchdown, we accelerated toward the end of the runway as the gear came up. With permission from the control tower, I zoomed the F-15 into a climbing left turn for the last closed pattern of my flying career. Starting my final turn for landing, I keyed the mic button and said,

"Warrior One, gear down, last stop."

Tower replied, "Warrior One, copy last stop. Best wishes."

As we pulled into the parking slot, I saw the fire engine pull into position. I knew I would get very wet in the fighter-pilot tradition of getting hosed down after one's final flight. As I climbed down the ladder, the fire truck and my squadron friends, who had filled fire extinguishers with high-pressure water, hosed me down from all sides.

Freezing in below-zero temperatures and beginning to turn into an icicle, I kissed my wife and children, and we all ran into the hanger to get out of the bitter-cold wind. I guess I deserved the chilling pain for making my family and friends wait an additional ten minutes as I wrung out my F-15 Eagle in the overhead pattern. I would have had it no other way.

Chief Dickens loved his ride in the F-15 and I had an awesome "fini" flight. As I celebrated with my family and fellow aviators, I was sincerely grateful for the twenty-six years I'd had on flight status as an Air Force fighter pilot.

The Pentagon would be my next landing.

11

Finding Osama bin Laden

Problems are to the mind what exercise is to the
muscles, they toughen and make strong.

— Norman Vincent Peale

AFTER THE CHANGE OF COMMAND at Elmendorf Air Force Base in late January 2000, I flew to Chicago to spend a few days with my mom and dad before heading to Virginia. It was wonderful to be with them again. As usual, my mother cooked all my favorite meals and I enjoyed discussing issues with my father.

We had decided that Judy would sell our old van, better known as a "beater with a heater," in Alaska after the school year was over. Therefore, Dad and I spent much of each day looking for a used car so that I would have family wheels when Judy and our children joined me in May.

Being an avid mechanic, my preference would have been to find a low-mileage car with a nice body and a bad engine. These cars were relatively inexpensive and I could generally repair or replace the engine in a few days for less than $1,200. In this situation, however, I did not have time to deal with the process of towing a car, nor did I have my tools. We finally found a great deal on a one-year-old Dodge Caravan that had been part of the Enterprise rental car fleet.

The next day my father and I drove to Virginia. Dad said he wanted to keep me company because he was afraid I would fall asleep at the wheel, given my last few hectic weeks in Alaska. Truthfully, we both were happy for an excuse to spend more time together. I had not given much thought to Dad's aging. He was now seventy-four years old. These moments were precious at the time, but have become even more precious over time.

Time flew by as we talked. I deeply valued my father's wisdom. He was well-read and could engage intelligently in a discussion on almost any subject. He also had sound judgment that comes from being able to quickly merge information and knowledge with context and experience. My dad's spiritual depth formed a solid foundation for his advice. It always reflected high ethical standards and strong Christian values. His life was a stellar example of a principled life—of someone who does what he believes is right despite any cost. All that, and his keen insight and broad perspective, meant that his advice in any situation was usually profound.

We drove straight through to Virginia in fourteen hours and stayed that night at Bolling Air Force Base outside of Washington, DC. The next morning, I took him to Dulles International Airport for his flight back to Chicago.

Twelve years later on January 29, 2012, my father passed on to his eternal resting place in heaven. I am very fortunate to have several other mentors in my life who continue to offer me wise counsel. But they will never replace my father. I will always miss him.

Pentagon: Second Time

This was not my first time in Washington, DC. I had spent a year here as a White House Fellow and I had returned in 1985 for a two year assignment as an international political-military affairs officer on the USAF staff in the Pentagon. In this job, I was responsible for Air Force plans and policy concerning the eastern side of Africa—from Egypt to South Africa.

It was during this last assignment to Washington that our daughter, Katherine, was born in September 1987 at Bethesda Naval Medical Center in Maryland. That part was easy. After considerable discussion, Judy supported my decision to finish the master's program at Georgetown University in sixteen months. It was hard to juggle work, school, and family activities, but we did it together as a team . . . most of the time.

I checked into the Pentagon and stopped in to see Brigadier General Bruce "Orville" Wright, whom I would be replacing on the Joint Staff. While I was waiting to see him, I reread my job description . . . the Joint Staff focal point for information operations, military information support operations, cyber operations, electronic warfare, special technical operations, and sensitive DOD support to government agencies.

Orville and I had a great talk—the job sounded very interesting. Some of the initiatives he discussed in the cyber operations and electronic warfare category were both futuristic and exciting. However, I was most interested in the high technology and ingenuity associated with the special technical operations. This was right in line with my problem-solving approach to difficult situations. While I knew I would face tough challenges in the "five-sided puzzle palace," I was eager to return to work in the Pentagon.

My official title was Deputy Director of Operations for Information Operations (J-39). My boss, Vice Admiral Scott Fry, was the Director of Operations (J-3) on the Joint Staff and he reported directly to General Hugh Shelton, the Chairman of the Joint Chiefs of Staff.

"And what time should I be here in the morning, Orville?" I asked as I prepared to leave his office.

"Five o'clock should be okay," he responded with a slight smile.

I didn't know if he was serious or just joking with me. I am a night person; 5:00 a.m. did not sound like an appealing time to be in the office.

"So, 5:00 a.m. Is that when you normally come into work?" I probed to get a better answer. I did not hear the words I was hoping for.

"Yes, we normally come in around 5:00 to 5:15 because we have to prepare for the 6:00 a.m. meeting where we brief Admiral Fry for his 6:45 meeting with General Shelton."

General Wright explained that I would attend two more regularly scheduled meetings each day—a J-39 office meeting at 7:00 a.m. and Admiral Fry's wrap-up meeting at 4:30 in the afternoon. Orville remarked that it was usually after 7:00 p.m. by the time he finished his J-39 duties each day.

Given this daily schedule, I was confident that my golf game would not improve during this assignment. And more significantly, I realized that my wife, despite living with me in the same house, would be like a single parent again.

This new job was nothing like my previous one, but it didn't take me long to adapt to the 5:00 a.m. reporting time and to shift from kinetic weapons to cyber warfare. Our J-39 team worked with technical centers around the Department of Defense to detect and prevent cyber attacks on military communications and data systems from outside the "firewall." We helped make sure our sensitive information was secure at all times.

As the director of information operations, my windowless office was located in a highly secure area, behind large metal doors that were protected with cipher locks and a video intercom system to control access. Special authorization was needed to enter the labyrinth of narrow hallways that connected our secret workspaces; everyone wore color-coded identification badges with pictures and special-access symbols at all times.

From this office, I also oversaw the military's unique and sometimes one-of-a-kind technical operations from the Joint Staff perspective. Our team was known for its very agile processes to solve real-world problems with rapid and innovative solutions. We specialized in finding practical solutions within months that would normally have taken the bureaucratic logistics cycle a year or two to resolve.

Mission Impossible

The White House and Washington's intelligence agencies were very frustrated that we still did not have good information about Osama bin Laden, also referred to as Usama bin Laden or UBL. Eighteen months had gone by since he orchestrated the US Embassy bombings in Kenya and Tanzania on August 7, 1998. Still we could not get consistent and reliable information on his whereabouts.[1]

Because some aspects of the unique surveillance program we developed are still sensitive, my discussion here is limited to areas that are now available in open sources.

Admiral Fry had just returned from a February 2000 meeting at the White House Situation Room. He shared with our small group of deputy directors about President Bill Clinton's growing frustration at not having reliable and actionable intelligence on Osama bin Laden. We knew UBL lived in Afghanistan, but he was constantly moving. Much of our intelligence about his location would be stale by the time reports arrived in Washington.

President Clinton reportedly said in the National Security Council meeting, "I can put my hand on the door knob, but can't open the door and walk in."[2]

And it was true; our covert collection programs in this region were inadequate. We all shared the president's frustration that the United States did not have enough reliable information to launch a strike against UBL. America needed real-time "eyes" on potential targets in Afghanistan.

I stayed behind after all my peers had left the J-3 conference room to reflect on President Clinton's words. After a few minutes, I knocked on Admiral Fry's open office door.

"Do you have a minute, sir?" He did not glance up; his eyes stayed on the papers on his desk. I took a breath and blazed ahead.

"Sir, I'd like to head up an initiative to find UBL and to give the president the lead time he needs to take action," I said.

Admiral Fry looked up with a slight grin.

"Come back when you have a plan on how to do what the entire US intelligence community and our allies have so far failed to accomplish," he chided gently.

I went back to my office, knowing that I probably should have kept my mouth shut and let the intelligence community continue to work on the problem. But that approach does not represent who I am or what I do. I always want to move things forward.

Confident we could figure out an innovative way to put our American eyes on UBL, I summoned the J-39 senior leaders to my office. I believed this team could help us reduce the unacceptably long time between sighting and striking, between detection and destruction.

"I've just taken on mission impossible," I began. "I told Admiral Fry we'd find Osama bin Laden and would reasonably predict his location for a six-hour period."

As I looked around the room, some officers wore quizzical stares of unbelief while others smiled as if this was some sort of practical joke.

"Our first problem is to figure out a way to verify human intelligence and build our confidence in its fidelity," I continued without pausing.

"I have some ideas, but I want you all to think about this problem set tonight. Let's brainstorm our way through this challenge tomorrow at the seven o'clock meeting."

There was dead silence in the room. After a few awkward moments, one officer stood up and stepped toward the door; others quickly followed. I am sure my colleagues believed they were now working for a megalomaniac or a raving lunatic.

Arriving at work early the next day to set up the room, I positioned a whiteboard next to my desk, drew a large tic-tac-toe grid, and enclosed it with a square to make nine boxes. Across the top of this three-by-three matrix I labeled the columns close in, standoff, and remote. Down the left side next to the three rows, I wrote physical, electronic, and perception.

My objective was to fill in each square with ideas to produce "actionable intelligence." We needed an architecture that could harvest and fuse all sources of intelligence in an innovative manner to reduce lag time and to establish consistency, reliability, and confidence. Knowing the places UBL frequented, I believed we should focus our collection efforts in eastern Afghanistan, around Kabul, Jalalabad, Darunta, Kandahar, and Tarnak Farms.

Starting the meeting promptly at 7:00 a.m., I gave a quick update to the J-39 senior staff and then launched into an overview of our new challenge. This would require everyone to think *far* outside the box as we filled in the nine little squares.

After an hour of free-flowing discussion, the close in column was empty. There were no realistic ways to get close to UBL, his entourage, and his facilities without risking detection or American lives. Yes, our laboratories had sensors and recorders that could be actuated by very sensitive motion detectors, but we did not have a battery that was strong enough to power these devices for the required surveillance time and yet small enough to conceal.

In the end, we ruled out close in thermal-imaging detectors that could "see" Osama bin Laden; electronic sniffers that could "smell" his special perfume; and acoustic, seismic, and vibration sensors that could detect multi-vehicle convoys and "hear" his Mitsubishi's missing engine cylinder. All these sensors would be very difficult to emplace and operate.

We discussed the standoff-capabilities column next. In the top standoff/physical box, I wrote "long-range telescope with laser-beam straightening, digital image enhancement, and bio-recognition." We added a drone with electro-optical and infrared sensors to put "American eyes" on areas of interest in Afghanistan for thirty hours at a time.

The next useful box was the standoff/perception square. We needed to understand UBL's historic patterns of movement and then draw predictive conclusions about his patterns of life. For example, if Osama bin Laden arrived at Kandahar before noon, what was the probability he would stay the night? If he arrived after 3:00 p.m., what were the odds he would remain overnight in Mullah Omar's guest house?

If we could gather accurate historical data, we could calculate the probabilities of UBL's patterns and predict locations where he was likely to stay for at least six hours. In 2000, applied social science was a new research field and social-network analysis was just becoming an operational art. Our team understood the statistical problem, but would need more time and expertise to find a solution.

We also explored the final category of remote capabilities, but found that our geosynchronous surveillance satellites were already fully committed to monitoring other hot spots, including Kosovo and Bosnia.

I dismissed the group, but asked Doc Hriar Cabayan, my go-to civilian employee with a very powerful mind, to stay behind.

Doc Cabayan, an American with Lebanese roots, was a very unassuming man who rode his bicycle to work and munched on fruits and vegetables throughout the day. A humble person, he was also a great patriot and unsung hero whose dedicated efforts had made our troops safer and more effective on the battlefield. Much of his work was highly classified and hidden from public view, but those of us who knew Doc were grateful to have him on our team.

"What do you think, Doc?" I asked "Is there enough here to justify a high-priority project?"

"I think we can do it," he said. "I believe we can find UBL."

I was pleased to hear that. "Please work with our team to flesh out these ideas into a prioritized list of options," I said. "I don't want a lot of details—just a single sheet of paper with options I can discuss with Admiral Fry this afternoon. I'll need it by four."

Privately, I believed a telescope and a remotely piloted aerial vehicle had the highest probability of success. After the 4:30 p.m. wrap up meeting, I entered Admiral Fry's office again. He invited me to sit down. I handed him the sheet of paper with J-39's options to find UBL and to give the president the time he needed to execute an attack.

Can We Use a Telescope?

A manned fighter or bomber attack was out of the question because the United States did not, at the time, have a way to rescue downed pilots in a timely manner. A Tomahawk cruise missile strike was still the best option, but this Navy missile needed about four hours to spin up its gyros, launch, and then fly to Afghanistan. With another two hours required for decision making, coordination, and communications, we needed to be relatively certain that the target would be in place for at least six hours.

We decided on two independent systems to physically track UBL's movements in real-time with "US eyes." The first surveillance option was an eleven-inch telescope with a twenty-mile range. The second was an unmanned aerial vehicle (UAV), such as the US Air Force's new RQ-1 reconnaissance Predator produced by General Atomics Aeronautical Systems.[3]

Admiral Fry and I discussed the J-39 proposals with General Shelton, the Chairman of the Joint Chiefs of Staff, and General Richard Myers, his vice chairman. Then we went over to the Old Executive Office Building next to the White House to brief the National Security Council staff, specifically Richard Clarke and Roger Cressey. They were pleased with the initiative and gave us the "green light" to proceed. Privately, I was delighted that my initiative was gaining traction beyond the Joint Staff.

With our concept sufficiently developed, we began to meet with the Central Intelligence Agency (CIA). Planning the surveillance operation over parts of Afghanistan was easy. The real challenge was trying to get funding from the CIA and the Department of Defense's coffers for this covert operation. I also encountered the usual bureaucratic resistance to new ideas as we circulated concept papers to get the requisite legal authority.

With solid support from a very small network of people who needed to know about our activities, I presented the final decision briefing to Admiral Fry, Clarke from the NSC, and Charles Allen, CIA's assistant director for collection. With their approval, we received funding to procure the requisite components to build the long-range telescope on May 24, 2000.

The military had developed electro-optical and infrared sensors a few years earlier to locate smugglers transporting their illegal drugs across US borders. We incorporated these and other new technologies into our high-tech telescope. After two months of construction and integration tests, we took the solar-powered telescope to a mountain near Tucson, Arizona. Here we could evaluate the equipment in approximately the same heat and dust conditions we would encounter when we positioned the telescope high up on the rugged mountain range near Torghar to look down at Darunta near Jalalabad.

Standing around a laptop connected to our large telescope, we could see two grainy figures unloading a vehicle about fourteen miles away. Observers watching larger video screens in Virginia were able to make out the shapes and sizes of the boxes, and discern the arms and legs of the individuals. I was confident we could use visual imagery enhancements, biometrics, and gait analysis to refine telescope imagery and to identify

UBL positively at that distance. He was six feet, four inches tall and he had a unique walk.

Building the final telescope in three backpack-sized sections, we planned for a small team to carry it up the rugged mountainside to the 12,000-elevation vantage point we had selected. From here, we would have an unrestricted view of the surrounding roads and towns—and UBL's movements. A solar-powered computer system would transmit just the changes to the previous picture back to our processing facility in the United States. Technicians and intelligence specialists would merge the new information with the saved background scenes, apply advanced image enhancements, analyze the activity, and then produce an actionable intelligence product for our national leaders.

Ahmad Shah Massoud, the powerful leader of Afghanistan's Northern Alliance, promised that his operatives would transport the telescope up the mountain. Unfortunately, our final negotiations stalled when internal political conflicts heightened tensions along Afghani tribal boundaries. Without the needed access and support from the local leaders, our efforts to deploy the long-range telescope also stalled. When two al-Qaeda assassins posing as Arab journalists killed Massoud on September 9, 2001 by detonating a bomb in his house,[4] the telescope project became just too hard to complete.

Of course I was very disappointed as we had spent over a year working on this innovative project. We now focused our attention on the other surveillance options. Two days later, the US political and military priorities would change, placing tremendous pressure on Washington for our initiative to be successful.

A Real-Time Look or Science Fiction?

Concurrent with efforts to develop the telescope, we had also been working very closely with representatives from Big Safari, the US Air Force's program office responsible for specialized special mission aircraft. This group was developing capabilities for remotely piloted vehicles that some called drones, including the brand new Predator unmanned aerial vehicle. I had requested three Predator airframes for our surveillance initiative, each with the same type of sensors used a year earlier in the Balkans conflict—an electro-optical and infrared camera, in addition to a semi-active radar system. To this reconnaissance configuration, we added a more robust

General Atomics RQ-1 Predator.
(Courtesy of the United States Air Force)

communications package and the capacity to conduct operations from a geographically separate site.

Until now, Predator pilots and sensor operators, along with the operations, maintenance, and intelligence support personnel, had all been located at the same airfield with the unmanned aerial vehicles. Wanting to limit the number of people we would have to deploy forward to conduct a Predator mission, Big Safari developed the command, control, and communications capability to conduct split operations. A small crew would deploy forward with the Predators to launch and recover the drone, while aircrew and the intelligence support team would stay in Europe or the United States to remotely conduct the missions—sometimes half a world away.

With the unmanned aerial vehicles ready, I worked with Joint Staff, Air Staff, and Central Intelligence Agency lawyers to have the three modified Predators "bailed" over to the CIA, under provisions of the "Economy Act,"[5] for covert operations. On August 11, 2000, the Principals Committee of the National Security Council agreed to deploy the reconnaissance-capable Predators to Uzbekistan to conduct CIA-sponsored surveillance.

Operating from Tashkent Airport, the CIA began flying Predator missions into Afghanistan on September 7, 2000. The ground crew in Uzbekistan would launch the Predator aircraft using line-of-sight communications that were good to about a hundred miles out.[6] When the remote control center had established a good satellite link with the Predator, mission pilots and targeting specialists there would take control of the flight for the next twenty or so hours. The video feed from the sensors was sent via fiber-optic cable to the CIA headquarters in Langley, Virginia, where intelligence analysts monitored the pictures and refined collection instructions. Upon the Predator's return to Tashkent, the local aircrew would take back control of the Predator and fly it to the airport for the landing.

When Richard Clarke, our White House point of contact, saw videos taken during those first flights, he became a regular visitor to the operations center in Langley, where we all sat watching the live feed from our "eye in the sky" after midnight. Afghanistan's time zone is nine and a half hours ahead of Eastern Standard Time.

Leaning forward in our chairs, we would sit with both excitement and anticipation—eyes glued to the large display. This experience bordered on science fiction as drones were not yet a reality for most Americans. It was hard to believe we were watching people in Afghanistan on our wall-sized television screen in real time, as if we were hovering right above them in an invisible helicopter. We had to keep silent about this unique capability and our early morning experiences, because our program was highly classified at the time.

Very excited about the drone program, Clarke went back to the White House and described the Predator imagery to National Security Advisor Sandy Berger as "truly astonishing."[7] He wanted to expand the program immediately so we could have Predators watching multiple targets for longer periods.

After a Taliban MiG-21 aircraft attacked our Predator, Berger became quite concerned that a Predator might be downed and warned Clarke that a shoot-down would be a "bonanza" for Osama bin Laden, al-Qaeda, and the Taliban. We needed a way to know when the Predator was under attack.[8]

The answer was simple and innovative. We knew the MiG-21's Russian-made radar operated in the same frequency band as a "fuzz buster" radar detector—that little device some speeders use to detect a police officer's radar gun. So we bought three "fuzz busters," the kind that are available at a local Radio Shack, and installed one in each of the Predators. Big Safari technicians then linked the transmitter signal to an indicator light on the Predator pilot's control console. We now had a way of knowing if a MiG-21 was in our vicinity so the operator could initiate some evasive maneuvering.

With the upgraded predator system working well, we watched the Predator live video feed night after night at the CIA headquarters. Our creative and innovative bootstrap efforts paid off when an analyst exclaimed over the intercom.

"Is that UBL?"

With hearts pounding, we sat in excited silence as a tall man dressed in a white robe walked between buildings with a security detail. Sensor operators had located an individual at Tarnak Farms near Kandahar that matched the notional description of our intelligence target.

We continued to search potential locations in Afghanistan for UBL. On September 28, we had another solid sighting of the "man in white," and our intelligence community analysts agreed this was likely Osama bin Laden.

We had proven our capability to put American eyes on high-value targets in conflict areas half a world away and to analyze the collected intelligence in the United States in almost real time. This new capacity opened up a wide variety of US options to locate, track, and potentially destroy our country's most dangerous enemies.

Our long-dwell surveillance coverage of selected targets in Afghanistan ended on November 8, 2000, when we terminated operations because of high winds, low clouds, and the ice that was beginning to accumulate on the Predator's wings when we flew through clouds. J-39 and America's Predator team had taken on a "mission impossible" challenge and had succeeded.

Nailing down UBL's Patterns

We woke on October 12, 2000, to breaking news that al-Qaeda operatives had used a small boat laden with explosives to attack the USS Cole. The blast had ripped a $250-million hole in the side of this US Navy destroyer.[9] When I arrived at the Pentagon, my bosses were already looking for me. There was a great sense of urgency to find Osama bin Laden and to give our commander-in-chief viable options to retaliate for this cowardly yet devastating attack that killed seventeen and wounded forty.

My boss was blunt. "Scott, you must accelerate your programs to find UBL and nail down his pattern of life."

Our J-39 team had already collected quite a bit of data about UBL's travel patterns, his comrades, and bodyguards. Two psychologists and a Bayesian statistical analyst moved into our J-39 spaces to pore over the data and model UBL's activities.

We needed to determine whether UBL was "rational" in his habits, where he slept when he traveled, how he communicated, and if we could externally influence his behavior patterns. We had just a few weeks to generate fact-based predictions for military operators, DOD leaders, and senior administration officials.

My professional reputation was at stake. I would need rigorous analysis and logical methodologies to convince combat-proven warriors that our "psych" conclusions about UBL's patterns of life were credible.

In a couple of months, these three analysts were able to predict UBL's probability of travel and overnight stays associated with medical appointments, religious activities, family meetings, and official business routines with uncanny accuracy. They confirmed a degree of regularity in his weekly schedule with as much as 70 percent predictability in some of his patterns. Our professionals also tried to determine the "triggers" for UBL's behavior patterns and analyzed his reaction to certain events with the goal of introducing artificial prompts to stimulate an anticipated and predictable reaction.

As good as our analysis was, I knew it would not produce a reasonable "probability of kill" using the cruise missile attack option. The uncertainties associated with the six-hour decision-to-impact timeline were just too long for attack planners and political decision-makers to accept our predictions. We had to figure out how to get a warhead on target in a significantly shorter time—within minutes of the decision to attack.

While we were still flying surveillance missions with the Predator in Afghanistan, General John P. Jumper, commander of the USAF Air Combat Command, decided to arm the Predator with two Hellfire missiles as a general combat weapon.[10] We believed this was an excellent option to shorten the attack timeline. Again, we worked closely with Big Safari to accelerate the arming process.

Who Pays?

In spite of our successful momentum, we did have one operational mishap that caused me a lot of extra work and some needless confrontation. One day, the CIA team at Tashkent was guiding a returning Predator to the airport for landing. To keep the landing environment in view while the Predator was bouncing around in the convection turbulence, the drone pilot slewed the eyeball sensor onto the approach end of the runway and locked it there so he could constantly "see" the landing zone.

Everything looked great until the Predator passed over the end of the runway. The visual sensor spun around to point backwards at that designated spot on the end of the runway. With no capacity to "see" forward, the pilot lost control of the Predator. It entered a nose-high stall and crashed about a third of the way down the runway.

The proper procedure would have been to switch the Predator's eyeball sensor back to the bore-sight mode a few miles away from landing. In this mode, the sensor would be looking straight ahead and the pilot would have a windshield-like view of everything in front of the Predator. But that had not been done.

After the crash, the question that made my life difficult was, "Who must pay the roughly three million dollars for the replacement Predator—my office or the CIA?" I thought the answer was straightforward, but it was obviously not in the minds of CIA lawyers. It would be months before this issue was resolved.

Thumbs Down on Armed Flights

In December 2000, our J-39 team drafted a strategy paper introducing the concept of armed reconnaissance using the Predator loaded with Hellfire missiles. This became a topic of hot debate after the holiday season as we continued to make the weapons platform reliable, should the president decide to deploy armed Predators to Afghanistan.

By February 2001, however, the Air Force had successfully fired a Hellfire from the Predator without the new sensor package that was still in development. Work continued through the spring and into the summer so we could conduct a real-time test of the weapons system against a realistic target. This process was not trivial—it is a credit to the innovation and dedication of the Big Safari team that they fielded this lethal unmanned aerial vehicle in a matter of months.

To ensure a convincing evaluation, we constructed a replica of our primary target on the China Lake complex in California using sundried bricks imported from Mexico. The first missile that was tested hit the target, but the warhead, designed to penetrate thick armor, pierced the adobe walls and buried itself deep in the ground. We worked closely with Big Safari and the Redstone Arsenal, the US Army's missile development and testing center, to modify the Hellfire fuse so the missile would detonate upon contact. We also developed a shrapnel sleeve for the missile so it would produce the larger fragmentation pattern we required.

I attended numerous meetings on operational issues, but the big elephant in the room continued to be the question of who would fund future operations and who would pay for any subsequent losses. In addition to the funding issues, we debated whether Executive Order 12333 (the presidential order against assassination of civilian leaders) applied to Osama bin Laden and Mullah Omar, the Afghan mujahedeen commander who was recognized as the leader of the Taliban.[11] An intelligence photograph showing a child's swing set in the front yard of Mullah Omar's house fueled passionate policy debates concerning the collateral damage.

On August 1, the National Security Council's Deputies Committee concluded that it was legal for the CIA to kill UBL and/or his deputies with a Predator missile. The United States considered these strikes to be acts of self-defense and not in violation of the Executive Order 12333 ban on assassinations. The operation now had specific approval to use the armed Predator to support CIA covert operations in Afghanistan.

There were long discussions in the National Security Council about sending the unarmed reconnaissance version of the Predator back to Afghanistan while Big Safari readied the armed version for deployment. National Security Advisor Condoleezza Rice ultimately sided with the CIA and the Pentagon and decided to cancel any further reconnaissance deployments until the Predator was ready for armed missions in Afghanistan.

Throughout this discussion, we continued to argue about funding. The Air Force was ready to loan Predators to the CIA for covert-action programs, but the Department of Defense was not prepared to bear the cost if another drone went down.[12] Unfortunately, this budgetary bickering cost us valuable time and energy, and was not resolved until the National Security Council principals finally decided to increase the Air Force and CIA budgets for Predator operations.

On August 28, the first group of CIA operatives left for Uzbekistan with portable hangars to house the weaponized Predator at the Tashkent airport. According to our plan, the first armed Predators would arrive at Tashkent on September 18, 2001, and the other Predator and Hellfire missiles would be delivered a day later. Operators planned to fly the first armed cross-border mission on September 25.

The principals committee met on September 4 to discuss final approval for this plan. After CIA Director George Tenet stated that the probability of taking out UBL with a Hellfire missile was low, Condoleezza Rice concurred that the warheads still were not lethal enough to guarantee a successful attack. The National Security Council principals recommended the Air Force continue to improve the lethality of the missile and gave the armed Predator deployment a "thumbs down."

None of us could have imagined the insidious events that Osama bin Laden and his team were finalizing at that very moment.

12

International Influence

What counts in life is not the mere fact that we have lived. It is what difference we have made to the lives of others that will determine the significance of the life we lead.

— Nelson Mandela

"TWO COMMERCIAL AIRLINERS CRASHED INTO THE TWIN TOWERS in New York City about twenty minutes ago," an Army major blurted through my partially opened office door. I saw just a slice of his face as he moved on, hollering, "That's all I know!"

I glanced at my watch: 9:23 a.m. My colleagues quickly concluded these were *not* bizarre accidents and dashed upstairs to assess information coming into the Pentagon's Operations Center. I decided to finish one quick task on my desk before joining them.

Ten minutes later, the scent of smoke and jet fuel drifted into the room. These smells did not make sense. Was I imagining this? These would be the dominant odors if I were standing in lower Manhattan where two airplanes had crashed, but I was in the basement of the Pentagon.

A muffled voice sounded from the building's loudspeaker system. Stepping into Corridor 6, I caught the tail end of the announcement. ". . . evacuate the building immediately."

Evacuate? What was happening? I had not felt a tremor nor heard an explosion. My brain tried to make sense of the conflicting information. Then another loudspeaker message interrupted my thoughts.

"An aircraft has crashed into the Pentagon midway between Corridors 4 and 5. Evacuate the Pentagon immediately. Avoid Corridors 3 through 6."[1]

My mind was racing now. If an airplane had just crashed a couple hundred yards to my left, people most certainly had been killed—but my life had been spared. Again. How close was I getting to those mythical nine lives?

I ran down a passageway toward the crash site. Thick smoke blocked my progress. Retracing my steps, I made my way outside to help from the exterior. Confused and frightened people were spilling from the exits and scattering in all directions. The parking lots, access roads, and grassy areas outside the Pentagon were a blur of disorganized commotion. Fire engines and ambulances rushed by with sirens wailing and red lights flashing. Police, Pentagon employees, and curious spectators crisscrossed in haste, compounding the pandemonium and sense of peril.

Several of us rushed over to the impact site to see if we could help in any way, but police officers told us to keep the area clear for the first responders. This directive made sense—they did not want untrained people going into areas of the Pentagon that were still on fire, where weakened building support structures could continue to collapse.

Feeling the need to be involved, I joined a small group that was attending injured individuals not yet in the care of paramedics. There was not much we could do beyond making people comfortable, stopping the bleeding on minor wounds, and providing water when we could find it.

The day crept by like a surreal nightmare. Recalling my experience after the bombing in Dhahran, I knew I needed to contact my wife and

Pentagon burning on September 11, 2001. (Courtesy of the US Department of Defense)

reassure her I was unharmed. Fortunately, I had had my car keys with me and my personal phone was in my car. I left it there each day because regulations prohibited personal communication devices in our offices that were cleared for highly classified discussions. But at this point my mobile phone was useless—all cell circuits were busy.

After a couple of hours, there was little I could do to help so I headed home. The traffic was snarled in all directions. I stopped at a gas station and used a landline telephone to reach Judy. The sixteen-mile trip that had taken twenty-two minutes to drive in the morning was now taking more than three hours.

When I finally got home, I collapsed on our living room couch next to Judy and started watching television coverage of the Twin Towers tragedy. I was stunned. I had not comprehended the extent of damage and destruction caused by the exploding aircraft, ensuing inferno, and the collapsing skyscrapers until I saw the chilling pictures on the television screen.

We heard about the smoking crater in a field near Shanksville, Pennsylvania, where the fourth hijacked aircraft crashed. Stories were beginning to surface about people on United Airlines Flight 93 making hurried telephone calls to friends and family members, telling them about the unfolding hijacking and the eventual decision to fight back. From media analysis, it appeared the airliner crashed after courageous passengers and crew members attempted to retake control of their Boeing 757-200.

Judy and I sat together in silence with our eyes glued to the screen while our children joined neighbors in our cul-de-sac discussing the news and trying to find answers. We were shocked by the devastation. I put my arm around my wife and drew her close when she cried after a commentator replayed a video clip of people jumping from windows to their deaths. She could not be comforted.

Camera crews broadcasted new images of terrified people running from "ground zero." A thick layer of ashen dust covered the panicked faces of escaping office workers; it looked like a mass exodus of living corpses. We felt helpless as America bled. Our hearts grieved.

We learned later that five al-Qaeda hijackers had flown American Airlines Flight 77 into the Pentagon at 9:37 a.m. In addition to the hijackers, one hundred seventy-nine innocent people had died just several hundred feet from where I was working at that time.

As I thought about the death and destruction of the four attacks, I could not help but recall that all of our Predators were parked neatly in a hangar at the General Atomics Aeronautical Systems facility at El Mirage, California, being readied to conduct unarmed reconnaissance missions in Afghanistan—even though the capacity to employ lethal weapons had been proven. UBL had just orchestrated the most devastating foreign attack on American soil since Pearl Harbor. Nearly three thousand people died and more than six thousand others were injured in the deadliest terrorist act in world history. I was deeply saddened and equally outraged.

The Drone Dilemma

The drone program expanded significantly after the 9/11 attacks, gaining more technical capability and additional support among Washington decision-makers. Eight years later, when the Obama administration looked for better options to fight terrorism besides the mired boots on the ground, the Predator program appeared to be a perfect solution. It was relatively low cost, covert, and effective.

For a generation that has grown up with video games, it was easy to comprehend that the Predator could insidiously remove reality from warfare. Admiral Dennis Blair, the former Director of National Intelligence, cautioned that the Predator strike campaign could be dangerously seductive.

"It is the politically advantageous thing to do—low cost, no US casualties, gives the appearance of toughness," he said. "It plays well domestically, and it is unpopular only in other countries. Any damage it does to the national interest only shows up over the long term."

Subsequently, in the first four years of the Obama administration, the number of drone strikes increased dramatically; Hellfire missiles killed many al-Qaeda operatives. Unfortunately, reports kept surfacing about the number of innocent civilians who were killed as "collateral damage."

I know that operators and decision-makers take the lethality radius of a Hellfire missile into strong consideration in the "shoot" decision matrix in order to avoid needless civilian casualties. However, the collateral damage caused by these weapons often alienates the very people we are trying to help and influence. The United States must continue to take tough measures to avoid collateral losses in drone missile strikes—even if we pass up an occasional shot. We must ensure the negative image of an errant drone strike does not compose the significant portion of America's foreign-policy face in a conflict zone.

While I am generally satisfied with the legal, moral, and political considerations and the decision-making rigor the US government uses to determine targets for drone attacks, I believe that the ease of use and effectiveness of this weapon, together with the detached fire-control mechanisms, make it a candidate for "mission creep" and an insidious expanded role. What started out as a weapon to target Osama bin Laden and top al-Qaeda leadership has killed well over 2,700 people—and the number continues to increase.

It is easy for drone strikes to become like the "Whac-a-Mole" game— an unending list of potential targets seem to pop up all over the globe. Drone targets now include Taliban foot soldiers, members of al-Shabaab in Somalia, foreign fighters, and more.

As a moral and principled nation, we must obey US and international laws that are in place to protect human rights. Before authorizing a Predator strike, the government has the responsibility to ensure that individuals in the Predator's crosshairs present a credible and imminent threat to American people and/or our national interests that cannot be captured or neutralized in a better way. Strict "shoot" criteria would rule out attacks against suspicious, but unconfirmed activities or gatherings.

I am still concerned about drone technology falling into the wrong hands in the same way the free world is concerned about chemical and nuclear weapons in the possession of those who may use them to wreak havoc. Many countries and organizations now have sophisticated unmanned aerial vehicles that could be armed and used against the United States and our citizens.

We need to ensure that our approach to remotely piloted vehicles considers a day when the United States and its allies are not the only countries regularly using lethal drones. No one wants to see video-game warfare played out around the globe with actual missiles. It may be time to consider an international policy or maybe a treaty on remotely fired tactical weapons that could silently roam the skies around the globe looking for targets.

As my mother used to say, "What's good for the goose is good for the gander."

We need to learn from the current debate about the capacity of Middle Eastern nations to produce nuclear bombs while possibly harboring veiled hegemonic intentions. It will be much easier to control the proliferation of armed drones now than to wait until we must pressure a country to surrender its lethal remotely piloted vehicles or face military action.

Recently, I was asked if I regretted my role in the early development of the Predator surveillance and weapon system. Paraphrasing J. Robert Oppenheimer, who had a major role in developing the atomic bomb, I said there was no mistake in creating a technical capability—mistakes only occur in the employment phase.

Dr. Oppenheimer said it best: "When you see something that is technically sweet, you go ahead and do it and you argue about what to do about it only after you have had your technical success."

The final chapter of the armed drone program remains to be written, but I believe we must control this capability with strict "shoot" criteria and strong international restrictions. While a few armed drones may not be classified a "weapon of mass destruction," swarms of these weaponized UAVs in the wrong hands—bloodied hands like those of another Osama bin Laden—could be just as frightening, indiscriminate, and destructive.

Information Warriors

My job tempo increased significantly because of this attack on America. The work we had done in secret for the past eighteen months and our team's efforts to track Osama bin Laden, Mullah Omar, and others now became a high-priority project in the Pentagon. My office was thrust right into the middle of the secretive planning for a military response. After the September 11 attacks, the bureaucratic bickering and petty funding feuds disappeared. The armed Predator soon became a weapon of choice in the war against radical extremists and al-Qaeda's terrorists.

The 9/11 attacks significantly changed my daily routine. Functioning with much less time for sleep, I learned to cope with chronic fatigue. I confess that I sometimes longed for my old "five-to-nine" workday. Now, I was working seventy days without a break. Many of my senior colleagues were doing the same.

The day started at 1:30 a.m. so that I could be at the Counter-Terrorism Center at the CIA headquarters building by about 2:45 a.m. to monitor Predator surveillance operations until 5:00 a.m. I would rush back to the Pentagon for the 6:00 a.m. meeting to give the J-3 a read-out on the Predator mission and an update on other J-39 activities.

Senior military leaders soon realized there would be a significant information warfare component to our new fight with al-Qaeda. To influence peoples' attitudes and reactions both domestically and in international media markets, we would need to put concise, consistent, and truthful messages on the street as expeditiously as possible. As the Director of Information Operations on the Joint Staff, it fell to me to establish and direct the Information Operations Task Force (IOTF). I had never seen evidence of an IOTF existing before this, but clearly the DOD needed a strategic hub to coordinate the information war.

Our first challenge was having a place from which to operate. We essentially commandeered a section of the Pentagon undergoing a major renovation, cleaned it up, and went to work. Our IOTF team filled the empty rooms with tables and chairs, whiteboards, photocopiers, and a video-teleconferencing system so we could exchange information with regional command posts around the globe.

Technicians set up a bank of televisions that would rival the electronics display at a Best Buy showroom and they hooked us into the Pentagon's cable network so we could monitor news broadcasts from around the world twenty-four hours a day.

Then we organized ourselves into four functional sections. The first group determined what we should be saying. The next monitored what others were saying. The third group did audience analysis to figure out who listens to what medium. The last group studied our options to get more effective penetration for our messages. We spent a great deal of time fine-tuning outgoing content and an equal amount of time disseminating messages.

Two months after IOTF was launched, the staff heard a terse message that made all sit at attention. "SecDef is on his way down." Secretary of Defense Donald Rumsfeld would soon be walking through the door.

I had met with Secretary Rumsfeld several times before and knew him to be pleasant and engaging—contrary to his reputation for being intolerant and quick-tempered. I understood his demand for unvarnished facts to support a recommendation, for sound logic during discussions, and for concise and correct answers to his probing questions. Wearing a grey sweater and looking relaxed, the Secretary spent forty-five minutes visiting each section to learn about our efforts. Because many of my staff believed the gossip about briefers being thrown out of his office, they were surprised by his genuine interest and friendly demeanor.

Not only did Secretary Rumsfeld make a very positive impression on our team with his impromptu visit, he later recommended that the White House build a similar information operation center to coordinate themes in all outgoing administration communications. The J-39 information warriors must have impressed him as well.

Information Coordination

To win the worldwide information campaign, we had to prevent alienation of the very people we needed to have on our side in the fight against terrorism. America was fighting an extremely small segment of the 1.5 billion Muslims in the world: a largely unseen and amorphous group of extremists who had hijacked religious concepts and used them to justify violent jihad. I was convinced that the administration had to stop communicating with polarizing sound bites that incorrectly defined and described our enemies. We risked alienating a far larger percentage of the Muslim world if the United States did not manage its strategic communications and national messages better.

To that end, our IOTF quickly became the model for incorporating and reinforcing consistent themes in senior leader speeches and the impetus for establishing information-coordinating structures throughout Washington to integrate politics and diplomacy. Soon, the White House had a network of Coalition Information Centers linking Washington, London, and Islamabad, capable of responding to breaking news within local news cycles.

Despite the measurable success the IOTF was logging, I sensed a turf battle was brewing between the IOTF and some of the Pentagon's civilian leaders. Unfortunately, I was right. After securing Secretary Rumsfeld's support, Under Secretary of Defense for Policy Douglas Feith handcuffed our Joint Staff IOTF team on October 30 by creating his own Office of Strategic Influence. In the Under Secretary of Defense for Policy announcement, he stated that his office would serve as the military's focal point for the "strategic information campaign in support of the war on terrorism." His objective "was to develop a full-spectrum influence strategy that would result in greater foreign support of US goals and repudiation of terrorists and their methods."[2] To us, this was a blatant move to take control of the Joint Staff-led IOTF and to include a propaganda element in DOD's messaging.

I was dismayed. Not because the Joint Staff could be sidelined. Rather, I was concerned that we were blurring the line between using factual information and distorting the truth with manipulated data as the new Office of Strategic Influence (OSI) took over the IOTF. Given the individuals Doug

Feith recruited to run his OSI, it was clear the psychological-operations community would have a significant voice in future information operations.

I had purposely excluded "psyops"[3] folks from IOTF "white world" operations. I had insisted that the IOTF stay away from disinformation and dark propaganda as I feared this "full spectrum" approach could undermine our credibility if we were ever associated with manipulated information.

While Victoria "Torie" Clarke, the Assistant Secretary of Defense for Public Affairs, initially viewed the IOTF as competition in her role as the principal spokesperson for the Department of Defense, she and I both agreed that the IOTF must be very careful to avoid black propaganda.[4]

Doug Feith and I differed on this and several other policy issues. I believed some neoconservatives in the Bush administration leaders, such as Doug Feith, Paul Wolfowitz, John Bolton, Elliott Abrams, Richard Perle, and Paul Bremer, were pushing America too fast toward military confrontation in Iraq. While I agreed with crushing the al-Qaeda network that attacked us on September 11th, I did not see the clear justification nor feel the same sense of urgency for invading Iraq to destroy Saddam Hussein's alleged weapons of mass destruction.

All the while, as my IOTF team and I were developing our innovative information operation, I continued to support the Predator surveillance program. After the Predator flew its last reconnaissance mission in early November 2001, my responsibilities for developing the drone program ended. While it was time for me to leave the Predator program, I missed being on the leading edge of this technology development.

Having served my two-year assignment on the Joint Staff, the Air Force assigned me in December to be the Director of Regional Affairs in its international affairs office at the Pentagon. As I transitioned out of the IOTF, Under Secretary Doug Feith was able to effectively marginalize my opposing voice in the Pentagon's internal debate on information operations. He eventually won and relegated the IOTF to the proverbial dark corner of his full-spectrum influence office. I was deeply disappointed, but accepted this ideological defeat.

Yet only four months after its inception, Secretary Rumsfeld dissolved the Office of Strategic Influence on February 26, 2002, stating "the office has clearly been so damaged that it is pretty clear to me that it could not function effectively."[5] While vindicated in my strong opposition, I sadly believe the rogue Office of Strategic Influence also diminished the effectiveness and influence of the Information Operations Task Force after my departure. That said, we had proven the value of coordinated US messaging to the outcome of a conflict. While future information operations might not be called an IOTF, the concept and function were here to stay.

Maybe because of my bent for fairness and justice, I was saddened by my perception that many Muslims, Arabs, and terrorists were being lumped into the same category: America's enemies. It was very bothersome for me to listen to the "you're either with us or against us" rhetoric that insidiously pitted America and Western Europe against parts of the Middle East, Eurasia, and North Africa.

Nineteen al-Qaeda terrorists from Saudi Arabia, United Arab Emirates, Egypt, and Lebanon attacked our country, supported by a network of another several thousand dedicated followers of Osama bin Laden. While the 9/11 assaults were devastating and required a swift and strong military response, we lost our way when the net we cast to catch al-Qaeda terrorists also targeted innocent Arabs and Muslims. Our expanded fight into Iraq set us on a course that further alienated many of the people in neighboring countries whom we actually needed on our side to win against this small group of terrorists.

Unfortunately, similar polarizing statements and unfair categorizations emerged in the 2016 Republican primary campaign. Some conservative candidates have painted Muslims with a broad negative brush that is not in line with America's values and is not useful in our efforts to defeat radicalized terrorists.

The IOTF team worked very hard to convey truthful messages about our unprejudiced intentions to the right audiences at the right time. I believe we did a lot of good in the early days after the September 11 attacks. Our band of dedicated information warriors did a superb job ensuring America conveyed consistent and correct messages about our new war on terrorists and their despicable activities.

Napoleon Bonaparte had it right when he said, "There are but two powers in the world, the sword and the mind. In the long run the sword is always beaten by the mind."

Culmination of a Lifetime of Training

Moving to the Air Force's international affairs office was the perfect assignment for me. I had been blessed with an international background from my earliest years. Traveling to new places, meeting interesting people, and learning about different cultures was very enjoyable. I had lived and traveled in Europe, the Middle East, and Africa; now I would have the opportunity to experience Asia and South America also.

Being the director of regional affairs put me right in the middle of all of the Air Force's foreign military sales, bilateral negotiations, and multilateral conferences. My office was also the focal point for coordination between Joint Staff, Office of the Secretary of Defense, State Department, and government agencies on international issues. I had been in training my whole life for this job and I loved every minute of it.

On top of that, this new position gave me more time with my wife and children, to work on my MGB sports car, and to serve in our community. One way in which I could do that was to put my barber skills to use.

I had been cutting hair for family and friends since high school. So when my schedule loosened up a bit, Judy agreed we should cut hair for disadvantaged people living in our northern Virginia community.

One elderly gentleman would lurch into my barber shop in Lorton Community Action Center every two weeks. He had served on Guadalcanal in World War II.

"Give me a number one, son," he would say as I helped him into the chair.

This frail, proud soldier had been out of the Army for almost six decades, but service to our country was still his defining accomplishment. I gave him the same haircut he got in boot camp in 1941.

"See you in two weeks, son," he would say as he bid farewell with a wave of his cane.

Another one of my favorite customers was an elderly woman from South America. In broken English, she would say, "Make me beautiful." She would then close her eyes and smile until her hairstyling was complete.

For two years I would post a calendar on the barber shop window, announcing which Saturday mornings I would be open for business. Customers of all sorts would fill my chair for three or four hours. Some became regulars. Judy would be there too, always prepared with a plateful of homemade cookies and juice and eager to play with the children and talk with waiting customers.

Judy and I were blessed to be able to encourage these people in a small way, some who worked so very hard every day just to get by. Their smiles, handshakes, and hugs were all the motivation we needed to make this service project a Saturday morning priority.

I enjoyed my weekday work just as much. SAF/IA was responsible for conducting most Air Force international negotiations, including software licenses, co-production agreements, military hardware and equipment, and international military education and training. Foreign military sales positioned us as a broker between foreign governments and US industries. We worked with foreign buyers and US suppliers to negotiate financial agreements and delivery commitments that complied with US export regulations and legal restrictions.

During my tenure, I was involved in the C-17 lease to the United Kingdom, the F-15K sale to Korea, the Boeing-767 tankers discussions with Italy and Japan, and the Global Hawk. My office directly participated in negotiations to sell new and refurbished F-16s and C-130s to Greece, Austria, Poland, Italy, Hungary, Czech Republic, Bulgaria, Slovakia, Egypt, Oman, Jordan, India, Bangladesh, Brazil, and Chile. I traveled to many of these countries to help close the deals. My colleagues and I were also very involved in helping the F-35 Joint Strike Fighter debut as the next generation F-16 replacement around the globe.

One project I enjoyed was making sure the United Arab Emirates' fourth-generation fighter, based on the reliable and proven F-16 airframe, was a success. This co-developed F-16 Block 60, also known as the Desert Falcon, incorporated many of the latest technologies from the F-22 Raptor and the F-35 Joint Strike Fighter. Interestingly, this deal represented the first in which the United States had sold an aircraft to a partner that was better than the fighters US pilots were currently using in combat.

I believed the US Air Force should have bought some of these F-16 Block 60s for our inventory, as I was not convinced the F-35 would match all the hype in USAF press clips nor meet cost estimates touted in Lockheed-Martin's media releases. I hope I am wrong about my concerns about the F-35's under-performance and over-budget projections because its stealth features are important. That said, I would not hesitate for a minute to fly the significantly less expensive F-16 Block 60 into most of today's combat environments.

Are We Going to War?

I was in Honolulu on January 15, 2003, giving a presentation about our plans for the region and SAF/IA's near-term engagement strategy. During the question and answer period in the conference center's auditorium at

Hickam Air Force Base, an officer asked me about the rumors that we were going to war with Iraq over weapons of mass destruction.

"I believe it's premature for the United States to go to war with Iraq," I replied. "The United Nations Monitoring, Verification, and Inspections Commission and the International Atomic Energy Agency inspectors are still conducting their examination of Iraqi facilities and so far they haven't found any weapons of mass destruction," I said.

Making sure the military audience knew I was expressing my personal opinion, I talked a bit more about clear differences between Saddam's tyrannical regime and the separate al-Qaeda terrorist threat. I suggested that the United States should use its military power sparingly to protect American vital interests, in support of a United Nations or NATO mandate, or to protect global citizens who were facing a severe humanitarian crisis or genocide.

As I was finishing, the moderator handed me a note. I glanced at it quickly and immediately transitioned to my closing comments.

The message read, "Lt Gen Moseley wants to speak with you ASAP on a secure line."

ASAP means "as soon as possible" to a peer. Since Lieutenant General T. Michael ("Buzz") Moseley was commander of US Central Command Air Forces, ASAP meant "you are already late."

13

Stopping the Scuds

*The very best way to ensure that people will
continue doing what you want is to give them
recognition when they do it. This is especially true
when it comes to practicing values.*

— Bud Bilanich

Wᴵᴛʜɪɴ ᴍɪɴᴜᴛᴇs, our classified phone conversation was under way from the military command post in Honolulu.

"General Moseley, this is Brigadier General Gration. I just got a message to call you."

"Yeah, thanks for calling back. General Franks wants you to be the commander of Combined Joint Task Force–West," he said. "You know all the players in Saudi, Jordan, Egypt, and he wants you to coordinate the special operations forces doing the Scud hunt." His tone conveyed no hint about his feelings; he was all business.

US Army General Tommy Franks was commander of the US Central Command (CENTCOM), overseeing military operations in a twenty-five-country region, including the Middle East. My mind was racing with questions. "I'd be pleased to serve wherever I can be used. When do I need to be in place, sir?"

"General Franks is visiting the countries in his AOR *[Area of Responsibility]* to have consultations with senior leaders. He'll be in Amman on Tuesday to see King Abdullah. He wants you to be there with him."

Tuesday, January 21, 2003. Less than a week away.

"When do you pin on?" Lt Gen Moseley asked.

"April first." Judy had already made elaborate party plans to celebrate my promotion to major general.

"We'll frock you this weekend. Show up in Amman wearing two stars. Plan to stay for a year. Any questions?"

When I replied "no," Lt Gen Moseley ended our cryptic conversation. I had spoken calmly, but knowing the huge task I was facing, calm was not my actual state.

As a fighter pilot, I knew a lot about the capabilities of the Scud missile. Developed and exported widely by the Soviet Union during the Cold War, this tactical ballistic missile could be used to attack our forces and terrorize population centers.

But Iraq had another use for the Scud missile.

During Operation Desert Storm, the first Gulf War, Saddam Hussein launched Scuds at Israel in an effort to bring Israel into the conflict. Many believed that an Israeli retaliation against Baghdad could have fractured the US-led coalition, because many member countries had large Muslim populations.

Our mission was unambiguous. The Combined Joint Task Force would have to find and destroy all of Iraq's Scud missiles before they could be launched.

This task was made considerably more difficult by the fact that Iraqi missile units had dispersed their Scud launchers—hiding them in

Scud missile on mobile launcher.
(Courtesy of the United States Air Force)

warehouses, culverts, ravines, and under highway bridges. They also used modern "shoot-and-scoot" tactics, hiding the launcher immediately after the missile had been fired.

It was late Wednesday afternoon in Hawaii. I would need to fly to Washington DC, get desert-camouflage uniforms, pack for a year, and be on a plane to Amman, Jordan, by Sunday evening.

Yes, it was doable, but I would need lots of help.

I called my executive officer, Major Steven ("Bick") Dutkus, and asked him to get two sets of uniforms sewn up with nametags, patches, and two-star rank. My duties could involve direct combat operations, so I would also require a full set of personal combat equipment—steel helmet, chemical mask and replacement filters, and a bulletproof flak vest.

This assignment was a good fit for me. I had lived in Saudi Arabia for a year and I knew Iraq from the air like the back of my hand. In addition, I had spent a lot of time in Egypt and had recently been in Jordan negotiating a deal involving F-16 aircraft and surveillance radars. These experiences had given me the opportunity to meet many senior military and government leaders in the region—some were still good friends.

I spent the weekend packing, changing the oil and transmission fluid in our two vehicles, and putting a new alternator in my daughter's car. Judy and I discussed the additional things she would have to do as a single parent again to keep the household running smoothly. Bick came by on Sunday with my new uniforms, combat gear, and airline tickets. I departed that evening with mixed emotions: excitement that I was going off to do the things I had trained almost twenty years to do, but apprehension knowing that no amount of training could fully prepare me for this new experience.

Creating an Organization

The US Central Command executive jet transporting General Franks and his staff touched down right on time at Marka Airport in Amman. After the official greeting time with our Jordanian hosts, General Franks sat down with me to outline my new duties. I quickly figured out that I had a very big job and very few guidelines.

He concluded with, "Get the job done and don't make me worry about you."

That evening the general invited me to his hotel room for an opportunity for us to get to know each other over French fries and a beer. He came across as a down-to-earth, say-it-as-it-is kind of leader. I appreciated his no-nonsense approach and believed it was a special privilege to work for him at such an important time in history.

The next morning, we stopped at the American Embassy for an office call with the US Ambassador to Jordan, Skip Gnehm, with whom I had worked in the Pentagon in the mid-1980s. We then drove to Baraka Palace, also known as Beit al-Urdun, to meet with His Majesty King Abdullah II. In all the meetings, General Franks introduced me as the US Central Command's regional liaison and single point of contact for military matters.

I clearly understood my role, my authority, my responsibilities, my classified geographic operating area, and my title. I would have to establish myself quickly as the commander of Combined Joint Task Force–West (TF-W) so that inbound deploying units would know from the beginning they had to coordinate everything through my office. The first couple of weeks would be interesting for sure.

At this point I was a leader of one with a staff of none, but that would change, according to Lieutenant General John Abizaid, the US Central Command's deputy commander.

"You'll end up with four special forces brigades—two from the United States, one from the United Kingdom, and one from Australia," said Lieutenant General Abizaid. "A British brigadier general will be your deputy. Personnel for your staff will be sent as reserve forces are mobilized."

My biggest challenge was that our organization and deployed personnel had to be hidden from public view as we operated around the region. We had a huge mission to accomplish with many aircraft, special operations shooters, and a significant support team. However, we were technically "not in the region."

The word, "Joint" in our organization's name meant that we would have personnel from each service—army, air force, navy, and marines. The word, "Combined," indicated that we would have service members from other military partners. The senior United Kingdom national representative, Brigadier General Adrian Bradshaw, arrived after a couple of weeks. He was very sharp and serious, and I was confident we would get along well as we put our organization together. The senior national representative from Australia, Lieutenant Colonel Robert DeRooy, filled out the task force's senior leadership group.

During the first few weeks, our growing team concentrated on installing adequate communications links and preparing our remote bases to receive personnel, aircraft, and support equipment. We built tent cities in the desert to accommodate 10,000 people, maintenance shelters, and ammo storage areas. Getting permission from the host-nation authorities for these activities was the easy part—the hard part was making sure daily routines and combat operations in the desert would be sustainable and adequately secure. TF-W would eventually have six desert operating locations, and all had to remain "invisible."

We estimated that our 140 aircraft and numerous vehicles would consume 375,000 gallons of fuel every day. Acquiring this daily supply was hard, but distributing this fuel each day to our helicopter pads, motor pools, and remote airfield fuel bladders was even harder. Working with CENTCOM logistics planners, we negotiated to purchase the required JP-8 jet fuel from several refineries in the region and agreed to lease fifty tanker trailers to haul fuel from the refineries to our various bases in the desert. CENTCOM logisticians negotiated for a tanker ship to hold our strategic fuel reserve in the Red Sea.

My focus during the first couple of weeks had been communications, logistics, and supplies, but now I had to think hard about my next concern—force protection. I probably spent half of my time in the early months ensuring that the TF-W facilities and our troops were protected adequately and appropriately.

As for my personal security, I often joke that I have both insurance and salvation—I will use the insurance if I end up in a hospital and the salvation if I end up dead. Obviously though, it always has been my goal to live a long life by taking all appropriate protective measures.

Having attended several military and CIA personal-security courses, I learned to be very aware of my surroundings so as to detect possible surveillance and recognize any impending attack. Whenever I was in a town or city, I varied my schedule day by day to present an unpredictable target for surveillance and I wore body armor whenever the risk made it appropriate. At the same time, I knew that a terrorist could kill me or anyone else given enough time to plan and a willingness to lose his or her life in the process. The devastation of the Khobar Towers bombing and the 9/11 attack on the Pentagon, both of which I had experienced firsthand, lingered in my mind.

Working the diplomatic side of our mission became increasingly important after initial set-up. Dealing with host-nation officials was challenging, yet rewarding. All of the leaders had high expectations about what their countries would get from the US-led coalition[1] and all wanted to collect user fees whenever we used their facilities. Drinking lots of tea, we built strong friendships and worked through the contentious issues. In general, the governments were supportive as long as we pledged to remain invisible to the international media. Issues of national sovereignty were always present, but usually unspoken.

In one month, we had gone from a task force of one to an organization with nine officers and twelve enlisted personnel. Our pyramid organization had a chain of command with specific offices for personnel, intelligence, operations, logistics, and planning. Our purpose was not to build a big organization; our job was to prepare for and execute the Scud hunt as part of CENTCOM's strategic plan.

On March 7, I sat alone in my room and watched the televised presentation by UN inspectors to the United Nations Security Council concerning the weapons of mass destruction in Iraq. From the rhetoric coming out of Washington and London, it was becoming clear that President George Bush and Prime Minister Tony Blair were ready to go it alone without an international mandate. In my heart, I hoped President Bush knew a lot more than I did about the reasons for this impending war, because I was confident that Osama bin Laden, al-Qaeda, and the 9/11 attackers were not connected with Saddam Hussein's regime.

I hoped and prayed that their decision would work out favorably for the military because these leaders would be using their nations' precious armed forces in a very bold way to fight a war in which the number of coalition and Iraqi casualties could be very great. We in the US military were just tools in the hands of our civilian leaders—we could only hope that our commander-in-chief had carefully considered our military advice, counted all the costs, and shouldered the serious responsibility for the significant blood and treasure that would likely be spent in this fight.

A Chalice Partially Filled

General Franks did a great job visiting all the heads of state in the US Central Command's area of responsibility to keep them apprised of military issues. On March 11, he asked me to accompany him to Jordan again, to see King Abdullah II, so His Majesty would fully understand what the coalition was planning to do and the possible ramifications for Jordan.

In Operation Desert Storm, Saddam Hussein's military had launched forty-three Scud missiles toward Jordan and Israel in 1991 and 1992. Because Iraqi civilians expected General Norman Schwarzkopf's coalition forces to continue to Baghdad after liberating Kuwait in 1992, thousands of refugees streamed to the Jordanian border seeking refuge. This time around, if we went to war, Iraq's neighbors would once again have to handle the difficult and costly indirect consequences of the coalition's combat operations.

As usual, General Franks was very warm and included me in all of his pre-meeting discussions with US Embassy and Jordanian leaders. We walked in to see His Majesty the King at 7:00 p.m. During our first meeting with His Majesty, General Franks had introduced me as Chuck. Now there was light banter about my real name.

"Is his name Chuck or Scott?" the King asked, smiling.

General Franks laughed and replied, "Well, I call him ___" and inserted a mild obscenity more often heard in boot camp than royal quarters.

Everyone laughed, including me, and the meeting started on a cordial note. During the hour-long meeting, General Franks discussed some of the military options he was considering. When he reminded His Majesty to contact me if Jordan needed anything from the coalition, the King looked at me, smiled, and nodded. We had already established a close working relationship.

During the ride back to the airport, the general's executive officer relayed that CIA Director George Tenet had spoken very highly of our task force in a recent National Security Council meeting at the White House, and also to Secretary of Defense Rumsfeld. I felt strongly that the credit belonged to the entire task force. This team was imaginative, innovative, resourceful, and awesome. I was fortunate to be a part of it.

As he departed, General Franks also praised our results. "Thanks, Scott. I've been able to prepare for war without having to worry about the southwestern flank."

Yes, there were a few conflicts between State Department employees and military officers trying to coordinate US Central Command's activities with the host-country officials. This was understandable. Embassy personnel had been in the country first; the US military was coming in with more money, greater access to host-nation military leaders, and a more urgent mission. We worked through the disagreements and hard feelings by putting "America first" and by talking about "one team, one mission."

The valuable lessons I learned here about interagency rivalries would serve me well later when I was a US diplomat in Sudan, and again when I served as the US Ambassador to Kenya.

Combined Joint Task Force–West now had thirty-six members and these individuals were jelling into a strong team. Two days after the visit with King Abdullah II, I convened an all-hands meeting in which I praised everyone for his or her significant contributions to the coalition's mission and for the superb reputation we were building. Because we had not yet reached our full manning and projected capabilities, some had described our organization as a glass half empty. I disagreed and explained to my team:

> We're not a half-empty glass. I choose to view us as a beautifully engraved chalice partially filled with the finest wine from the very best vineyards of United States, Britain, and Australia. We're our nations' best.

Negotiating Host-Nation Permission

As we approached the probable start date for combat operations, I felt increasingly squeezed between "Iraq and a hard place." Host-nation interlocutors were beginning to balk at the number of foreign troops in their countries and to complain about the massive amount of military equipment accumulating in the region's deserts. At the same time, US Central Command was pressuring me to bed down even more coalition forces after the Ankara government refused to allow US forces to use their bases in southeastern Turkey.[2]

By mid-March, the number of personnel in the region was up to 8,330, and the figures kept increasing despite my strong recommendations to hold them down. The growing coalition presence was making some host-nation officials very nervous, especially as the international press began to follow the situation in Iraq with more interest. I kept drinking tea with my host-nation friends.

With the war only about a week away, one fuel refinery cut our allotment of jet fuel by 90 percent. The superb TF-W staff and our effective logistics team at CENTCOM headquarters evaluated realistic alternatives and resolved this seemingly insurmountable challenge in a few days. This experience reinforced what I already knew about successful combat campaigns: operators get the praise, but logisticians win wars.

My next challenge was to get permission for our combined special operations forces to cross host-nation borders prior to the beginning of the coalition's ground invasion. One of the governments had already informed me there would be no cross-border operations from their country before the Saddam regime had fallen. While I certainly understood the concerns about sovereignty and historical nonaggression policies, our forces needed to conduct certain aspects of the Scud hunt before the coalition forces entered Iraq from Kuwait.

I sat down with each of the senior leaders of our host countries and described our urgent requirement for crossing the Iraqi border. I presented the US Central Command's operational constraints and planning considerations, and then put my requests on the table for each government to consider.

On the evening of March 17, 2003, President George Bush gave the Iraqi government an ultimatum. In a public statement he said, "Saddam and his sons must leave Iraq within forty-eight hours. Their refusal to do so will result in military conflict."[3]

There was no question in anyone's mind any more. The coalition was going to war in two days.

The next morning, two of my host-nation contacts called and asked for a joint meeting. Seated in comfortable leather chairs in the senior commander's office, we sipped sweetened black tea and I listened for twenty minutes as each government official explained the reason behind his government's refusal to concur with my earlier request. Scooting to the edge of my seat, I looked into each man's eyes while carefully laying out the requirements and rationale for our appeal. After several hours of discussion, they collectively agreed to the coalition timing.

The War Begins

Combat operations were ready to start and everyone's heart was beating just a little faster as we made final preparations. The weather was quite nasty and we all thought we might have to cancel our operations because of the high surface winds—helicopter transport was an integral element of successfully completing the first night's activities.

I called Lieutenant General Abizaid at 5:30 p.m. to let him know that we had just received the last host-nation approval and helicopters would be able to fly—everything was "green" from TF-W's perspective. He thanked me for all the work the task force had done and acknowledged that our team had overcome many "make or break" hurdles en route to this big day. He concluded by saying that the US Central Command had received the execute order and everything was a "go."

Two large video screens were mounted on the side wall of our small operations room. The one on the left showed the ground picture. Aside from the yellow political borders, this screen was blank because there were no ground forces in Iraq. The other screen showed the air picture—the real-time display of all aircraft flying in and around southern Iraq, primarily to enforce the UN-mandated no-fly zone.

Knowing Operation Iraqi Freedom was about to kick off, our team had gathered quietly around these screens. We watched the ground picture as electronic trackers attached to each of our ground units generated symbols on the screen showing our forces crossing the yellow border markers en route to their tactical mission objectives. Over the next few days, we continued watching the dots indicating coalition vehicles were moving deep into Iraq while the air picture screen displayed symbols of our aircraft supporting combat operations on the ground.

The television news channels were not reporting anything yet, which made us all feel a little better that our operation was still invisible to the public.

Reflecting on my previous combat experiences, I mused that we could see almost too much activity—the days of being able to hide in the desert's sandbox or in the big sky were over.

We were now carrying our chemical protective gear with us all the time. There was a real threat. Iraqi soldiers had already fired three missiles toward Kuwait. So far, our sensors had not detected any "slime or bugs," but we were not taking any chances with chemical or biological threats.

By March 28, coalition forces in southern Iraq were resupplying, consolidating, pounding the enemy from the air, and getting ready for the big battle to take Baghdad. While we didn't see many reports on coalition casualties and aircraft losses, I did learn that the US Air Force lost an F-15E during a combat bombing mission near Tikrit on April 7 and an A-10 was shot down by an Iraqi Roland surface-to-air missile the next day. Unfortunately, the pilot and weapon systems officer in the F-15E had been killed.

Like my colleagues in the military, I had taken an oath to support and defend the Constitution of the United States against all enemies, foreign and domestic. As active-duty service members, we willingly and faithfully followed the orders of our Commander-in-Chief George W. Bush. As he had made the decision to invade Iraq we had to believe that he understood the security and political situation and consequences of this war better than we did. We had to trust that our leaders had defined America's vital interests in this conflict and had answered the "then what?" question before deciding to go to war.

I have always believed that America's blood and treasure should be used to defend US vital national interests and to stop violent genocide and war crimes against global citizens. While the debate continues about the definition of "vital national interests," I thought it was probably a stretch to include intervening in sectarian violence or supporting an armed rebellion against a regime we did not like (for example, Libya) in that highest category of US interests.

I kept my feelings about the decision to go to war with Iraq to myself. I had a job to do for my country. That said, I prayed that the United States precious military resource would not be squandered in battles against adversaries whose threat to America's vital national interests was questionable.

Organizing Humanitarian Assistance

By late March, my efforts shifted from combat operations to planning for the post-hostilities period. The Jordanian Ministry of Interior and the Hashemite Charity Foundation were planning to build two refugee camps on Jordan's eastern border. It was not clear what Saudi Arabia would do about the potential influx of refugees across its border with Iraq. It made sense to move our humanitarian assistance operation to Amman, Jordan, as this would likely be the center of activity for this next phase.

I offered to set up a humanitarian assistance coordination center and requested personnel to work on the expanding humanitarian assistance issues.[4] It was interesting to watch the US State Department's policy offices and humanitarian assistance agencies working with various local and international aid groups to resolve the same humanitarian problem with such varied priorities, different approaches, and dissimilar solutions. Fortunately, the military was on the periphery of most contentious policy debates concerning the incoming refugees—our job was to help make things happen to care for these displaced people. I would experience this discord again in Darfur as the US Special Envoy to Sudan, and in northern Kenya when dealing with Somali refugees when I served as the US Ambassador to Kenya.

Upon request from the Iraqi ambassador to Jordan, the Jordanian government decided to move one of their forty-bed field hospitals to Al-Fallujah. We coordinated all the timing details, armed escort change-over points, and media coverage for the eleven-truck convoy. This was just the beginning. We coordinated refugee issues with a myriad of agencies and offices from the United Nations, diplomatic community, non-governmental organizations, and private volunteer groups. Although this was complicated and sometimes frustrating, it was a very rewarding mission.

One evening, my wife sent me an email with the news that the pilot of the F-15E that went down on April 7 was Captain Eric Das.[5] He had been a pilot in the 90th Fighter Squadron at Elmendorf Air Force Base in Alaska when I was the wing commander there. His wife, Nikki, was an Air Force operations support officer at the base and had become close friends with my wife, Judy, when they served together in a chapel program for military youth.

My heart ached for Nikki and many other spouses like her. I was painfully reminded that the sacrifice of service continues to be great for so many who have lost family members, friends, and colleagues in combat. I am deeply grateful for each man and woman who has volunteered to serve in the US Armed Forces and who has willingly gone into harm's way in order to protect our nation's freedoms and the ideals we cherish so dearly.

Throughout my time as the commander of Combined Joint Task Force–West, I had spent almost an hour of my "free time" every day writing thank you letters, making certificates of appreciation, and signing birthday cards to my staff. I have given birthday cards to individuals who have worked for me since I was a major.

At Elmendorf, I signed an average of twenty-five cards a day with the individual's name, and included a personal note whenever I knew the individual well enough to be able to highlight something about his or her service. I kept an eye out to catch people doing the little extra things so that I could recognize them in staff meetings with a certificate of recognition or appreciation.

In my last few assignments, I wrote letters home to a spouse, parents, or children expressing my gratitude for their family member who was serving our country as a member of our team. I did the same in TF-W. The program was received extremely well. Family members back home were naturally worried about their loved ones serving on unknown front lines in the deserts of the Middle East, so far away from home. A warm letter of gratitude from the commander meant a lot to both our team and their families.

We Were Not There

On May 1, 2003, the US Secretary of Defense announced the end of the combat operations in Afghanistan, and President Bush declared an end to major combat operations in Iraq. My next job was to come up with a plan to get all of the remaining coalition forces out of the desert smoothly and to restore all of the host-nation facilities we had used during the conflict. In the next month, we would have to move some forces to their new bed-down locations in Iraq and redeploy everyone else and their equipment back home just as invisibly as they had come into the Middle East.

My last day in the region was June 5. This assignment reinforced some important lessons for me. First, winning the battle for hearts and minds of civilians is usually just as important as winning the battle against your adversary. Second, take good care of your logisticians and suppliers, for an operator cannot do much without their products and services. Third, look for people doing the little extras so you can recognize them appropriately—even in combat. Fourth, even though pragmatists and ideologues see solutions to the same problem in very different ways, they both get up in the morning trying to do the right thing for their organization and our country. Finally, the US Armed Forces and US State Department are fortunate to have volunteers who willingly go into harm's way when directed by the president to protect our nation's freedoms and the ideals we cherish.

Maybe the rest of this six-month story will be declassified someday and someone will be able to fill in the remaining operational details. Until that time comes, you will just have to accept that the Scud hunt was successful, even though we were technically "not in the region."[6] My next assignment would be more visible.

14

Military Diplomacy

*Destiny is not a matter of chance, it is a matter of
choice. It is not a thing to be waited for,
it is a thing to be achieved.*

— William Jennings Bryan

A PROMOTION TO AN ELEVEN-WORD TITLE might sound as if it wouldn't be much fun. But this promotion was. Back in Washington, DC, I was to serve as the Deputy Assistant Under Secretary of the Air Force for International Affairs. I learned early in my military career that long titles were not indicators of important assignments. In fact, promotions to shorter titles usually meant more leadership responsibilities. Fortunately, this lengthy title came with an important and challenging job description.

My operational background and diplomatic experience equipped me to represent the Air Force around the globe, serving as one of the faces of America to presidents, prime ministers, chiefs of staffs, and other senior government officials in the many countries I visited.[1] Having already served as the director of regional affairs, my promotion to the deputy position enabled me to build on the international relationships I had cultivated previously. I spent almost a third of my time on international travel—closing deals on sales of US aircraft and munitions, fostering closer bilateral relations and promoting cooperation with partner countries, and speaking on behalf of the military at trade shows, conferences, and academic seminars.

Then in July 2004, it was time for the summer shuffle of senior Air Force officers. I was assigned to the US European Command (EUCOM) in Stuttgart, Germany. We loved being back in Europe as a family.

At EUCOM I was to be the Director of Strategy, Plans, and Policy in the J-5 Directorate, one of the nine departments that make up the headquarters staff. I also would lead the J-8 Directorate, responsible for assessments, capabilities, and transformation. I was going to enjoy the responsibility for planning US military activities in ninety-three countries in Europe, Asia, and Africa. Each continent had its own interesting set of challenges.

The United States military environment in Europe had benefited greatly from past cooperation. However, we now encountered a new strategic environment. We had to deal with regional instability, fledgling democracies, a new relationship with Russia, and the growing challenges associated with weapons of mass destruction, terrorism, HIV/AIDS, and hydrocarbon security.

During the Cold War, the United States was focused on Europe. With forces amassed in numerous posts and bases throughout Western Europe, we were a reactive force—poised and ready to stop Soviet aggression at a moment's notice. In the new operating environment, we needed a proactive force with a smaller permanent footprint in Europe. We would now use forward-deployed forces to project power against potential threats in Southeast Europe, the Caucasus, and in Africa.

To adjust its force structure and combat capabilities to the new threats, the US European Command would cut its forces by 39 percent, from 112,000 to 68,500 personnel. We focused on building indigenous capabilities within regions, including growing an integrated airspace and maritime surveillance capability, strengthening border-control mechanisms, training quick-reaction forces, and upgrading command and control centers. EUCOM helped to reform old-style militaries in former Warsaw Pact countries and worked to resolve frozen conflicts through peaceful means.

Our directorate also led the thinking and planning on issues such as theater security cooperation projects, protection of the oil and gas infrastructure in Africa and Eurasia, and a variety of interesting initiatives throughout the region. We even tackled the outbreak of avian flu. I had a staff of one hundred thirty officers at Stuttgart and needed every one of these individuals to keep up with the changing issues and challenging matters in the ninety-three countries we had to be knowledgeable about at all times.[2]

While we had detailed documents that laid out the US vision, objectives, and approach for Europe and Eurasia, there was very little reference material on US policy toward Africa. We needed a strategic US policy document to guide our long-term plans and to help us set near-term priorities.

I had a discussion on this subject with the deputy EUCOM commander, General Chuck Wald, who directed me to take action. "Scott, I need you to draft a document to propose a new US Africa policy as a baseline for discussions in Washington," he said.

While the assignment was daunting, I was excited to get started. First, I recruited a small team of the individuals most knowledgeable about Africa's issues, including members of my J-5 Africa Division and key representatives from the intelligence, operations, and logistics directorates. At our first meeting, we wrote an outline for the white paper and identified US priorities, constraints, threats, risks, and desired outcomes. I volunteered to write the first draft over the weekend.

After two days of bleary eyes, stiff shoulders, and minimal sleep, I produced a five-page document. It described the military challenges of terrorism in Africa—the spawning grounds for the terrorists created by socio-economic hopelessness born of institutionalized poverty and governments that were unable or unwilling to provide for even the most basic of human needs. It was against this grim backdrop that I believed the United States would have to focus its current and long-term attention, efforts, and investment.

Our proposed vision statement for US policy was to see a continent where democratic ideals were valued, economies were vibrant, and the fifty-three sovereign nations were secure, stable, and at peace with their neighbors. To achieve these ends, Africans would need to have representative governments that were accountable to citizens through transparent electoral processes, the rule of law, free-market economies, and civilian control of militaries.

The white paper was relatively easy to write, but its vision and desired outcomes seemed a bit naive and unrealistic to me. Given Africa's harsh realities and daunting challenges, it would be nearly impossible for the US European Command to implement our ideas while dealing with our current full plate in NATO and Eastern Europe. Maybe that is why previous US administrations had turned their focus toward Europe and Asia, hoping that Africa's problems could be contained or benignly neglected.

Was it possible to change this historical paradigm to make a tangible difference? I believed America had no option but to engage proactively with measured optimism in Africa in an effort to bend the course of history toward the aspirations and objectives outlined in the white paper.

US Africa Command

US interests in Africa were changing fast, primarily because of the legitimate concerns about international terrorism and the increasing flow of African fighters to hotspots in other regions, especially Iraq, Afghanistan, and Yemen. We also were seeing more terrorist sympathizers and African mercenaries, in need of money, moving around Africa to fight in the conflicts in Algeria, Chad, Sudan, and Somalia.

During my orientation to EUCOM in June 2004, my predecessor, Major General Jeffrey Kohler, had given me some advice on work priorities. "You'll spend about 70 percent of your time on Europe and Eurasia, and 30 percent on Africa. Get smart on the European Union and NATO."

Only a year later that proportion was flipped: I was spending about 70 percent of my time on Africa's issues. Broad expanses of minimally governed areas in Africa were havens for terrorists and criminals. The trans-Sahara region offered sanctuary to Islamic extremists, smugglers, and various insurgent groups. Vast maritime areas provided havens for smuggling, piracy, and illegal oil bunkering.

But I was concerned that the terrorist lens through which many senior US decision-makers seemed to view the world was blurring the potential of nonmilitary solutions. I believed socio-economic programs could be equally as effective in the long run—maybe even more effective than military operations.

It seemed to me the international community could not continue to ignore the living conditions of nearly one billion Africans. Insufficient food production, illiteracy, inadequate healthcare, inequitable distribution of wealth, and the disintegrating social infrastructure continued to pose seemingly insurmountable challenges. Because the oppressive plight of Africans provided breeding grounds for extremist sentiment and terrorist activities, these humanitarian issues were at the same time global security issues.

As I studied this herculean challenge facing the US European Command, a couple of things became very clear. First, the United States had to mesh its efforts with those of our partners in the international community. We just did not have the resources, experience, access, or moral mandate to take on Africa's challenges by ourselves. Secondly, the Department of Defense was not organized for success in Africa. We needed a separate organization focused on managing US military and socioeconomic strategy in Africa's five economic regions.

This new organization would have to help integrate all the tools of statecraft and coordinate the activities of other US Departments and Agencies that were involved in security, stability, peacekeeping, and the fight against terrorism. Its personnel would have to spend most of their time building capacity, preventing conflict, and helping the countries of Africa do the same if America was going to make a difference on this emerging continent.

I knew that previous attempts from Washington to establish a separate US military organization focused on Africa had not succeeded. Nonetheless, I was undaunted. Through well-placed emails and private discussions, I passionately championed the idea of establishing a new Africa Command. The concept became a topic of discussion within EUCOM directorates and senior leaders talked openly about the idea. One of the critical supporters was Andy Hoehn, the deputy assistant secretary of defense for strategy. He saw the value of Africa Command right from the start of our email exchanges on the subject and worked to generate traction for the idea in the Pentagon.

This time, the response was different. EUCOM commander, Marine Corps General James L. Jones and Hoehn convinced Secretary Rumsfeld to consider a change to the Unified Command Plan.[3] In the end, the Department of Defense decided to establish a separate Geographic Combatant Command, named Africa Command (AFRICOM). It would be responsible for all US military operations on the continent of Africa and would coordinate America's military assistance and US involvement in Africa's security challenges. I was delighted.

Most of us who were involved from the beginning believed AFRICOM would foster a regional orientation to US efforts in Africa, as opposed to the State Department's organizational focus on individual countries. We expected that it would integrate efforts of the various US agencies more effectively. We envisioned that AFRICOM would coordinate regional initiatives with our international partners and the African nations.

Unfortunately, while AFRICOM is certainly better than the old three-way division of responsibility for US military efforts in Africa, it has not

met our initial expectations. Most AFRICOM activities in Africa appear
to be bilaterally fragmented rather than continentally coherent. I realize,
however, that this large organization is in a maturing process; there is still
hope.

Negotiations with Spain

I was working in my EUCOM office one afternoon in September 2005
when the operator patched an incoming call to my desk. On the other end
was my boss, EUCOM commander General Jones.

After providing background information, he said, "I want you to take
over the negotiations with Spain concerning US access to the tanker ramp
at Morón Air Base."[4]

My response was automatic. "Yes, sir. I'd be happy to do so."

Previous negotiations had failed. We had not been able to reach an
agreement on sharing the geo-strategic ramp with the Spanish Air Force in
over six years. Drawing on the negotiation skills I honed as a child in the
dining room at Rethy Academy in Belgian Congo,[5] I would seek to find a
mutually beneficial outcome that would bring an end to the standoff.

To prepare, I spent the next two weeks studying the history of
US-Spanish relations, both country's perspectives on Morón Air Base, and
possible scenarios for a mutually beneficial solution. When I understood
the legal terminology that had caused earlier efforts to fail, I called my
counterpart—Lieutenant General Pedro Pitarch Bartolome in the Spanish
Ministry of Defense.

Thanking him for Spain's generous contributions in the wake of
Hurricane Katrina and expressing my condolences to the Spanish military
and families who had recently lost nineteen soldiers in a helicopter accident in Afghanistan, I tried to lay the foundation for a friendly relationship.
After more discussion, I asked if the EUCOM team could come to Spain to
meet him and negotiate a mutually beneficial memorandum of agreement.
He agreed.

On September 16, our US team of five joined our Spanish counterparts
for the first negotiation session in Madrid. After greeting the Spanish team,
I took my seat across from our host, General Pitarch. Mr. Donald Timm,
EUCOM's legal advisor, sat on my right and the other US team members
took their places along our side of the long conference room table, across
from the Spanish delegation.

After General Pitarch and I gave our short opening remarks, we listened as the chief lawyers from each side laid out their tedious points in legalese. The first hour of negotiations had some tense moments. It became very clear that General Pitarch was not prepared for our arguments; he threatened to terminate the discussion several times. He finally left the negotiations after two hours, but authorized his deputy, Rear Admiral Enrique Perez Ramirez, to continue negotiating in his place.

The next day started out the same way. The US and Spanish teams were seated on opposite sides of the table, drinking coffee from a never-empty urn and still debating the appropriateness of "shall" or "will" in the list of each nation's responsibilities. By late morning, I couldn't take it anymore.

Turning to Admiral Perez, I said, "Do you have a draft access and ramp-sharing agreement you wanted us to sign?"

With a surprised look, he turned to the lawyer seated next to him and they spoke in Spanish for a minute. Their side of the table immediately began to buzz as team members hovered over a white loose-leaf binder, flipping quickly through the tabs and pages. Soon the binder clicked open and my counterpart handed me a six-page document. I suggested we could break for lunch and I asked him and my team to stay behind for a few minutes.

The admiral and I had already developed a friendly relationship because I had taken the time during coffee breaks to learn about his career, his family, and his hobbies. Holding the Spanish agreement, I asked if we could get a digital copy of the document and large-screen monitor or a projector so we could display this document on the front wall. My friend graciously agreed and we decided to reconvene at 2:00 p.m.

Huddled with the US team around one end of the conference table, I outlined my two objectives for the afternoon.

"First, I want to get away from the 'us' versus 'them' dynamics. We should put the admiral and me together at the end of the table, opposite the screen, and make the other seating more informal. Second, I want to demonstrate by our example that the United States will be good and respectful guests in their country, just as we expect the Spanish military to be generous and gracious hosts to us."

After a short discussion, I handed Spain's ramp-sharing agreement to our chief lawyer and asked him to highlight all the language the United States would find objectionable. We adjourned to the cafeteria for lunch with our Spanish hosts.

Before the afternoon session began, Mr. Timm, our legal advisor, whispered to me, "Most of this is okay. Unfortunately, the three or four problematic issues that stopped previous negotiations are still in their memorandum. Unless we can crack these, it will never fly in Washington."

"If that's all you have, we're in there," I said with a smile, taking my new seat at the end of the table.

We used a small projector to display the proposed Spanish documents on the front wall. After reviewing the text line by line and highlighting the major areas of disagreement, we identified four issues we would have to resolve over the next few days in order to produce the new, amenable memorandum.

It was great to hear both sides collaborating to suggest alternative wording that would make the new document agreeable to both Spain and the United States. After two more days, we reached final agreement on all outstanding issues. While not "perfect" for the United States, we now had an agreement that was fair and reciprocal. It facilitated US daily operations of our air-refueling tanker fleet and provided access to the entire Morón Air Base ramp in contingency situations.

General Pitarch and I initialed the memorandum of agreement privately in his office and celebrated the new access and ramp-sharing arrangement. Washington and Madrid reviewed the memorandum of agreement for legal sufficiency, translated it into Spanish, and high-level defense representatives from Spain and the United States formally signed the document in Madrid—a record-breaking two months after the negotiation process began.

A New Relationship with Libya?

In the twenty years since the United States bombed military targets in Libya in 1986, not one US general officer[6] had visited the North African country. While still assigned to EUCOM, I was asked to go to Tripoli to reestablish the US military relationship with the Libyan government.

The 1986 air strikes had been in retaliation—after years of Libyan sponsored terrorism against American troops and citizens—for the April 5 Libyan bombing of the La Belle nightclub in West Berlin that killed three individuals and injured two hundred twenty-nine people. Among them were US Army Sergeant Kenneth Ford, who was killed instantly in the blast, and seventy-nine American military personnel who were injured.

Investigators obtained communication transcripts of Libyan agents in East Germany and concluded that Tripoli was directly involved. On April 15, US F-111F aircraft bombed an airfield, a frogman training center at a naval academy, and the Bab al-Azizia barracks in Tripoli.[7]

For the next two years, there were no other major terrorist attacks linked to Libya until Pan Am Flight 103 was destroyed by a terrorist bomb over Lockerbie, Scotland, in 1988. In an effort to ease United Nations sanctions, Muammar al-Qadhafi agreed in 1999 to turn over the suspects in the Lockerbie attack to Scotland and eventually accepted responsibility for the bombing. In 2001 Qadhafi denounced al-Qaeda, and in 2003, he opened the country's weapons of mass destruction program to inspection and promised to dismantle it. While my eyes were wide open, I recognized that the United States and Libya could be poised for a new military relationship.

Major General Ahmed Azwai, my Libyan host whom I had met previously in Europe, welcomed us at the airport. He was very warm and friendly, which set the tone for the rest of the visit.

Entering the comfortable office of Libya's chief of staff of the air force and air defenses to kick off our three days of meetings, General Azwai and I accepted General Rifi Sharifi's gesture to sit around his coffee table. Our staffs and US Embassy representatives took their seats in the outer ring of chairs. After a warm "ice breaker" conversation, we had open, honest, and frank discussions on Libya's expectations for a new military relationship with the United States. The three of us talked about constraints and restrictions on our activities, along with potential areas for cooperation, as our staffs scribbled cryptic notes to document the discussions. We left with the clear understanding that the Libyans wanted to establish immediate military-to-military relations with the United States.

In the afternoon, our entourage drove west of Tripoli for about thirty minutes to visit the Libyan naval academy, which had been bombed in 1986. We were impressed with the strong leadership, dedicated staff, and excellent facilities. This institution graduated the officers for the Libyan Navy and civilian engineers for the Merchant Marines. The commandant expressed a desire for Libya to become a naval training center for the African Union.

During the next day's office call with the minister of foreign affairs, we discussed Libya's efforts to assist Darfur, to resolve the dispute in the Western Sahara, and to support the African Union. The minister outlined Libya's need for peacekeeping training, and offered to assist with socio-economic roots of terrorism, including activities to slow illegal migration, to improve health programs, and to increase literacy and employment opportunities throughout the continent. I believed his suggestions to improve bilateral cooperation offered several good opportunities to initiate a building-block program to reestablish and strengthen US-Libya military relations.

There was one last place I wanted to visit while in Libya. An American cemetery in Tripoli cradles the remains of at least five, and possibly eleven, sailors who lost their lives on the USS Intrepid during the Barbary War in 1804.[8] The outer walls were beginning to crumble as the ocean's waves continued to erode the foundations and the interior was in a sad state of disrepair. Several embassy personnel had recently spent a weekend reassembling the gravestones and removing weeds, but more needed to be done.

I strongly believed that America should care for the resting place of these brave veterans who blew up their ship and gave their lives to prevent the ship's valuable cargo of gun powder from falling into the hands of the enemy. However, my efforts and the efforts of others to honor these sailors and to generate funds to move or rehabilitate the current cemetery received little interest in Washington, DC.

As my team and I climbed the stairs of our military aircraft, we had great hopes that we could begin a new chapter of positive US-Libya relations, especially with the military. We had been given access to very high-level officials in the Libyan government during our visit and I had been pleasantly surprised by the realistic expectations of our Libyan counterparts. The Libyans showed us warm hospitality that we reciprocated with open friendship and appreciation.

A Missed Opportunity?

Fast-forward five years. After a call with Germany's Chancellor Angela Merkel on Saturday, February 26, 2011, President Obama stated that Colonel Qadhafi had lost the legitimacy to rule and should step down. This statement was accurate, but it did not help facilitate a peaceful, face-saving way for Qadhafi to leave power. The window for a negotiated settlement slammed shut when the White House and other key members of the administration, including Secretary of State Hillary Clinton, joined senior European and NATO officials in using fiery rhetoric to demand Qadhafi's immediate exit and a total regime change.

After the multi-nation coalition initiated a massive air attack against government forces and facilities in Libya on March 19, Qadhafi had no way in which he could step down and still save face. When the internationally supported band of armed rebels from Benghazi pushed the Qadhafi regime into a proverbial corner with their efforts to overthrow his four decades in power, Qadhafi and his loyalists likely believed they had no remaining honorable option but to fight to the death.

If our intervention in the Libyan conflict was about saving lives under the "responsibility to protect" doctrine, then US efforts were a catastrophic failure. In 2011, Libya's National Transitional Council put the losses at 30,000 dead and 50,000 wounded during the battle for Tripoli, and some experts believe the actual casualty numbers were higher.[9] The number of lost lives has grown much larger since that time as civil war continues to rage in many parts of Libya—government leaders, militia members, and innocent bystanders die daily with no end in sight. Libyans continue to flee their country to escape the bloodshed and miserable living conditions that still exist today.

While I did not like the way Qadhafi ruled Libya, repressed much of his population, jailed and shot demonstrators, and misappropriated the country's wealth, I believe we could have helped to negotiate a peaceful transition of power within Libya. From my perspective, the Obama administration's foreign policy ideologues rushed too quickly for their "sticks," exacerbated the situation with unbending rhetoric, and removed the more peaceful alternatives for a regime change.

Supporting armed rebels in a civil war or masking a coup d'état as a democratic movement seldom produces good results. We can see this in the continued political divisions, devastated infrastructure, and weak economy that characterize Libya today. In addition, the country-wide unrest gave the Islamic State of Iraq and Syria (ISIS) an opening in Libya that they have exploited against western interests. Militants in Libya pledged allegiance to ISIS leader Abu Bakr al-Baghdadi and formed the Libya Province branch on November 13, 2014.

As I look back on my ground-breaking trip to Tripoli in 2006, I remember that I had such high hopes that the United States could help bring security and stability to North Africa through a better relationship with the government of Libya. Today, my heart aches for the people of this nation who have endured so much suffering and loss since the fall of Muammar Qadhafi's government.

Scott retired as a Major General
on October 1, 2006.
(Courtesy of the US Air Force)

I believe we missed a significant opportunity to make a difference in this country . . . an opportunity that might have offered practical options to avoid the turmoil and bloodshed we have witnessed daily since 2011. We could have done better; we should have pursued a peaceful regime change in Libya.

Taking Off My Boots

A few months after I returned to Stuttgart, Germany from the Libya trip, I made the difficult decision to retire from the military I had served for thirty-two years, effective October 1, 2006.

My daughter, Katherine, had graduated from the local high school in June. We knew that she needed a stable platform in the United States as she started college, so Judy and I considered all of our options. It appeared my next job in the military would be very demanding and likely take me overseas again. After praying and seeking counsel from military leaders, peers, and family, we decided it was time for me to hang up my uniform.[10]

I had enjoyed serving America as an Air Force officer, and would not want to give up even one day of active duty. But it was time to move on. This was the right choice for my family and me. I have never regretted the decision.

The military gave me a superb background in security issues. It gave me the opportunity to hone my diplomatic skills, and it gave me insights and perspectives on numerous cultures and on US international relations. Military service was the perfect classroom for my next career.

15

Obama Goes to Africa

Leadership is practiced not so much in words as in attitude and in actions.

— Harold Geneen

"SENATOR BARACK OBAMA would like General Gration to accompany him to Africa."[1]

I received this message from the Pentagon in July 2006, a few days before my scheduled retirement ceremony at Patch Barracks in Stuttgart, Germany. My official retirement date was October 1, but I had planned to take leave in August and September before starting work at Millennium Villages International in October.

The Senator wanted to travel over his congressional break in late August, which was right in the middle of the time I was scheduled to take leave. Unable to move my official October retirement date, Judy and I decided that I should use my allocated vacation days to accompany Senator Obama and ensure that he would have an enjoyable and profitable trip to Africa.

As Director of Strategy, Policy, Plans, and Assessments at the US European Command (EUCOM) in Stuttgart, I periodically had returned to Washington to update congressional leaders on our military activities and new initiatives, especially when the legislative branch was appropriating funds for Department of Defense programs.

One senator took a special interest in EUCOM's activities. That was Senator Obama, the newly elected Democrat from Illinois who was on the European subcommittee. He was working closely with Richard Lugar on counter-proliferation issues in former Warsaw Pact countries, and he had a personal connection with Africa.

At my first meeting with Senator Obama, I remember noticing that he had a different demeanor and approach than many of the other senators I met with on the Hill. First, he listened. He did not lecture me about his agenda and objectives. Second, he wanted to go beyond just hearing a report about what we were doing—he wanted to understand why we were doing it and what we hoped to gain as an outcome.

Walking toward the door of his office after one of my last meetings with the Senator, he said, "When I go to Africa, I want you to take me."

I had no idea if he was serious or not, but of course I responded. "I'd be happy to."

Now this trip was actually happening.

Mark Lippert, Senator Obama's Senate staffer, planned the trip with assistance from military and State Department professionals. We coordinated with the US embassies in South Africa, Kenya, Chad, and Djibouti to arrange high-level meetings with a wide spectrum of officials and local representatives in each country. Working through many challenges, we put together a packed itinerary that flowed well logistically and strategically.

I met up with Senator Obama and his team in Amsterdam on August 19. We would continue to South Africa on a commercial flight that departed at 10:00 a.m. and would not land in Cape Town until 8:30 p.m. Africa is an enormous continent—flying from the northern coast of Algeria to the southern tip of South Africa is about the same distance as flying from New York City to Honolulu, Hawaii.

The next day, Sunday, we started with a poignant trip to Robben Island. The impenetrable fortress on the small land mass five miles off the southern tip of the continent served as a government prison during the apartheid period.[2] During the twenty-minute boat ride from Cape Town, we sat on plastic seats in the partially enclosed cabin section of the ferry boat and tried to hear our tour guide over the rumbling engines and blowing wind. Ahmed Kathrada, known for twenty-six years as Prisoner No. 468, provided insights about his captivity as well as that of Nelson Mandela, the first black president of South Africa.

Once inside the penitentiary, Kathrada escorted us to the small room where the government of South Africa incarcerated Mr. Mandela for eighteen of his twenty-seven years of imprisonment.[3] Senator Obama and I stood in this cell, looking out from behind the same bars that secured Mr. Mandela's window, reflecting quietly on these almost three lost decades of Mr. Mandela's life.

Inside that room, I was reminded of the words of nineteenth century poet Frederick Langbridge which my father often quoted to me about keeping a positive attitude. "Two men looked out from prison bars; one saw mud, the other saw stars."

Nelson Mandela was one who looked out from behind bars and saw stars. He developed a vision for his country while he was in prison—a vision where whites, Boers, Asians, and Africans could live together peacefully in one country. Mandela envisioned a strong country that could be the economic engine for Africa's southern region and he shouldered the responsibility of bringing that vision to reality someday.

Watching photographers capture the image of Senator Obama looking out from behind the bars that once fenced South Africa's first post-apartheid president, I saw more than a well-composed picture. I believed I was looking at a man who had the potential to do for America what Nelson Mandela had done for his country. I was observing an individual who had the potential to unite the different ethnic groups in America, someone who could ignite the economic engines of our country. I thought that Senator Obama, with his African father and American mother, biracial yet identified as black, reared both in the United States and overseas, could be a transformative figure. That morning on Robben Island, I realized that perhaps I was traveling with a future president of the United States.

Senator Obama looking out from Nelson Mandela's cell. (Reuters photo/Howard Burditt)

Returning to Cape Town, Senator Obama wanted to have his trip blessed with a word of prayer by Cape Town's Anglican archbishop. I was impressed. We stayed on at the St. James Anglican Church to attend a multi-faith meeting where we saw Muslims, Jews, and Christians working together to resolve issues and to foster better communication in their communities.

One of the experiences that touched me most was the Monday morning tour of a hospital in Khayelitsha Township. Walking through this crowded facility, I saw the suffering of these individuals in a more personal way. The head nurse relayed stories about the medical and emotional needs of families dealing with HIV/AIDS. We learned that sixty-two percent of the infected people in South Africa were women. The Senator and I had the opportunity to go into a private room—behind closed doors without doctors, tour guides, or reporters—and listen to the heart-wrenching stories of some of these women.

As we departed, Senator Obama gave these women hugs and expressed his gratitude to them for having shared their life stories. He did not see these ladies as statistics; he viewed them as special people who had endured much physical and emotional pain. He saw them as individuals who needed our continued love, compassion, and medical support.

Senator Obama publicly criticized the South African government as being in "denial" of the HIV/AIDS epidemic, specifically because they were advocating for nutritional treatments over medical alternatives. Yet HIV/AIDS continued to claim as many as one thousand lives a day. His courageous stand likely kept us from being granted a courtesy call with South Africa's President Thabo Mbeki.

That evening Senator Obama and I went for a long stroll down the cement walkway that separated the sea from the rows of beautiful townhouses and condominiums in this predominantly white Victoria & Alfred Waterfront neighborhood. Afterward, we met Mark Lippert and the Senator's communications director, Robert Gibbs, at a nice restaurant in Cape Town's modern waterfront shopping center. Joining us was our military escort officer, US Navy Lieutenant DeVere Crooks.

During the meal, Senator Obama asked me what I thought about the war in Iraq and about US foreign policy toward Africa and the Middle East. While eating my way through a delicious South African steak dinner, I told him that I believed it was time to get out of Iraq and to remake the image of the United States in this part of the world. At the end of the evening, he asked me to write down the ideas I had shared, in addition to any more thoughts and suggestions I might have about Iraq, our national defense, and US foreign policy. It was clear that we held similar convictions regarding these national issues.

Even though it was after eleven o'clock when I returned to my hotel room, I took out my computer. After playing around with themes and key words, I wrote *ARISE*. This would serve as both the title and outline for the paper. Recognizing the United States must use all elements of national power—diplomacy, economic influence, military strength, and informational advantage—in a coordinated, synergistic, and effective manner to accomplish its objectives internationally, I decided to limit my think piece to foreign policy concerns and national defense priorities.

The first section, "A," was about our ARMED FORCES and the need to rebuild and reshape the US military's capabilities to meet today's challenges and likely future threats. My discussion included a section on asymmetrical threats, such as cyber attacks and the information security issues I struggled with while serving as director of information operations on the Joint Staff.

Next, the "R" section discussed the RELATIONSHIPS we had to restore around the globe. The Bush administration's you're-either-with-us-or-against-us rhetoric had alienated many people, as had US bluster about the "axis of evil." Some of America's generalizations about the 1.5 billion Muslims and the roughly 200 million Arabs had damaged our relations with many of these people and the countries where they lived. We needed to make a special effort to rebuild enduring partnerships with these and other key nations that could eventually contribute more to our mutual security.

In the third section, "I," I wrote about reestablishing America as a nation of global INFLUENCE. We could not just rely on US military presence or economic dominance. America needed to regain influence that was based on reciprocated respect, a foundation of shared values, a common vision of the future, mutually beneficial objectives, agreed-upon common goals and collaborative solutions, and a trusting relationship that was continually reinforced by deed and word. This approach to international influence was easy to talk about, but hard to accomplish. Nevertheless, it had to be a foundational concept of US foreign policy and our national defense. I was careful to express my firm belief that the policies of the departments of

State and Defense had to reflect the United States of America—not just the political agenda of the Republican or Democratic Party.

The "S" section was about ways we could increase SECURITY to protect Americans and US interests at home and around the world with a special emphasis on addressing the root causes of instability and insecurity. I believed our foreign policy had to have a strong socio-economic component in order to be effective, especially in the Middle East and Africa.

The final section, "E," contained my thoughts for an EXIT strategy to disengage safely and prudently from Iraq. I also expressed my perspective that the United States should use its military power to defend our critical and vital interests—not to intervene in civil wars or religious conflicts. In my view, focusing on these five ARISE priorities would give us a good start on improving America's national security and US foreign policy.

During our trip to Cape Town, I witnessed a US leader, guided by a spiritual compass and a genuine compassion for his fellow human beings, moved by the heart-wrenching stories of those who had experienced so much pain and suffering. I saw Barack Obama as a frontrunner who had the moral courage to criticize wrongs when he saw them and to condemn society's injustices. This was just the beginning of my professional respect for this man and our personal relationship.

A Credible Candidate

After an enjoyable visit in Cape Town, we boarded our US European Command C-20B aircraft and flew to Pretoria on August 22. This plane, the military version of the commercial Gulfstream III, would serve as our transport for most of the remainder of the trip around Africa. Except for the upgraded military satellite communications, the C-20B was very similar to a commercial executive aircraft.

On the flight, Senator Obama and I sat across from each other in comfortable VIP seats in the forward executive cabin. Our staff and security detail were in the aft cabin. With a pull-out table between us, we talked about our families and about current events in Western Europe, Asia, and Africa. I was a lifelong Republican and he was a liberal Democrat, yet we shared similar worldviews and pragmatic approaches to problem solving. These were interesting discussions.

The next day's trip to Soweto, southwest of Johannesburg, may have been the most impressive and surprising for me. My mental images of this township dated back to the Soweto riots of the mid-1970s—people running through white clouds of teargas, plumes of black smoke billowing up from blazing tires, and white policemen patrolling the dark slums with loaded weapons and armored personnel carriers. As we drove down the street that had produced two Nobel Laureates—Nelson Mandela and Desmond Tutu—beautiful flowers, manicured green lawns, and brightly painted houses splashed vivid colors all over my mind's outdated white and black pictures. The former slum had transformed into a diverse neighborhood and vibrant community.

The Hector Pieterson Museum was our first stop. This facility was named in honor of the first student killed in the Soweto uprising. The displays and framed pictures poignantly conveyed the pain that began with protests led by high school students on the morning of June 16, 1976. These demonstrations escalated into fierce clashes between armed police and unarmed students. Hector Pieterson was a thirteen-year-old student at Orlando West High School when he was shot and killed. It was this and other ensuing deaths that focused the international community's bright spotlight on South Africa's apartheid policy and its strict racial separation laws.

Antoinette Sithole, Hector's sister, led us on a tour. The museum's images and memorabilia vividly recreated the tensions on both sides of the conflict and the still-painful emotions of those who witnessed the dreadful events thirty years before. I can remember being behind Senator Obama as he stood with his arm around Mrs. Sithole's shoulder, studying the details of a large black-and-white photograph hanging on the museum wall. The iconic picture captured the anguish and urgency on the faces of Antoinette and Mbuyisa Makhubo, the lanky teenager carrying a dying Hector in his arms as they ran to get medical attention.[4]

Our time with Archbishop Emeritus Desmond Tutu was the most memorable of all our meetings with government and community leaders.[5] I had met him before and always appreciated the archbishop's positive attitude and infectious laugh. We enjoyed an insightful discussion about South Africa, the continent, and global issues.

"You are going to be a very credible presidential candidate," Archbishop Tutu told Senator Obama with confidence as we were departing his Soweto residence. We all just laughed, but I quietly believed the archbishop was right on the mark in his insightful prediction.

Back Home in Kenya

During the long flight from South Africa to Kenya, Senator Obama and I discussed various topics. He asked lots of questions and then summarized his conclusions in a very succinct and thoughtful way. I perceived that Senator Obama used exercises like this to hone his problem-solving skills and to further develop his gift of asking the right questions in order to get useful and relevant information.

We touched down at Jomo Kenyatta International Airport just after 6:00 p.m. It was great to be back in Kenya. Even the air had a smell of home as I took a few deep breaths while descending the aircraft stairs behind Senator Obama.

Ambassador Michael Ranneberger and his staff escorted us into the awaiting convoy of Toyota Land Cruisers. With sirens blaring and lights flashing, we made our way through Nairobi's snarled rush-hour traffic to the Serena Hotel. The last time he had traveled to Kenya, Senator Obama carried a backpack and walked without recognition.[6] Fourteen years later, he arrived as a US senator and a Kenyan hero.

Michelle Obama, along with their daughters Malia and Sasha, joined the Senator for the Kenya portion of our trip as a personal vacation and not at government expense. Auma Obama, the Senator's stepsister, and her young daughter linked up to be part of the family activities. It was obvious they enjoyed being together.

Our schedule was packed. Starting right after breakfast, we had meetings at the American Embassy and with several cabinet ministers, followed by a courtesy call on Kenya's President Mwai Kibaki at State House. While the 2007 national elections were still a year away, it was obvious that the country was already beginning to polarize along tribal lines.

A 12:30 p.m. meeting with opposition leader Uhuru Kenyatta was followed by lunch with a group of members of Parliament. Then Michelle Obama and the girls joined our entourage to participate in a remembrance ceremony at the site of the former US Embassy.

Eight years before, on August 7, 1998, al-Qaeda operatives reduced the six-story US Embassy building to a pile of twisted metal and concrete rubble. The attack killed two hundred and eighteen and wounded more than 4,000 people.[7] The twelve US citizens who lost their lives that day fortunately were the last Americans to date to be killed by terrorists in Kenya.

As we entered the guarded gate, crowds of Kenyans pressed against the perimeter iron fence straining to see Senator Obama. People gathered on rooftops, peered from windows of adjacent buildings, and joined the sea of humanity crowding nearby streets, many with no view at all. Some wore colored T-shirts saying *Obama for President*; others just chanted, "O-baaa-ma, O-baaa-ma."

After Senator Obama wrote a note in the condolence book, the entire family walked slowly to the curved marble wall inscribed with all the names of those who died in the bombing. They solemnly placed wreaths in front of the memorial and bowed for a short moment of silence and remembrance.

As we departed, the Senator moved toward a low police barricade to shake some hands. The crowd surged toward him, trying to touch his hand. With the situation rapidly moving toward pandemonium, the security team pushed the Senator and his family toward a silver Toyota Land Cruiser. We all scurried to our cars while the local police cleared a narrow corridor through the masses for our convoy to depart. As we drove away, a few members of our team still had lingering signs of panic on their faces as they replayed mental videos of well-wishers mobbing their boss.

Despite the intense schedule, Senator Obama was up early every morning to exercise, and he frequently was awake after midnight working on a new book, *The Audacity of Hope.* Yet he was always prepared for every meeting—he had read all the background papers and was able to get quickly to the core issues in each discussion.

I provided additional background between meetings about the individuals we were going to see and offered an "ice breaker" statement or question for him to use to start off the meeting. He hardly needed my assistance, but Senator Obama always made me feel useful.

Family Time

Throngs of people lined the roads as we drove by and entrepreneurs took advantage of the event by hawking brightly colored tee shirts with the silk-screened image of Senator Obama emblazoned on the front. This was our welcome to Kisumu, the heartland of the Luo tribe and the homeland of Senator Obama's father.

Arriving at a regional HIV/AIDS testing center, Barack and Michelle Obama went through the counseling and testing steps together for all to see and hear, including having their blood tested. When the process was complete, the Senator gave a compelling speech, pleading for everyone to know their status. This public HIV/AIDS test by both of the Obamas encouraged Kenyan couples to be tested together and gave a very positive boost to the fight against the spread of this deadly virus in Kenya and East Africa.

Our convoy of Toyota Land Cruisers pulled up to the front of Mama Sarah's modest house in the tiny village of Nyangoma-Kogelo. Standing by the porch was Senator Obama's eighty-five-year-old grandmother, greeting us with open arms and a warm smile—Sarah Hussein Onyango Obama was obviously delighted to see her now-famous grandson. This visit was intended to give the Obamas some family time, especially since Malia and Sasha were visiting the burial site of their Kenyan grandfather and meeting their great-grandmother for the first time.

While this trip to Kisumu had been hectic, it was a great day for Kenya and for the Obama family. Before passengers boarded the commercial flight to Nairobi, I asked permission to enter the cockpit to greet the pilots. To my delight, the senior pilot had been in the Kenya Air Force when I served as the US instructor pilot assigned to the Kenyan military in the early 1980s. It was nice to get the latest news on many of my former fighter-pilot trainees.

Experiencing the "Other Side"

While most of Nairobi was waking leisurely to a beautiful Sunday morning, Senator Obama and I boarded a USAF C-130 cargo aircraft for the flight to Wajir, a rural town in northeastern Kenya. Severe drought in the Horn of Africa had caused many nomadic pastoralists in this region to teeter on the knife-edge of survival as many of their animals starved to death.

Gathered in the community center, a simple structure made of corrugated iron sheets nailed to a wooden frame, we sat around a long table, chasing away thirsty flies that would quickly return to continue exploring our warm brows for moisture. As we drank sweet milky tea, local leaders and government representatives took turns telling us about the political situation, the spillover effects from the conflict in Somalia, and the economic dynamics at work in this semi-arid region.

After an hour of discussions, our team visited the local camel and sheep auction. Although it was very hot in the desert's sun, we enjoyed the scene as old men examined the animals and bargained for the best deal. Noticing the reddening complexions of some in our group, our Kenyan host walked us to the shade of a solitary tree where a group of younger men and women told us about their economic struggles.

Before leaving, community leaders presented Senator Obama with a parting gift of local garb—the traditional white cloth Somali men use to wrap themselves. After significant prompting, he agreed to try it on with the help of our hosts. Someone in our group captured this act of kindness and generosity on the part of our hosts and Senator Obama's reciprocal appreciation on camera.

Whether inadvertently or with malicious intent, the photograph of Senator Obama trying on local robes over his plum-colored golf shirt and khakis hit media outlets with a splash. It became a *Drudge Report* headline and many newspapers and television commentators across America used the story to portray the Senator as a Muslim.

I spent a lot of time during the 2008 campaign defending his decision to try on the community's gracious gift. To a reporter's typical question, I would explain that Senator Obama was merely being a great guest. I have learned that logic is not always persuasive in politics. The story of Obama being a Muslim continued to circulate widely, especially in right-wing blogs and on conservative websites.

After returning to Nairobi, we made our way down narrow shop-lined streets to the outskirts of Kibera, the largest slum on the continent.[8] Within

Senator Obama accepts gift of local robes.
(Anonymous photo)

an area of less than two square miles, about one million people live in abject poverty, crowding into small shacks with little access to running water and other basic services.

While we were inside a community center listening to a presentation on micro-finance assistance for local entrepreneurs and small businesses, news spread that Barack Obama was in Kibera. The crowds mushroomed rapidly. By the time we were ready to depart, the streets were packed with those wanting to catch a glimpse of the Senator.

Mark Lippert was able to clear just enough room for our vehicles to get repositioned next to the doorway. Safely inside the vans, our drivers carefully inched forward through the mob of jubilant Kenyans. We watched as smiling faces pressed against the tinted windows and waving hands slid slowly past as people from Kibera peered into our SUV to get a look at this man with Kenyan heritage who had become successful and famous.

Parking a few minutes later, we stepped out of our upscale vehicles into widespread squalor. Walking single file down a shoulder-wide path that wove between shacks and under hand-washed clothes hung out to dry, we jumped over open sewage drains and avoided plastic bags of excrement, known as "flying toilets." Our destination was a progressive HIV/AIDS-prevention program affiliated with the University of North Carolina. The public health officer there, in a sobering presentation, told us that one in five of the slum's population was HIV positive.

Twenty minutes later, we were back in the opulence of the Serena Hotel. Except for mud and filth on our shoes, no one would have known we had been to the slums on the other side of town. While separated by only a few miles, it was hard for me to reconcile the enormous disparity between Kibera's poor and the Serena's wealthy. We all share the responsibility to help those stuck in the seemingly perpetual cycle of poverty, to provide more job opportunities, and to give these individuals a genuine hope for a brighter future.

Take Care of Barack

Wangari Maathai stepped forward from the line of dignitaries to greet us as we arrived at Nairobi's Uhuru Park on Monday. The overcast skies did not dull Kenya's Nobel Peace Prize laureate and world-renown environmental-ist's bright yellow dress or diminish her passion as she presided over the tree-planting ceremony.[9] Senator Obama and his family planted an African olive tree and an evergreen tree native to Africa.

After lunch, our convoy headed toward the University of Nairobi's auditorium. A rousing welcome from the standing-room only crowd greeted us before Senator Obama gave a "tough love" speech.

He said that Kenya would never find its true economic potential unless the nation abandoned its entrenched government corruption and deep-seated tradition of tribal politics. During his speech, which was carried live on all local television stations, Senator Obama challenged his listeners to reject the assumption that corruption is part of Kenyan culture, and to stand up and speak out against injustices. He said that the Kenyan government should reduce patronage jobs, pass laws and regulations to prevent individual bureaucrats from twisting the rules to suit their own desires, and end ethnic-based politics.

While he could have chosen to say things in Kenya to make everyone feel good, Senator Obama again showed that he had the courage and conviction to recommend a tough remedy. Only someone of Barack Obama's stature in Kenya could have delivered this strong and candid message.

Soon it came time for Michelle Obama to return with the children to Chicago. Her husband would be continuing to Djibouti and Chad. As she was saying good-bye she had a simple request. "Take care of Barack," she told me.

"You know I will," I said. I gave her a hug. "It's been a real pleasure to travel with all of you."

Commander-in-Chief?

Looking out of our aircraft's window, I could see the dimly lit but familiar shapes of fighter jets parked inside sun shelters. It was 1:30 a.m. when our C-20B shut down its engines on Camp Lemonnier's airfield parking ramp in tiny Djibouti, on the coast of the Horn of Africa.[10] This military installation housed the headquarters of CENTCOM's Combined Joint Task Force-Horn of Africa and was the temporary home to about 1,200 men and women from all branches of the US Armed Forces.

Senator Obama did not have an obvious connection with the military, so I was not sure how this visit was going to turn out. We met for breakfast at the dining facility and soldiers willingly came over and sat at our table.

The Senator, always smiling and friendly, soon learned about their jobs, families, and hardships in service to America.

Shortly after the briefings and a walking tour of the facilities ended, Senator Obama was on the courts, participating in a pick-up basketball game. That evening, there was a basketball tournament and the Senator's team was right in the middle of it. During our meals at the dining facility, military personnel continued to flock around him. Senator Obama was keenly interested in what each military member was saying and expressed his and America's sincere appreciation for what these service members were doing. Clearly, my fears about the Senator's possible inability to relate to the US military were unfounded.

I Can Work With This Guy

Chad, in central Africa, was the last country on our itinerary. Arriving at the Kempinski Hotel in N'Djamena at 9:30 p.m. on September 1, I remember walking to the elevator with Senator Obama after checking in. As we waited to ascend to the seventh floor, we discussed one's motivation for public service—whether it be aspiring to show oneself as a person of stature or having the opportunity to make a difference. I have always known my motivation was in the latter category, and after our conversation, I confirmed the Senator's was also. We had many philosophical talks throughout the trip, and the more we talked, the more I liked him.

Using two United Nations' aircraft, we flew the next morning to a dirt airstrip near a remote refugee camp on the Chad-Sudanese border. Here, UN and humanitarian organizations in the Mile Refugee Camp at Guereda were caring for refugees from Darfur who had escaped the killing and raping perpetrated by the Sudan-backed Janjaweed. We listened to African Muslim refugees tell of the heartbreaking violence they had experienced in Sudan. This was an opportunity for Senator Obama to see the humanitarian crisis in Darfur with his own eyes.[11]

After a very long day in the Mile Refugee Camp and in Darfur, we raced back to the planes so we could take off before official sunset. By the time we arrived back at our hotel, it was just after midnight. Ready to enter our rooms and get some much-needed rest, each of us encountered the same problem—our room keys were not working. The key codes in the electronic door locks had expired at midnight.

We had been up for more than eighteen hours. Everyone was tired and we could not find the duty manger. When I told Senator Obama I was working on the problem, I received a reply I did not expect.

"Don't worry about me, Scott. I'm going down to the lounge to sleep there. When you get the key to my room, just come wake me up," he said.

I thought to myself, *I can work with a guy like this.* I soon found a manager to make new key cards and we entered our rooms for a few hours of rest.

The trip was almost over. We boarded our military aircraft for the last flight at 7:30 a.m. en route to Frankfurt, and then we both took the United Airlines flight to Chicago.

Exhausted, but satisfied, I sat in my exit-row aisle seat and reflected over the last couple of weeks. I liked the way Senator Obama thought about issues. His was not a partisan approach; instead, he wanted to do the right thing for America and the world. He viewed issues from a strategic perspective, but then drilled down quickly to determine what was tactical and practical. Senator Obama was always thinking about how to make our country more economically competitive, safer, and more secure—better for future generations of Americans. I was also very impressed with his integrity, judgment, honesty, and the way he treated his staff.

When we started this five-country journey, I believed that we were different in terms of our perspectives. After all, I was a Republican who had been in the military for thirty-two years and he was a community organizer and a Democrat. I soon learned that we had much in common; it started with a deep love for our country. We shared a strong desire to serve our country, to safeguard our democratic institutions, and to protect our American values.

When I said goodbye to Senator Obama at O'Hare International Airport after seventeen days in Africa, I did so not only as a traveling companion, Kiswahili translator, and debating partner, but as a friend.

16

Service, Faith, and Family

I'm convinced more than ever that man finds
liberation only when he binds himself to God and
commits himself to his fellow man.

— Ronald Reagan

First, let me share a bit about my faith, my family, and my commitment to service. Those subjects are at the center of this memoir because they are the center of everything in my life. Relationships in my family and service to God, my community, my country, and my fellow global citizens are central to my childhood, my experiences as a warrior-diplomat, and who I am as a person.

Growing up as a missionary child, faith was an important and everyday part of life. My parents lived out their faith in authentic ways. They taught us to love God and to give back to our society. I made a personal decision to follow Christian teachings when I was seven years old. My faith is solid and its influence on my life is strong.

The desire I have to serve and my motivation to "do the right thing" were both instilled in me as a child. My mother and father guided me by their example. They modeled "service before self" and encouraged me to live according to my principles, no matter what the consequences might be.

My paternal grandparents immigrated to the United States from England and my grandfather worked as a gardener and caretaker on several

of New Jersey's large estates. Emulating my grandfather's strong work ethic, my father studied hard and earned his PhD from New York University.

Guiding me through word and example, my parents modeled the core
values of integrity, service, and excellence. They were intolerant of lying,
stealing, and dishonesty, and made it hard to live by anything other than
high ethical standards. On top of this, my mother and father made sure that
I understood the biblical foundations for integrity. They lived their faith
every day.

Service was a calling for my parents. My father joined the Navy in
World War II in answer to our nation's call to serve. After his time in the
Navy, he felt a call to serve God in Africa as an educator. Judy's parents
followed a similar path. Her dad served in the Army for three years, and
then her parents completed graduate school before departing for Africa as
missionary teachers.

My two younger sisters, Barbara Harbert and Judy Kohl, and I were
reared in a close-knit family environment. We always felt that we were
richly blessed with possessions even though we did not have much compared to our peers in the United States. Losing our belongings during the
evacuation from Congo reminded us that possessions are really not all that
important. We had so much to be thankful for: family, friends, and life itself.

My Second Priority

While I do not remember meeting my future wife, Judy, when I was just
three years old, I am grateful that we were able to grow up together in
Africa—to share faith, friends, experiences, and memories. Our families
picnicked together in the Great Rift Valley where Judy and I chased giraffes
before eating grilled hamburgers under the setting sun. We enjoyed hiking
along animal trails almost hidden in the lush vegetation and thorny acacia
bushes. The Gration and DeYoung children held a tradition of trekking
into the woods each December to cut down a Christmas tree. We spent
vacations together on Diani Beach near Mombasa, and our families toured
parts of the Middle East and Europe together when we traveled back to the
United States in 1963.

Judy's support and encouragement was a tremendous boost to my
military career, and she deserves much of the credit for my promotions

Scott (left) and Judy (right) cutting a Christmas tree in 1964.

beyond the rank of captain. My wife has been the rock of stability in our home. Judy made our home a wonderful place for our four children while coping with seventeen moves across America and around the world.

My Air Force career did demand a lot of my time and, given my type-A personality,[1] I typically put in long hours at work. Yes, there were times I shorted my home responsibilities in order to accomplish my military duties. Not only did Judy have to cover the logistics of parenting, such as making sure the children arrived at their activities on time or received the medical attention they needed, she also had to be emotionally strong and resilient. Looking back, I regret that I sometimes was not available to be the husband and father I should have been. I am grateful to Judy for her unwavering commitment to God and our family that overcame the exhaustion and loneliness that can be part of military life.

My "love language"[2] is serving others by repairing their broken things or doing something special for them. My family has learned to accept my way of expressing love, but I am sure my wife would have rather had more quality time together, especially since quality time is her dominant "love language." At some point, I had to learn to speak a language that others would best understand. So for much of the last decade, my tools have been in storage; I have made it a priority to share more time and activities together with my wife and family.

Our oldest son, Jonathan, was interested in flying from his early years. He loved airplanes and kept a watchful eye out for aircraft flying overhead from the tender age of two. Jonathan is now a pilot with FedEx in Alaska, while still flying the F-22 Raptor in the US Air Force Reserves. He and his wife, Julie, are parents of twins, a boy and a girl.

Jonathan was attending the Air Force Academy in Colorado Springs by the time I was assigned to Incirlik Air Base, as the wing commander. Those years in Turkey are memorable as being wonderful for our family. Picnics, sightseeing, bargaining for perceived treasures, and enjoying Turkish cuisine were among the highlights. Jennifer graduated from high school in Turkey and one of my fondest memories was watching her walk across the stage with not only high marks academically, but more importantly as a woman of character, strong values and a deep faith. She and her husband, Brian, a US Army officer she met in Germany, have four children.

Our two younger children have chosen very different career paths from the military life. David quite naturally combines his strong work ethic with a fun loving, adventurous spirit to succeed in business. He married his best friend, Jocelyn, and they recently had a baby boy—our seventh grandchild. Katherine is innately creative and expressive with everything she touches, especially in her art. She seems to have the ability to discern various dimensions to life, nature, and relationships that most of us miss or simply take for granted. Passionate about taking care of children, she finds great joy working as a nanny.

Like most parents, Judy and I experienced some difficulties guiding our children through the teenage years. We sought immensely valuable counseling to help us along as we struggled with some tough issues. There are no perfect families and we certainly were not perfect parents. We thank God for the extended family, friends, and youth workers at church who positively influenced our children, especially during their teen years.

While our immediate family is very important to Judy and me, we have always shared a love and concern for the greater "family" we live and work with every day. We have a special compassion for orphans, the disabled, and the vulnerable. We have often said that the prayer of Saint Francis of Assisi was written just for us as we try to make service a daily priority.[3]

Lord, make me an instrument of your peace.
Where there is hatred, let me sow love;
where there is injury, pardon;
where there is doubt, faith;
where there is despair, hope;
where there is darkness, light;
and where there is sadness, joy.

O Divine Master, grant that I may not so much seek
to be consoled as to console;
to be understood as to understand;
to be loved as to love.
For it is in giving that we receive;
it is in pardoning that we are pardoned;
and it is in dying that we are born to eternal life.

Wearing a Suit to Work

When I retired from the Air Force on October 1, 2006, I wanted my next career to allow me to directly implement the words of Saint Francis's prayer. I accepted a position as the first CEO of Millennium Villages International, an organization committed to help bring an end to extreme poverty.

On May 8, 2007, I was seated at a large conference room table in New York City along with members of Millennium Promise's board of directors (Millennium Promise provided the operational platform and mobilized resources for Millennium Villages). As part of the formal program, I gave these distinguished individuals an update on our village clusters and then forecasted our priorities and projects for the next quarter.

The discussion that followed was disheartening to me as the conversation turned to ideas about how to produce quick results in order to generate positive reports and upbeat brochures. It seemed that there was little concern about whether the results would be sustainable in the long term or not. The new priority for our organization was to get additional funding from existing donors and to recruit new funders. I understood the realities of fundraising, but this approach was in direct conflict with my beliefs about sustainable development.

Following the board's discussion on finances, I said, "If that's our new focus, then I'm not the right person to be CEO." The meeting soon adjourned and I left immediately.

I walked back to my office and closed the door. Picking up the phone, I dialed my wife's telephone number.

Judy's cheery greeting did not last long. "I just resigned. I'm coming home now." She was not pleased.

I was passionate about addressing the problems of poverty, health, gender equality, and disease around the world, and I believed that much more could be done to achieve the United Nations' Millennium Development Goals.[4] Our organization's aim was to improve access to education, basic health care, clean water, sanitation, and efficient food production.

I was proud to have been a part of this dedicated team that was helping African communities develop sustainable ways to lift themselves out of the poverty trap. My fundamental disagreement with Dr. Jeffery Sachs and the board over sustainability issues was not personal—we just saw things differently. I believed it was better for me to move on without disrupting the efforts of the Millennium Villages team.

Given the organization's upcoming merger with the United Nations Development Programme, this was a good opportunity for me to leave quietly without causing ripples among the donors or in the field. My last day at work was May 10. While I missed being surrounded by passionate professionals who were dedicated to making a difference in Africa, it was the right move for me and Millennium Villages.

A few months later, I joined Safe Water Network as an engineering consultant and eventually served as the chief operating officer. Formed by a group of philanthropic investors, this nonprofit organization is a collaboration of leading global institutions dedicated to advancing sustainable and scalable approaches to provide safe water to people in Asia and Africa.

Using low cost technologies, our company removed fluoride from drinking water with reverse-osmosis systems, sponsored rain-water harvesting programs, and constructed safe-water points for communities in India that lacked adequate access to potable water. These projects made a difference in community health one bucket at a time.

In Ghana, we built five safe-water kiosks to provide potable water. These water purification systems used a series of filters and an ultraviolet-light purification system to kill bacteria. Not only did community health improve from drinking safe water, but there was a 91 percent drop in the incidence of schistosomiasis because women and children no longer had to enter lakes and slow-moving streams to fetch water to meet their household needs.[5]

Judy and I continue to give community service a high priority in our lives. Judy has helped in orphanages, nurseries, and churches. She serves as a mentor to young women and new mothers, and has been a Bible study leader in each of our assignments. We enjoy entertaining and building new relationships with people that we meet from all walks of life.

The company I helped start in Kenya, Champion Afrik, was designed to create more jobs for East Africans and provide business opportunities for small and medium enterprises. We are currently investing in mining, large-scale agriculture, and medical tourism.

Saint Francis was correct in saying, "For it is in giving that we receive." The years with Millennium Villages, Safe Water Network, and now in Kenya have been fulfilling—not so much because of what we did, but because of what we saw: lots of smiles from those whose lives have changed for the better.

While I enjoyed my two years of humanitarian work, my association with Senator Obama that started on our trip to Africa in 2006 evolved into campaigning for him in 2008. In February 2007, I became a part-time volunteer working on the Senator's presidential election campaign as a member of the foreign policy and national security teams. Still a volunteer in 2008, I took on greater responsibilities as a national surrogate, representing the "Obama for America" campaign in many venues across the United States. Even though I believed he was on his way to the White House, I knew the road ahead would be long and tiring.

17

Trek to the White House

Success in any endeavor does not happen by accident. Rather, it's the result of deliberate decisions, conscious effort, and immense persistence—all directed at specific goals.

— Gary Ryan Blair

THE TAXIING V-22 OSPREY stirred up a storm of sand and dust as it pulled up to the VIP terminal at Marka Air Base in Amman, Jordan. Senator Obama stepped off the rear ramp of the lead Osprey as Senator Chuck Hagel and Senator Jack Reed each disembarked from the other two tilt-rotor aircraft. Just finishing a visit to Iraq as part of a congressional delegation on July 22, 2008, Senator Obama would now begin a campaign-sponsored trip that would take him to Jordan, Israel, Germany, France, and the United Kingdom.[1] I was in charge of the advance preparations and logistics for the Jordan portion of the campaign trip and I would continue on to Israel and Europe as a foreign policy advisor.

Scott welcomes Senator Obama to Amman, Jordan. (Associated Press photo/Jae C. Hong)

After some down time, we departed for the historical area known as the Citadel, situated atop one of Amman's many hills. The long shadows drawn by the setting sun on the ruins in the foreground and stone dwellings on the distant hills provided a stunning backdrop for the forty-five-minute press conference. After Senator Obama's interview with Katie Couric of CBS news, we jumped into a waiting armored Toyota Land Cruiser for the trip to Beit al-Urdun, the palace of His Majesty King Abdullah II and Queen Rania.

During the drive, I previewed the activities that were planned and mentioned issues that might come up during the dinner conversation. His Majesty King Abdullah was waiting on the front steps as we pulled up to the royal residence. I introduced Senator Obama. After a private meeting with the King, we later joined Her Majesty Queen Rania al-Abdullah, Senator Hagel, Senator Reed, and four other local guests for a private dinner.

As we were saying good-bye, His Majesty offered to drive Senator Obama to the Queen Alia International Airport in his new black Mercedes 600. The Senator agreed and our convoy spent the next twenty minutes racing though Amman trying to keep up with the King. His Majesty King Abdullah II has a penchant for fast action—he is a helicopter pilot, motorcyclist, free-fall parachutist, racecar driver, and scuba diver. The high-speed drive to the airport was the perfect ending to a great visit to Jordan.

A few months earlier, Denis McDonough had asked several members of the Core Group, a group of high-level volunteers having significant foreign policy and national security experience, to head up preparations in each country that Senator Obama planned to visit on this trip. I was delighted to spearhead the activities in Jordan, a country I knew very well and appreciated.

As Amman would be the first stop on our campaign swing through the Middle East and Europe, I wanted to ensure the trip generated positive momentum and great press reviews. Helping to establish a warm personal relationship between the Senator and the King was another key objective for the visit. I believe we successfully achieved all of our goals.

The Next Leg: Israel

Senator Obama's event-loaded schedule for Israel included more media interviews, a meeting with Labor Party leader and Defense Minister Ehud Barak, and a visit with opposition leader and Likud Party chairman Benjamin

Map of Sderot.

Netanyahu in Jerusalem. We also toured the Yad Vashem Holocaust History Museum where the Senator laid a wreath at the Holocaust Memorial, followed by a private meeting with President Shimon Peres at his residence.

While the rest of us took a scenic bus ride to the border town of Sderot (near the northeastern boundary of the Gaza Strip), Senator Obama traveled by helicopter to the Palestinian city of Ramallah for meetings with President Mahmoud Abbas and Prime Minister Salam Fayyad. The Senator joined us in Sderot at 4:30 p.m.

Surrounded by tight security, we climbed the cement stairs to a second-story apartment to meet with the Amar family, long-time residents of this community located less than a mile from Gaza. Mr. Amar described hearing a Palestinian rocket slam into his home in December 2007, destroying part of his house and his family's peace of mind. Walking back to the Sderot Police Station, we paused to examine a display of Qassam rocket casings and other projectiles that the security forces had collected over the past seven years.

Senator Obama capped the day with more media interviews and a private dinner with Prime Minister Ehud Olmert at his residence.

The Swing Through Europe

It was now July 24, 2008. I took my assigned seat in business class in the Obama campaign's Boeing 757-200ER for the four-hour flight to Berlin. The aircraft had business and coach seats assigned to members of the Senator's campaign staff, the Secret Service detail, and selected members of the press corps. *Change We Can Believe In* was painted prominently on the fuselage and Senator Obama's campaign logo was emblazoned on the aircraft's tail.

After a quick ride from the airport, Senator Obama met with German Chancellor Angela Merkel, taped an interview with NBC's Brian Williams, and attended a meeting with Foreign Minister Frank-Walter Steinmeier. The rest of us joined the campaign staff that had been in Berlin for more than a week as they finalized preparations for our main event—a globally televised speech in front of the city's best known landmark, the 200-feet high Victory Column.

The gates had opened mid-afternoon and by 7:30 p.m., when Barack Obama addressed this enthusiastic audience, the crowd stretched at least a mile up the avenue as far as I could see toward the Brandenburg Gate.[2] I had attended large campaign events in the United States, but this special evening was different. We witnessed excited people of all nationalities shouting, clapping, and chanting "Obama" as we stood on German soil. I believed this event increased the Senator's international stature and would be a turning point in the way people in America and around the world would view our presidential candidate.

I had been working hard to set up Senator Obama's planned visit to the Landstuhl Regional Medical Center in Germany (LRMC).[3] He wanted to see some of the returning wounded warriors from the Iraq war—quietly, privately, and without any media.

The day before the visit, I got a call from the hospital's public affairs officer.

"Sir, you won't be permitted on the LRMC premises," he stated after a short greeting and introduction.

"But I have a military ID card," I objected.

"I understand, sir." He continued, "Military police will only allow Senator Obama into the hospital."

Calling the Pentagon, I learned that the McCain campaign headquarters had put out a statement accusing Senator Obama of exploiting wounded soldiers for his election campaign. Senior military officials in Washington, DC, decided to bar anyone directly associated with the presidential campaign from entering the hospital; Senator Obama would be allowed in as a member of Congress. While very disappointed that we would not be able to express our sincere appreciation for the dedicated and heroic service of our soldiers, we all believed it would be best to skip the planned visit to Landstuhl and avoid any possible political fallout.

The remaining stops in Paris and London went well and the meetings with French and UK leaders were very productive. In each country we visited in the Middle East and Europe, Senator Obama was well-prepared for each event, engaged his counterparts flawlessly, and burnished his image as a credible presidential candidate.

The Democratic National Convention

My journey with the Obama presidential campaign began in early 2007. Senator Obama had decided to run for president while on vacation in Hawaii in December 2006. By the end of January, the campaign had its lean start-up organization in place. Soon after, Mark Lippert and Denis McDonough invited me to be a member of the initial "Core Group" that was formed in February 2007.

In that capacity, I helped to write some of the initial speeches and drafted some of the early background papers on counter-proliferation, counter-insurgency operations, reorganizing the Pentagon, and a safe exit strategy from Iraq. Since several Republican candidates in the GOP primary had national security experience, I believed it was extremely important for Senator Obama to stake out strong positions on security and defense issues. This would be especially important if Rudy Giuliani, Duncan Hunter, or John McCain became the GOP candidate in the general campaign.

Mark Lippert was the critical daily link between the campaign, the Senate staff, and Senator Obama. He had been on our August 2006 trip to Africa and had accompanied Senator Obama on other international trips. His fingerprints were on everything during the campaign's early days, especially the Senator's speeches and statements on international affairs.

Lippert, former National Security Adviser Tony Lake, and former State Department official Susan Rice headed up the Core Group, but we all contributed equally. Other members included Brooke Anderson, Greg Craig, Mike Froman, Jeh Johnson, Denis McDonough, Samantha Power, Daniel Shapiro, Gayle Smith, Tara Sonenshine, Mona Sutphen, and Chris Weideman.

By June, several new members had joined our group, including Richard Danzig. I had been reaching out to general officers and flag officers (GO/FO) in an effort to persuade retired senior military personnel to endorse Senator Obama. Having served as a Secretary of the Navy, Richard Danzig's assistance was invaluable to gaining more GO/FO endorsements.

By April, I was serving as a representative of the Obama campaign. This included giving interviews to print media reporters and doing radio and television interviews. My first major campaign event was the "Commander-in-Chief Tour" across Iowa in mid-July 2007. I joined a small team of "Obama for America" state organizers in Des Moines. Over the next week, these energetic and enthusiastic young adults nearly wore me out—we would get up early in the morning and arrive at the next hotel late. Traveling across Iowa, we had events in ten cities and stopped at many American Legion halls and other veterans' facilities.

As the campaign progressed, I continued to represent Senator Obama on television and radio shows around America. I went on sixteen campaign trips to thirteen states, including five visits to Iowa. In addition, I spoke at numerous house parties and rallies in the New Jersey and New York area. Meshing the campaign schedule with my work at the Safe Water Network resulted in a lot of seven-day work weeks and many late nights, but I loved it. Being able to make my voice heard through the democratic political process was both exhilarating and gratifying.

A month before the Democratic National Convention, I received a call from the campaign headquarters in Chicago, asking me to be one of the speakers at Mile High Stadium in Denver. I would be speaking on behalf of the Armed Forces.

"Why don't you ask General McPeak, General Wesley Clark, or former Secretary of the Navy Danzig?" I asked. "These individuals had achieved higher positions in the military," I reasoned to myself, still disbelieving that I was on this phone call.

The caller replied, "Because the Senator wants you."

Well, that was that. How could I say no?

The time slot was about twenty minutes before the Senator would accept the Democratic Party's nomination for president. A week later, I received a very nice letter from Governor Howard Dean, the chairman of the Democratic National Committee. It said:

Dear General Gration:

At the recommendation of Senator Barack Obama, I am pleased to invite you to participate as a speaker at the 2008 Democratic National Convention.

This year's Convention will truly be like none other in our nation's history. Our country is at a crossroads, and the Convention is our opportunity to show the American people a new path toward peace and prosperity. Your speech will be an important part of that effort.

This is a unique moment for our country, and all eyes will be upon us at this Convention. It is going to be exciting and historic, and I am delighted that you will be a part of it. On behalf of Senator Obama and all of us at the Democratic National Convention Committee, thank you for your participation.

A follow-up letter explained that I would have six minutes to speak. A group of thirty distinguished generals and admirals would form a semi-circle behind me on the stage.

This was a big honor and I sincerely appreciated the Senator's kind endorsement of my position in the campaign. Without seeking advice from family or friends, I wrote my remarks the following week. While I expected them to be edited in Denver, I wanted my words to convey a sincere message without it sounding as if the remarks were penned by a ghostwriter. I wrote:

> I'm honored to share the stage with those who have served our country with distinction, Veterans who share my commitment to making Barack Obama our commander-in-chief.
>
> I'd like to ask everyone in this stadium who has worn the uniform of the United States to please stand and be recognized. Join me in a round of applause in appreciation for their service.
>
> Before I go any further, I have a confession to make. Until recently, I was a Republican. But you'll be happy to know that I'm looking forward to voting for Barack Obama.
>
> In 2005, I was director of strategy, plans, and policy at United States European Command. That's when I met a leader unlike any I had met before. That's when I met Barack Obama. Senator Obama asked tough questions and he didn't settle for easy answers. It was this same way of thinking that led him to get it right when he opposed the war in Iraq, when he warned of its consequences.
>
> In 2006, I went with Senator Obama to Africa and experienced firsthand the leadership that America needs. In the shadow of Nelson Mandela's prison cell, I saw a leader with the understanding to build new bridges over old divides. That leader is Barack Obama.
>
> In Nairobi, I saw a leader with the courage to confront corruption directly with the President of Kenya. In Chad, I saw a leader who listened to the stories of refugees from Darfur—a leader committed to end that genocide.
>
> In Djibouti, I saw a leader who relaxed with our troops on the basketball court, who won their respect in discussions around the

dinner table, and who appreciates their service. That leader is Barack Obama.

Leadership does matter and we can't afford four more years of more of the same. When I consider who should be commander-in-chief, I ask four questions.

First, who has the judgment to make the right decisions about when to use force? In his opposition to the invasion of Iraq and in his consistent calls for more force against al-Qaeda and the Taliban, Barack Obama has shown the judgment to lead.

Second, who grasps the complex threats of the 21st century? Barack Obama understands these challenges. He has a strategy to use all elements of our power to keep America safe.

Third, who has the integrity, vision, values, and patriotism to inspire Americans to serve? I have seen firsthand this man's capacity to inspire. It is second to none.

And fourth, who has the dedication to take care of our wounded warriors, veterans, and military families? Barack Obama is a friend of our military. He stood up for the 21st century GI bill. He improved care for wounded warriors. As President, he will fully fund the VA and make it more effective. Yes, leadership does matter.

I cannot forget that night in 1996 when terrorists attacked our barracks at Khobar Towers. Nurses, doctors worked frantically to save lives. I saw a medical technician putting stitches in a patient before tending to his own head wound. Our men and women at Khobar Towers made me proud to be in the military, proud to be an American. Nineteen men died that night—eighteen of them worked for me. It was a poignant reminder that "life itself is a gift," and, no, freedom is not free.

I have served under six commanders-in-chief. We're here because we know that leadership does matter. That is why we are enthusiastically supporting Barack Obama to be our next president. He is the leader our military needs. He is the leader our country needs.

Thank you and may God bless America.

I stared at these words. My friendship with Senator Obama and my participation in his presidential campaign had changed me politically. I had been a Republican while serving as a White House Fellow under President Ronald Reagan in 1982–83. Twenty-five years later, I would endorse Barack Obama at the Democratic National Convention. Yes, I had changed, but

America's two political parties had changed too. Still conservative when it came to fiscal policy and several social issues, I struggled with some domestic policy positions of the Democratic Party. But I had decided that America needed President Barack Obama at this critical time; I wanted to be aligned with him.

A few weeks before the Democratic National Convention, I walked into the Essex County Clerk's Office in Newark and changed my party affiliation from Republican to Democrat. Judy continued with her registration as an Independent.

While I did not perceive my political affiliation as a personal ideological transformation, some of my military colleagues and personal friends were surprised and others were disappointed with my decision. Judy and I both received passionate messages from a few of our Republican friends, but we had expected this political venting would accompany my public endorsement of Senator Obama. We were still the same Scott and Judy Gration.

The convention was an amazing experience for Judy and me. Denver was a wonderful city, the daily convention speeches were motivating, and the camaraderie was contagious. Thursday was the last day and the convention would end with Senator Obama's nomination and his acceptance speech.

By mid-afternoon, we made our way to Mile High Stadium. Approaching Invesco Field, I could hear the thundering fans above the music. Judy and I sat in the enclosed box-seat area enjoying the impressive view. I was a bit nervous as I looked out at the red, white, and blue decorations and the crowd, many waving American flags. My apprehension faded as I greeted my senior military colleagues, some of whom I had not seen for years.

I also felt at ease about my remarks. Ben Rhodes, a very competent campaign speechwriter, had edited the text to make it fit into my shorter than originally planned for time allocation. In a session with Rhodes, I had been able to practice giving my remarks using a teleprompter similar to the one I would be using in the stadium. I was ready for the eighty-three thousand people in the stadium and the forty-four million watching on television.

Approaching the time slot in the program for my speech, our group of military leaders headed down to the multistory stage with its Grecian columns and massive podium area. As Michael McDonald sang his moving rendition of "America the Beautiful," we formed a line in the holding area.

Scott speaking at the Democratic National Convention at Invesco Field.

At the coordinator's signal, we all filed onto stage as the announcer introduced our group of men and women. I was last in line and peeled off to stand behind the solitary microphone in the middle of the stage. Looking up, I saw huge Jumbotrons, each carrying my picture. In front of me, I saw the infield crowded with cheering Americans, many waving our beautiful flag. Across the stadium, I saw the large teleprompter and I began to speak with a strong, confident voice.

"What a great night! I'm honored to share the stage with those who have served our country with distinction. . . ."

Yes, We Did

Totally engaged in the political race and committed to Senator Obama's election, Judy and I had spent the last eighteen months of the presidential campaign watching every daily twist. We took it personally when the Clinton campaign captured another state victory during the primary elections and we monitored John McCain's events as much as we watched our children's activities.

We had been invited to Illinois to attend the election night events with other high-level campaign workers. Sitting in the VIP tent in Chicago's Grant Park as the critical states began reporting the early returns, we anxiously monitored the tally board. Then we heard the announcement projecting Barack Obama as America's next president. The entire venue went wild with cheers and hugs.

As we waited for the Obamas and the Biden family to address the audience of dedicated supporters that crowded tightly around the raised platform, the atmosphere was electric. Some people were crying, others were shouting, "Yes, we did." The people surrounding the stage had put their hearts, souls, and resources into getting Senator Obama elected as our next president. These individuals truly believed in change and were persuaded this leader would make the greatest difference. We all were there because we were convinced Barack Obama could lead America to a brighter future.

Transition to the White House

Senator Obama was now the president-elect. Judy and I flew back to New Jersey on November 5 and put our house up for sale that day, knowing that it was not a good housing market for sellers. I had committed myself to be part of the Obama administration and we would need to live in Washington, DC.

The Obama-Biden presidential transition team served during the period of time between the end of a presidential election and the inauguration of President Obama to prepare for the smooth change over from the Bush administration. During this time, President-elect Obama pulled together his team to select new government personnel, including new Cabinet secretaries and government department or agency heads. He also established a team of professionals and confidants that could move seamlessly into the

White House at noon on January 20 as the Bush administration's personnel were leaving. This smooth transition was important as the United States was fighting two wars and was experiencing a severe economic crisis. America could not afford to skip a beat at this critical time.

Housed in a government building located at the corner of Sixth and E Streets in Washington, DC, the presidential transition team recruited staff and set up offices that the Obama administration would need to have in place in order to conduct business in the West Wing and the Eisenhower Executive Office Building on January 20. My first task was to help set up the transitional National Security Council staff. This job kicked off my service as a civilian leader in national government.

One of the more enjoyable assignments was to work with Samantha Power and Mark Lippert to set up a dinner with President-elect Obama and eight unconventional thinkers. This very informal, closed event would give Barack Obama some different perspectives on the major foreign policy challenges he would face in two months.

We selected strategic thinkers who had unique backgrounds and international experiences, and with whom President-elect Obama would not normally have the opportunity to interact. During dinner, the guests shared their views on the next set of troubling global issues. America's next chief executive listened carefully to the lively discussion, stopping a few times to ask for clarification. At the end of the dinner, he summarized what we all had heard. Actually, President-elect Obama took what the guests had said to a higher level in his powerful conclusion.

One distinguished participant remarked to me as we were leaving, "I've just been to the mountain top."

On November 19, I moved to the transition team's Presidential Personnel Office to help fill political appointments in the national security organizations. This involved sorting through resumes of applicants, paring down the list of candidates for each job, doing the requisite background screening, and submitting the top candidates to the new department leadership for final selection.

Filling political job openings in the Department of Defense (DOD) was a bit complicated because President Bush's Secretary of Defense, Robert Gates, would be staying on to work for the Obama administration. While it made good sense to keep some of the Defense Department's leadership in place for continuity because the United States was fighting two wars, it complicated personnel issues because Secretary Gates would still be serving in the Republican Bush administration until January 20. We couldn't wait until then to begin the selection and confirmation process for the new political appointees.

My responsibility, therefore, was to screen candidates for the DOD political appointments in lieu of the Secretary of Defense and to find the best nominee for each position in the Pentagon. While Secretary Gates could veto a selection if he had an issue with my proposed candidate, I understood his hiring priorities and he accepted all of our recommendations for the Pentagon's top leadership billets.

During this period, I completed the administration's interview process to be the next administrator of the National Aeronautics and Space Administration (NASA) and now I was the informal nominee. Aviation and space had captured my interest since the Soviet Union launched the sputnik satellite in May 1957 and I chose my college major to be able to participate in space-related activities. As described in chapter six, I had served at NASA as a White House Fellow and continued to follow space news with great interest while in the military. I was excited about this possibility to serve at NASA.

The nomination process stalled abruptly, however, when the administration's legislative-liaison staff learned of a clause in the National Aeronautics and Space Act stating that the NASA administrator "shall be appointed from civilian life by the President." My nomination would require a congressional waiver because, as a retired General Officer, I remained on a roster of civilians subject to military recall.

I understood the law. It made sense to have a clear separation between the military and civilian space activities. Even as my nomination was being worked by the White House Office of Legislative Affairs, I knew the president was frustrated with the congressional delays he was experiencing as he filled his cabinet. Given the administration's confirmation priorities, I sadly withdrew my name from consideration for the NASA administrator, offering to serve the Obama team in another leadership position.

Working as a special assistant to the President for Presidential Personnel until May 2009, I, along with our small team of former campaign workers, found and vetted names for over 80 percent of the 278 "Plum Book" positions in the Department of Defense.[4] My time on the presidential transition team and in the White House was a daily learning experience. In addition to having a front-row seat to the democratic transition of power, I was able to see how decisions were made in the "engine room." I saw the

Scott with President Obama in the Oval Office. (White House photo/Pete Souza)

terrible economic situation the president had to deal with on his first day. I witnessed both the informal and formal decision-making processes, and was grateful that we had superb, smart, and dedicated Americans who stepped into huge shoes when they had been figuratively barefoot only a few months before.

I was caught by surprise when, sitting in a cramped office on the lower level of the West Wing on March 13, 2009, I was given my next assignment. Would I accept it?

18

"Save Lives," Said the President

Service is the outer expression of your inner values.

— Angela Perkey

"Pʀᴇꜱɪᴅᴇɴᴛ Oʙᴀᴍᴀ ᴡᴀɴᴛꜱ ʏᴏᴜ to be his Special Envoy to Sudan."

I was surprised by Denis McDonough's statement and took a moment to answer. Chief of Staff for the National Security Council, Denis was tall, handsome, and smart—a former football player at St. John's University in Minnesota and one of the President's most influential advisors. But more importantly, we were close friends: I could be very honest and frank with him. Denis and I had worked together closely on the 2008 presidential campaign trail and we shared a loyalty to the President, a sense of duty to our country, a love for our families, and a strong faith in God.

"I don't think so." All the reasons why such a job would not be a good fit for me or the White House were flooding my mind. Besides, the pictures drawn with crayon by his children, taped to the wall behind his desk, were reminding me how significantly this job would take me away from my family.

"Well, think about it over the weekend," Denis said, taking a folder off the top of his overflowing inbox. I knew he was responding to my lack of enthusiasm by giving me another chance to do the right thing.

"Let's talk again on Monday." The conversation was over and I stood to leave.

That weekend, my wife Judy and I discussed the job offer. It did not take long for me to realize I had no option. I had to accept. It is a lot like the military; when the President of the United States of America asks you to take a tough job, the answer is, "Yes, Sir." Besides, all of my life experiences had been preparing me for this job.

I jotted down some of the prerequisite qualifications the President's Special Envoy should have to be successful: a relationship with the President; diplomatic experience; an understanding of humanitarian assistance and rural development; experience with security challenges and stability operations; and a good knowledge of the region, its people, and their cultures.

Serving as the President's Special Envoy to Sudan was a natural fit, given my childhood experiences in Africa and my professional activities on the continent. My wife and I had been associated with Africa literally all our lives. Judy was born in Nairobi's Queen Elizabeth Hospital just three months after my introduction to Kenya as an eighteen-month-old in January 1953.

It was clear that my objections were unfounded. I would accept the job.

After driving straight from New Jersey to the West Wing of the White House on Monday, March 16, I met with Denis again. Sitting forward in the straight-backed chair beside his cluttered desk, I told Denis I would be proud to serve as the President's Special Envoy to Sudan.

Denis called an hour later. He wanted me to meet the Secretary of State for an interview. We call these "sniff checks" in the Air Force. When Secretary Hillary Clinton came out of her meeting with the President, I met her in the hallway and introduced myself. We then walked to a small conference room adjoining the White House Situation Room.

Seated opposite me at a well-polished wooden table, Secretary Clinton was relaxed as she asked questions about my background and experience. I began by reminding her that we had met several times when I was the Wing Commander at Elmendorf Air Force Base in Alaska. Air Force One often stopped at our base when transiting to and from Asia—Elmendorf was a convenient and secure midway refueling point.

The memory of one presidential visit stands out. En route to China for the 1998 state visit, President Clinton stopped on June 24 to address our Arctic Warriors—the name given to US military personnel serving in Alaska. We held this "town hall" meeting in one of our large maintenance hangars. I introduced the First Lady to the cheering crowd and then the president followed with a speech that resonated with the troops. Ten days later, the Clintons returned to the base for a brief refueling stop before heading back to Washington.

While taking a walk with her special assistant before boarding Air Force One for the long flight back to Andrews Air Force Base, the First Lady strolled past the tail of the presidential aircraft and onto a taxiway leading to the main runway. Even though we did not have many flights scheduled to land on this Saturday afternoon, I called the control tower and asked the supervisor to close the runway until further notice. In this situation, it was a lot easier to shut down airfield operations for fifteen minutes than to curtail Mrs. Clinton's walk. She never knew.

While she probably didn't remember my face from Alaska, Secretary Clinton had read my biography and knew all about my childhood and professional experiences in Africa. Even though the Obama and Clinton campaign staff had battled fiercely for their candidate during the 2008 Democratic Primary, Mrs. Clinton came across to me as extremely focused, yet very pleasant and professional. I believed I would enjoy working with her—we seemed to connect personally and appeared to share a common view on Sudanese issues.

Satisfied that I understood the challenges of the Sudan assignment, Secretary Clinton vented her frustration over the recent expulsion of the thirteen non-governmental organizations (NGOs) from Sudan.

"In my mind, any person who dies because they did not have adequate food, health care, sanitation or water will be a genocide victim," she stated with conviction.

Secretary Clinton strongly believed the United States and the international community should hold President Omar Hassan al-Bashir and his cronies responsible for the genocide in Darfur. I listened carefully. Closing the interview with a warm smile, she welcomed me to the job and to the State Department, subject to the President's final approval.

The next day Denis called to say I had the job. My title would be the President's Special Envoy to Sudan.

Back to Sudan

News of my new assignment spread quickly through the White House. Some called to express their congratulations, but many others phoned to pass their condolences. A few even said I was crazy for accepting such an impossible mission.

To give me a proper "blessing," the White House organized a rollout ceremony in the Roosevelt Room. Key members of Congress and the advocacy community, along with senior White House representatives, sat around the table and filled the chairs against the wall. Part way through the meeting, President Obama joined us to say nice things about me, to highlight the current challenges in Sudan, and to reiterate my mandate—which was to "save lives".

The International Criminal Court (ICC) had indicted President Omar al-Bashir of Sudan for war crimes on March 4, 2009; the next day he had expelled thirteen international aid agencies.[1] Sudan's president believed the foreign "spies" in these non-governmental agencies (NGOs) were responsible for giving the ICC the information it needed to build the case against him.

Seated around the large table in the White House Situation Room on March 23, I participated in my first Deputies Committee meeting on Sudan. To my left and to my right, grim-faced leaders from key departments and agencies listened as intelligence analysts and senior government officials painted a dire picture about the deteriorating situation in Darfur. Without the presence of international organizations to deliver needed humanitarian assistance, at least 1.2 million people were in risk of death in the coming rainy season from malnutrition, diarrhea, and acute respiratory diseases.

I left the Situation Room even more convinced that disaster was right around the corner if we were not able to reverse President Bashir's decision to expel the non-governmental organizations. We had to get these humanitarians back into Darfur and the areas along the border with Southern Sudan: Abyei, South Kordofan, and Blue Nile.

Wanting to send a strong message about the gravity of the impending crisis, I decided to depart for Sudan within a week. Every day wasted could translate into more lives lost to hunger and disease. The situation teetered on a knife's edge.

I had been assigned to Sudan before. In mid-1985, Sudan received twelve F-5 aircraft from America, and the US Air Force was looking for a fighter instructor pilot to go to Wadi Seidna Air Base, about ten miles north of Khartoum. I was selected to be that instructor who would teach Sudanese MiG-21 pilots to fly their new fighters.

Always ready for an exciting challenge, Judy and I had jumped at this interesting assignment and decided to move our family to Omdurman. We would be able to explore the interesting historical sites in this ancient city

Map of Sudan.

and wander through the famous Arab *souqs* and markets located across from Khartoum on the western bank of the Nile River.

The US relationship with Khartoum had been improving since the late 1970s. Washington's deep concern about the spread of communism in the Horn of Africa began after Ethiopia pivoted squarely into the Soviet sphere of influence. The United States viewed Sudan as a critical bastion against communism in the region. Both the Carter and Reagan administrations nurtured the friendship with Sudan's President Jaafar al-Nimeiri as he backed the Camp David Peace Accords in 1979, supported the airlift of some seven thousand Ethiopian Jews to Israel, and openly clashed with Soviet-backed Libya.

Given its geostrategic location on the Nile River, many Westerners viewed Sudan as Egypt's soft underbelly. To protect Sudan and Egypt, the Reagan Administration believed that keeping Muammar Qadhafi at bay in the north and John Garang's new rebel offensive subdued in the south should be US priorities. My assignment to train Sudanese pilots to fly their new F-5 fighters was in line with America's pro-Khartoum policy.

US-Sudan diplomatic relations began to deteriorate, however, after President Nimeiri was toppled by a military coup in April 1985. Sudan's new military leader, General Suwar al-Dhahab, began to develop closer ties with the Soviet Union. Relations between the United States and Sudan reached a low point in November 1985, when Washington announced that the country had become a base for Libyan and other known terrorists. My assignment to Wadi Seidna was cancelled and my household goods, already en route to Sudan, were recalled. A few days later, the US Air Force reassigned me to the Pentagon to serve as a Middle East and Africa politico-military affairs officer.

Twenty-Four Miracles

Knowing I was following in admirable footsteps, I called each previous special envoy to Sudan and asked for their advice and perspectives on my new duties. The State Department's Sudan Programs Group soon became part of my leadership portfolio and our team eventually became the Office of the US Special Envoy to Sudan (USSES), responsible for all internal and external issues relating to Sudan.[2]

But my duties were different from other special envoys working in the Foggy Bottom neighborhood of Washington, DC. Our office was also responsible for the State Department's day-to-day administrative activities involving Sudan. The USSES office was an autonomous island inside the department's Bureau of African Affairs. While I got along well with Assistant Secretary of State for Africa Johnnie Carson, I was in a professionally awkward position because his bureau was responsible for every country in sub-Saharan Africa—except Sudan.

I did my best to keep him apprised of all our activities and initiatives in Sudan, and was careful to ask for his approval when I needed to visit countries in Khartoum's neighborhood. I did this because it was the right thing to do—I had no idea that before long, Johnnie Carson would be my immediate boss.

Religious and ethnic conflicts in Darfur and Southern Sudan[3] were "hot-button" emotional issues. Each region had well-organized and passionate constituencies in the United States that would judge my approach and evaluate my results. I spent lots of time listening to these advocacy organizations and church groups.

Even within the Obama Administration, I had to deal with vocal officials who advocated for no-fly zones, additional economic sanctions, and military solutions as "sticks" to pressure Khartoum to comply with US demands. Some high-ranking officials were publicly calling for an immediate regime change in Sudan. I knew I would have to walk a political tightrope, balancing pragmatic life-saving solutions with domestic politics, especially with White House staffers concerned about elevating the President's poll numbers and wooing the ideological constituencies in Congress and in the left-wing base of the Democratic Party.

My mission was unambiguous: I had to save lives immediately and help Sudan get through the next two years peacefully. At the strategic level, our team at the State Department developed a mix of incentives and disincentives designed to achieve three objectives.

First, we had to pursue a definitive end to conflict, gross human rights abuses, and genocide in Darfur. At the same time, we had to help both the north and the south implement the Comprehensive Peace Agreement (CPA) to achieve a peaceful and united post-2011 Sudan or an orderly transition of two separate and viable states at peace with one another.[4] Finally, we sought a Sudan that did not serve as a safe haven for terrorists, but that contributed to a safer and more stable continent.

Sitting in my office one evening after all the USSES staff had gone home, I started to write down all the milestones that would need to be accomplished in order to resolve the Darfur situation and implement the Comprehensive Peace Agreement. My list grew into twenty-four consecutive miracles that we would need in Sudan:

1. Foster a productive US relationship with Sudan.
2. Ensure Sudan is supporting the global war against terror and is controlling transit of foreign fighters.
3. Restore/improve unhindered access to Darfur for NGOs, international aid organizations, and UN/AU forces (UNAMID).
4. Negotiate a ceasefire and cessation to hostilities in Darfur, followed by a lasting security framework to stabilize the region, protect IDPs (internally displaced persons), and control the border areas.
5. Unify the Darfuri rebel movements in order to develop common negotiation positions for the next round of peace talks.
6. Give voice to Darfuri Arabs and civil society so they would have an equitable role in the peace process.
7. Support the UN-AU-Qatar peace talks in Doha and help to negotiate the Darfur Peace Agreement.
8. Support creating a judicial system of accountability for war crimes and crimes against humanity, and seek compensation and justice for the people of Darfur affected by the conflict.

9. Work with Sudan's neighboring countries to support the peace process in Darfur and to facilitate lasting security.

10. Mobilize the international community to support the peace process in Darfur and post-conflict reconstruction and development in Darfur.

11. Develop sustainable livelihoods and safe areas so displaced people, refugees, and nomads could return home voluntarily.

12. Restructure and reorient humanitarian operations towards normalizing life for the people of Darfur and reducing dependency on humanitarian agencies in IDP and refugee camps.

13. Facilitate and support reconciliation amongst the Darfur community for normal, productive relationships between all segments.

14. Demarcate the January 1956 north-south border and Abyei boundary demarcation; resolve border disputed areas, in accordance with the 2005 Comprehensive Peace Agreement.

15. Get both parties to recognize the national census and proposed allocation of seats in the National Assembly.

16. Prepare for and support popular consultations in South Kordofan and Blue Nile per the CPA.

17. Support passage of election reform legislation, encourage suspension of elements of criminal laws that conflict with free elections, and promote democratic transformation.

18. Assist National Election Commission to conduct a free, fair, and credible national election in 2010.

19. Support national security reform (pass a new administrative detention law; field integrated security forces for the border areas; implement security protocol calls for a lasting ceasefire; redeploy both Sudanese Armed Forces (SAF) and Sudan People's Liberation Army (SPLA) from their forward-deployed positions along the north-south border; form Joint Integrated Units comprised of both SAF and SPLA to deploy in the south, Khartoum, and parts of South Kordofan and Blue Nile; disarm, demobilize, and reintegrate northern and southern soldiers; and create an international peacekeeping force to monitor the ceasefire and peace agreement).

20. Prepare the south for possible independence to include agreements on the choice of citizenship after independence, using the same currency or creating new currencies after independence, renegotiating international conventions and treaty obligations,

splitting assets and debts, sharing oil wealth, using the interstate oil pipeline to Port Sudan and resolving the status of displaced minorities and their wealth.

21. Prepare for the Southern Sudan referendum, including acquisition of polling materials, determination and registration of eligible voters, and preparation of polling centers.

22. Prepare for the Abyei referendum, including resolving voter eligibility and diffusing tensions concerning the Misseriya and trans-boundary migration.

23. Monitor the referendum on Southern Sudan's independence.

24. Monitor the referendum on Abyei's future—to stay with the north or join the south.

Yes, we would need miracles indeed.

Experts had already warned me that national elections and the referendum on Southern Sudan's independence would be impossible due to the wide gap between negotiating positions and the political intransigence on both sides.

I was told the situation in Darfur was equally unsolvable. Since 2005, the United States Government had pumped approximately six billion dollars to Sudan and eastern Chad, but the situation remained essentially frozen as we tried to keep the plight of refugees and internally displaced persons from getting any worse. There had been almost no lasting political progress in the previous four years.

My job was simple: just work miracles and accomplish the impossible mission. Right!

Fostering a Productive US-Sudan Relationship

Just three workdays after being sworn in at the State Department, I left for Sudan. We needed a working relationship with Khartoum, even if the United States did not approve of Bashir's government. My first objective was to get to know key interlocutors (dialogue partners) as a prerequisite and foundation for subsequent negotiations. This relationship with Sudan was the first miracle I needed.

Having been a White House Fellow in the Reagan Administration, I was very familiar with President Reagan's arms-control negotiation mantra, "trust, but verify." Modifying this a little, our office adopted an "agree, verify, then trust" approach with the Sudanese government.[5] I knew we would need some initial confidence-building dialogues and a few positive engagements to create the trust necessary to negotiate the important Darfur and CPA-related issues—resolving the worsening humanitarian crisis would be a good start. At my initial news conference after landing in Khartoum, I began by speaking some Arabic.

"*As-Salaam-Alaikum. Ana ahib Sudan wa Sudaniyiin.*" I said as I greeted the audience These words served to announce that I liked Sudan and the Sudanese people, and that I had come to see, listen, and learn.

While I never met with President Bashir, I knew we would need a good rapport with Sudanese leaders from Bashir's National Congress Party. I chose my words carefully and took deliberate actions to be a good guest and to convey the message that the United States would strive to produce positive outcomes in Darfur and to mediate the remaining issues of disagreement between the north and south.

The next morning, we filed into a large, well-ventilated room on the top floor of the Foreign Ministry Annex to begin the negotiations. Standing on the far side of a long double-wide table, covered with a white cloth and decorated with small arrangements of flowers, were seven members of Bashir's National Congress Party government. After formal handshakes, our small team took our seats across the table from our interlocutors. Dressed in loose-fitting, long-sleeved, white jalabiyas topped with the traditionally wrapped white headgear, these men represented key ministries in the Khartoum government. All were highly educated, spoke perfect English, and articulated the party's positions well.

Our chatter was silenced when the Sudanese Presidential Advisor, Dr. Ghazi Salahuddin Atabani, opened the dialogue with a warm welcome. Lean and fit with a closely cropped moustache and beard that had begun to turn grey, Dr. Ghazi's serious and often formal demeanor masked a

Press conference in Khartoum as special envoy. (Agence France-Presse photo/Ashraf Shazly)

gentle spirit that was visible only to those who knew him well. A medical doctor with a PhD in clinical biochemistry from the University of Surrey in England, he was also a dedicated family man—he and his wife, also a medical doctor, were very proud of their children.

Over the two years when he was Khartoum's primary point of contact for US-Sudan negotiations, I gained a deep appreciation for Dr. Ghazi's keen intellect, knowledge of world history, and ability to put debates and decisions into a sound strategic context. While he was a tough negotiator, we developed a personal relationship of trust and were able to communicate professionally with the requisite honesty and frankness needed to overcome many challenges.

Restoring Unhindered Access to Darfur

I responded to Dr. Ghazi's warm opening welcome by expressing my appreciation for the Sudanese hospitality and telling my counterparts that I wanted our relationship to be one of friendship and trust.

Taking the room by surprise, I added, "We fully respect Sudan's national sovereignty and recognize President Bashir's political right to decide who can work in this country." Continuing, I cautioned, "Expelling all the non-governmental organizations has not only put millions of Sudanese citizens at risk, but has further isolated Sudan from the international community."

After several hours of hammering out a framework agreement for the negotiations and taking a lunch break, I asked the Sudanese delegation, "What if you hold firm to President Bashir's decree to expel the thirteen NGOs, but allow some different NGOs to come into Darfur to carry on humanitarian efforts?"

After some discussion on their side, the lead negotiator said that this option might be possible.

"Would it then be possible for some of the departing NGOs to have their staff return to Darfur under one of the new organizations?" I queried.

After another long discussion, the Sudanese Government representatives agreed to permit the staff of six US non-governmental organizations back into Darfur, Abyei, South Kordofan, and Blue Nile, but under new management and with different organizational names. This arrangement immediately restored about 75 percent of the critical programs that provided food, shelter, medical care, and other life-sustaining assistance to millions of vulnerable Sudanese. This was a good start on accomplishing miracle number three on my list.

By finding a face-saving way out of the NGO-expulsion crisis, we were also able to avoid an immediate confrontation with the government of Sudan and to focus pressure from the international community where it was needed—to resolve the Darfur conflict, implement the CPA, and to make progress toward overall justice and accountability.

> It is not the critic who counts, not the man who points out how the strong man stumbles or where the doer of deeds could have done better. . . .
>
> The credit belongs to the man who is actually in the arena, whose face is marred by dust and sweat and blood, who strives valiantly, who errs and comes up short again and again, because there is no effort without error or shortcoming, but who knows the great enthusiasms, the great devotions, who spends himself for a worthy cause; who, at the best, knows, in the end, the triumph of high achievement, and who, at the worst, if he fails, at least he fails while daring greatly, so that his place shall never be with those cold and timid souls who knew neither victory nor defeat.
>
> — Theodore Roosevelt

19

Serving in Sudan

*It's not the things we get but the hearts we touch
that will determine our success in life.*

— Mac Anderson

Mʏ ᴛɪᴍᴇ ᴀs sᴘᴇᴄɪᴀʟ ᴇɴᴠᴏʏ was spent managing two fronts: keeping Washington and the advocacy groups on my side and resolving the Darfur and Southern Sudan challenges. Each was a full-time job, equally unpredictable and full of surprises.

Improving security in Darfur[1] so that we could expand humanitarian operations was a high priority for the United States. The US special envoy to Sudan team[2] hoped that Darfuri communities, if safe and empowered, would not only tackle their own local problems but would pressure leaders of armed rebel movements to enter into serious negotiations with the Sudanese government. We wanted civil society to take a greater role in finding a permanent political solution to the conflict (miracle number six).

Unifying Rebels and Giving Voice to Darfuri Arabs

Many of my predecessors working the Sudan portfolio, including Senator John Danforth, Deputy Secretary of State Robert Zoellick, and Special Envoys Andrew Natsios and Rich Williamson, had tried to secure a lasting Darfur Peace Agreement (DPA). When I began my tenure as the special envoy, the African Union and the United Nations, together with the government of Qatar, were already facilitating a peace process in Doha, the capital of Qatar. I believed that process would be unproductive as long as there was no unified voice representing Darfur at the negotiating table.

Our strategy for Darfur was straight-forward, but complicated. We would have to unite the fragmented rebel groups—there were twenty-nine different factions by one count. In addition, we needed to increase humanitarian assistance capacity, end the indirect Chad-Sudan conflict fought by sponsored rebel forces, improve local security, and give voice to civil society. We also had to support the Doha peace process and plan for eventual voluntary returns of Darfuri internally displaced persons and refugees to their home areas. This would entail establishing the requisite social infrastructure, creating opportunities for wealth creation and sustainable livelihoods, and providing psychological and emotional support.

Enabling Voluntary Returns

Concerned that we were spending too much of our time on Darfur's day-to-day challenges of survival, I wanted to put more of our effort into addressing the underlying causes of the conflict. We had to end the continuous displacement that forced people to live in the fragile conditions of camps established for internally displaced persons and refugees. My first challenge, therefore, was to stop the proxy war and constant skirmishes between Chad and Sudan's surrogate fighters—the major cause of displacement in the Darfur region.

Visiting N'Djamena, we met with Chad's President Idriss Deby Itno in his office and later over dinner to discuss ways to end the Chad-Sudan conflict. President Deby and I shared a few things in common. We were about the same age, both of us had completed a full career in the military before getting into politics, and we both were military pilots. Communicating with a blend of my limited French, his broken English, and our hand gestures and smiles, we carried on an animated conversation throughout the meal. I felt we understood each other.

We adjourned for coffee to a quiet room. Using an interpreter to ensure accurate translation, we engaged in a long discussion about the security situation in eastern Chad and Darfur. President Deby finally assured me that he would curtail the flow of material and financial support to the Justice and Equality Movement (JEM), the rebel group he used as Chad's proxy force in Sudan.[3]

We also wanted Chad's president to use his influence to push the JEM back into the Doha negotiations and to improve his nation's bilateral relations with Sudan. Before taking these steps, President Deby said he would need assurances that Sudan and its neighbors would support him in this new stance because the JEM had been his surrogate military force for years.

Coordinating with Sudan's Neighbors

With approval from the State Department, I traveled to Libya, Ethiopia, Egypt, and Qatar to secure their backing, in support of Miracle 9. On my last day in Libya, July 3, 2009, senior Libyan officials dispatched an aircraft to take the US Ambassador to Libya Gene Cretz and me to the city of Sirte for discussions with Libyan leader Muammar Qadhafi.

Dressed in a beautiful gold-colored robe with matching headgear and surrounded by his senior staff, Qadhafi welcomed the US role in Sudan, endorsed our joint approach, and stressed that we had to seize the opportunity to bring peace to Chad and Sudan. The meeting got off to a cordial start. He had obviously been briefed on my previous meetings with senior members of Libya's government—maybe he knew about my successful trip

Gaddafi at the African Union conference in 2009.
(Wikimedia Commons)

to Tripoli as an Air Force general officer in July 2006. Fully aware of his reputation as a cruel and capricious despot in the region, I nevertheless noted that in our discussions, he was approachable, hospitable, and pleasant.

Qadhafi asked that the United States and Libya work together to end the proxy war in Darfur and to address the underlying causes of the conflict in Darfur. He promised his nation's close collaboration with the United States toward promoting regional peace. This was not the tone or message I expected from Libya's leader, nor was it a picture of Qadhafi I believed Washington would readily accept.

Throughout my time as the US Special Envoy to Sudan, senior Libyan leaders continued to be of significant assistance to me as we worked together to push rebel groups to the negotiating table. Qadhafi was serious about helping and had given clear instructions to his staff to work closely with me.

This encounter with Qadhafi and previous personal meetings with Libya's leaders gave me a different picture than that portrayed by some US government officials who had never traveled to Libya or talked with him. I had received clear indications from several sources that Qadhafi was ready to hand over power in Tripoli in a peaceful manner if he believed his legacy would remain intact in the process. I passed the details through classified channels, but my friends in Washington held firmly to their hardened perceptions.

Negotiating a Ceasefire in Darfur

In my first months as the special envoy, our team concentrated on building the requisite relationships in Sudan and stabilizing the humanitarian situation after non-governmental organizations were expelled on March 5, 2009. After being largely successful in restoring the needed food, medicine, shelter, and sanitation for people displaced by the persistent skirmishes, we had to deal with the root causes of the insecurity and fear in Darfur.

After five months of intensive shuttle diplomacy, the governments of Chad and Sudan agreed in January 2010 to implement a ceasefire, to form a joint border force, and to reestablish normal diplomatic relations. This was miracle number four on my list. To make these agreements official and binding, we convinced Chad's President Idriss Deby Itno to fly to Khartoum to sign a ceasefire agreement and non-aggression pact. He did so on February 8, 2010. We also needed President Omar Hassan al-Bashir of Sudan to travel to N'Djamena for a second ceremony in which he would do the same.

I went to N'Djamena shortly before President Bashir was to travel to Chad. While resting in my hotel room, I received a telephone call from a confidant in Washington, DC. She told me a group of my more ideological colleagues in the State Department and White House had sent a démarche[4] to N'Djamena.

"They want to nab him," she said. I was stunned.

Not wanting to discuss potentially classified information on the telephone, I drove to the US Embassy and read the cable. It instructed the US ambassador or deputy chief of mission to convey to the government of Chad that it had the responsibility to arrest the Sudanese leader and send him to the International Criminal Court (ICC) in The Hague to stand trial for crimes against humanity.

In July 2008, the prosecutor of the ICC had accused President Bashir of genocide, crimes against humanity, and war crimes in Darfur. The court then had issued an arrest warrant for Bashir on March 4, 2009, on counts of war crimes and crimes against humanity, but had ruled that there was insufficient evidence to prosecute him for genocide.

There was an irony here. The United States had refused to join the International Criminal Court since it was founded in 2002. I had personally supported the ICC and argued that the international community needed a court with the ICC's mandate. Yet now, some among Washington's elite were leveraging this very ICC that the US government did not recognize in order to prematurely arrest President Bashir and sabotage our diplomatic efforts toward real peace.

Yes, my approach to resolving Sudan's challenges since becoming special envoy in March 2009 was a pragmatic one. Yes, some in the Obama administration who leaned ideologically left had taken issue with that approach. But this was the first time a difference of opinion had not been resolved through debate and dialogue. It would not be the last time we clashed.

I was well aware that President Bashir had been indicted by the ICC and he needed to be held accountable for his crimes against humanity. At the same time, an agreement between Sudan and Chad could mean the beginning of a new period of peace in the region, opening the possibility of safety and prosperity for millions. We needed that agreement signed—by President Deby *and* President Bashir!

To say I was frustrated when I received that call stating our government's intentions would be an understatement. I am sure my blood pressure must have spiked off the charts.

I immediately wrote a short but pointed email to the White House. I explained that my staff and I had arranged President Bashir's travel to Chad as part a major ceasefire agreement designed to bring stability and more peace to Darfur. It would not be helpful, I wrote, to arrest one of the principals as he prepared to sign the implementing document.

My advice was heeded. A few days later, Sudan's president signed the agreement in N'Djamena as planned. We viewed it as a miracle. It was another miracle ticked off in the list of the twenty-four we needed in order to achieve "mission impossible."

Pursue Justice Now or Restore Peace?

While conditions for many in Darfur were miserable and had to change, some of the terrible things that occurred during the height of the rebellion and the Sudanese government's counterinsurgency operations from 2003 to 2005 were no longer taking place on such a large scale. The fighting was increasingly more localized and inter-tribal in nature—as opposed to being government sponsored. Still, there was no question that those responsible for atrocities had to be held accountable for their actions and those found to have committed war crimes and crimes against humanity had to be punished appropriately.

This caused a real dilemma for me. While we all agreed that international justice had to be achieved, some in the Obama administration and the NGO community were advocating for an immediate regime change—their mantra was "justice now!" However, it was President Bashir's administration that had signed the Comprehensive Peace Agreement (CPA) with the south's leader, John Garang.[5] A leadership change would leave no assurance that a new regime would be more just and accommodating, and a political upheaval in Khartoum would certainly disrupt the tight timelines required to complete the referendum for Southern Sudan's independence in less than two years.

As I had mentally calculated, we really had no choice but to continue working with the ruling Sudanese National Congress Party to accomplish the remaining milestones by January 9, 2011, as stipulated in the 2006 Comprehensive Peace Agreement. Despite what my detractors argued in public, the consecutive miracles in my long list, including the southern Sudanese decision on independence and the future of Abyei, required Khartoum's direct participation if they were to be accomplished.

Supporting the UN-AU-Qatar Peace Talks

As we worked with the United Nations and the government of Sudan to improve security in western Sudan, we also labored to unify eight factions of the Darfur armed movements under the umbrella name of the Liberty and Justice Movement and to ensure that they participated fully in the Doha negotiations . . . miracle number five. While we all wished the Justice and Equality Movement had been part of the final deal, the unification of these eight rebel groups was another major miracle.

Eventually, the African Union-United Nations Joint Mediator on Darfur negotiated a political settlement between the Liberty and Justice Movement and the government of Sudan . . . miracle number seven. Signed in July 14, 2011, this agreement formed the Darfur Regional Authority, a governance structure that still exists in Darfur today. Unfortunately, three rebel factions[6] refused to participate in the final negotiations and they continue to disrupt and destabilize the region.

Ongoing Genocide in Darfur?

Led by the US Ambassador to the United Nations Susan Rice, several administration leaders continued to talk publicly about the "ongoing genocide in Darfur." President Obama had said to me, as we traveled in Chad during our 2006 trip to Africa and during the 2008 campaign visit to Israel, that it is the responsibility of global citizens to stop genocide wherever it was occurring. I agreed. Therefore, I decided that before I could do anything else, my first task would need to be stopping this genocide.

Researching the latest United Nations-African Union Mission in Darfur (UNAMID) reports, I noticed that UN officials recorded only sixteen fatalities in June 2009 and none were linked to the conflict between Sudanese forces and the rebel groups. All fatalities were Arabs killed in criminal-related activities.

While any violent death is one too many, there was a significant difference between the reality reflected in this UN report and widespread perceptions in America concerning the ongoing bloodshed in Darfur. From my observations, the intensity of the conflict in Darfur had decreased significantly since my first visit to the region in 2004.

While it was not a popular thing to say publicly, US intelligence experts confirmed my impression of the significant downward trend and agreed that the violent death rates in Darfur had dropped well below several thousand per year since 2005. UNAMID leadership also stated that 80 to 85 percent of Darfur's populated areas were now free of combat operations.

UN officials in western Sudan told us that the insecurity in Darfur was primarily due to violent criminal activity. Women continued to fear for their safety while they collected firewood away from the security of IDP camps. Arab militias, once armed by the government and since untethered, continued to threaten Darfuri communities at will. We had to stop them.

Ongoing Debate in Washington

I struggled with the phrase, "ongoing genocide in Darfur." I needed to say these words to be in lockstep with other vocal leaders within the Obama administration, but no other nation had yet described the situation in Darfur as genocide. The United Nations had been very careful to call it "crimes against humanity." Even the International Criminal Court rejected the genocide charge, citing a lack of sufficient evidence on intent, when it issued an arrest warrant for President Bashir on charges of war crimes and crimes against humanity.

There are two necessary and sufficient conditions for genocide. There must be widespread systemic violence and there must be the expressed intent by perpetrators to destroy specific ethnic groups. Since attacks in Darfur had decreased significantly over time, I ascribed to the compelling argument that the necessary condition of widespread violence against civilians was no longer present in that region of Sudan. I believed the primary reason IDPs were not returning to their homes was due to local insecurity—not genocide.

On the other side, however, many were convinced that the intent toward genocide remained. Administration officials, such as Susan Rice and Samantha Power, were opposed to any efforts to change the "ongoing genocide" narrative. Their position was that an immediate regime change in Khartoum was required for resolution.

While I certainly understood why Secretary of State Colin Powell labeled the Darfur conflict as genocide on September 9, 2004, and agreed that the United States should do everything within its power to end death and displacement in Darfur, I had not used the genocide label to describe the situation I saw in 2009. At one State Department news conference, a reporter asked me why I had not portrayed the current situation in Darfur as "genocide."

"I believe we are dealing with the consequences and remnants of genocide," I responded.

I elaborated by saying that insecurity persists in many parts of the region because of increased crime, banditry, and rebel-related conflict. In my numerous visits to Darfur, I had not seen evidence of a "coordinated" campaign of mass murder against Darfuri civilians.

My press statement and the associated media attention resulted in public criticism from the advocacy community and a flurry of interagency emails and rapidly convened meetings in Washington, DC. I could have saved myself a lot of grief if I had joined the administration choir by publicly describing the situation in Darfur as an "ongoing genocide." But I just did not see evidence of the continuing genocide when I was traveling in Darfur.

President Obama ended the debate in June 2009 when he referred to "genocide that's taking place" in Darfur. He went on to say that the United States must find solutions to immediately alleviate the suffering of the people of Darfur.

My focus had not been on labeling the crisis in Sudan; it had been on reversing the dire ongoing human consequences of genocide—disarming local militias, enabling displaced persons to return home, and ensuring Darfuris who had suffered so much could live in peace and security . . . miracles ten through thirteen on my list. President Obama and I were perfectly aligned in our focus to reverse the appalling living conditions and to resolve the continuing injustices we found in Darfur. That is what we worked every day to remedy while I was the President's Special Envoy to Sudan.

Implementing the 2005 Peace Agreement

Sudan had experienced four decades of conflict and suffered nearly two million casualties before the 2005 Comprehensive Peace Agreement (CPA) opened a pathway for the south to decide if it would remain unified with the north or become an independent nation. Not much had happened politically since that historic signing in Naivasha, Kenya, because the period of genocide in Darfur had overshadowed the CPA and north-south issues. In

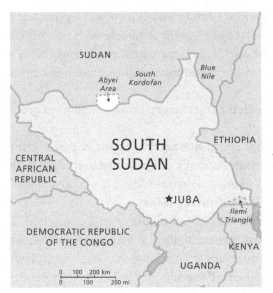

Map of South Sudan.

addition, the leadership in the south was largely ineffective as they continued to focus on preparation for fighting the north if the CPA's mandated referenda should slip away. We needed more miracles—and quickly.

I knew we only had twenty months left until the referendum on unity or independence was to be held. If we could not ensure a smooth and on-time referendum, I was confident Sudan would again become a bloody battlefield. Most people knowledgeable on Sudan agreed.

While I continued to be optimistic, many of my professional colleagues doubted whether it would be possible to negotiate a peaceful transition to independence if the south chose to be independent. Given the decades of war and the north's dependence on oil revenues, Africa experts and academics believed that the National Congress Party would never agree to a separation and that people living in Southern Sudan would fight to the last person to be free from Khartoum. But I was not deterred from my mission, despite the dire predictions and dismal prospects for success.

Resolving the CPA Standoff

The next miracle we needed was a free, fair, credible, and peaceful national election. In my view, this was an undisputable prerequisite to pulling off a peaceful and credible referendum on January 9, 2011. But we had a lot of work to do. First, the north and the south needed to reach agreements on the twelve CPA issues that remained unresolved. Second, we would have to unite the international community behind our efforts. We focused on building a broad multilateral team to make Sudan a political priority in key capitals around the globe so we could deliver common, strong, and timely messages to Sudan.

We began by organizing and facilitating the first trilateral talks with key participants from the National Congress Party, the Sudan People's Liberation Movement, and the United States. In our first meeting, I wanted the Sudanese interlocutors to move beyond the rigid professional relationships put in place during the past five years of stagnated negotiations.

"I want each of you to share some details about your families and hobbies," I said, asking the Sudan People's Liberation Movement official seated closest to me to begin.

They needed to perceive each other as fellow Sudanese who desired what was best for their people, their children, and future generations. It was very interesting to see both sides open up and begin to view each other as fellow citizens of Sudan rather than long-time adversaries.

On September 10, 2009, we witnessed leaders of the Sudan People's Liberation Movement and the National Congress Party initial a bilateral agreement in which the two parties laid out points of agreement on ten of the twelve yet-to-be-resolved issues in the CPA. This was another wonderful

Malik Agar and Ghazi Attabani celebrate the CPA bilateral agreement.
(Courtesy of the US State Department)

miracle. Now, all we had to do was to ensure both sides implemented these agreements.

My staff, comprised of career foreign service officers and experienced professionals from other departments and agencies, and I were quite upbeat in the fall of 2009 about the progress we had made in just six months. Then things turned sour. Mistrust and polarization between north and south Sudan increased. On December 7, 2009, National Congress Party security forces in Khartoum beat up demonstrators and injured several prominent opposition leaders. The situation in Sudan's capital was deteriorating fast. We had to regroup and try a new strategy.

Sudan's Counter-Terrorism Support

I believed that we needed to offer concrete rewards for positive actions and outline the pathway to sanctions relief and to Sudan's removal from the State Sponsor of Terrorism list. I had been working with Sudan's national intelligence bureau in efforts to accomplish miracle number two. It was clear to me that Sudan's intelligence was helping the United States and our allies significantly in the war against global terrorism and in the control of foreign fighters transiting the region. My approach ran counter to that of many in Washington, who still believed we needed to bring out the "sticks" to punish Khartoum.

Cookies, Gold Stars, and Smiley Faces

My efforts to communicate our negotiating strategy took a setback when I allowed several members of the media to accompany me on a trip to Juba, Darfur, and Khartoum in September 2009. I let them attend all my meetings and I gave many interviews during the five-day trip. One evening, Stephanie McCrummen, the *Washington Post* reporter, asked about our diplomatic efforts in Sudan and how I planned to accomplish the US objectives.

I responded that all US diplomatic efforts use incentives and pressures. While I don't like the analogy of influencing a donkey, I mentioned that some call this the use of "carrots and sticks."

"This isn't a difficult concept to understand. Businesses, the military, teachers, and parents use the same techniques to attain desired outcomes or achieve behavioral changes. Bonuses and promotions, military medals and ribbons, gold stars and smiley faces on good school papers, and cookies if children eat their green beans are all forms of positive reinforcement," I said to the reporter.

"On the other hand, pink slips, demotions, no recess, and time-outs can be used as pressures and punishments," I added.

Soon after, *Washington Post* published a negative story that overlooked my most important messages. Taking my comments out of context, they quoted me as saying: "We've got to think about giving out cookies, gold stars, and smiley faces." While I had told the reporter that I intended to initiate the US-Sudan relationship with incentives—handshakes and engagement—rather than disincentives, she grabbed my allegorical illustration and conveyed it as a simplistic and literal plan. I don't know if it was naiveté or malice, but the effect was traumatic.

I was beyond frustrated with the headlines and the not-so-subtle slams on my competence as a negotiator, but White House and State Department public-affairs officers advised me to remain silent and let the demeaning story die. However, it did not die—the headline instead seemed to grow strong legs and follow me to congressional hearings and around the world for the next two years.

Throughout my time as the special envoy to Sudan, I met regularly with advocacy groups and included their leaders in my decision-making process. Unfortunately, I failed to convince the majority that we were toiling for the same results in Sudan—lasting peace in Darfur and full implementation of the 2005 Comprehensive Peace Agreement.

Frankly, I expected negativity and derogatory stories from advocacy groups; positive stories about real progress challenged the popular assumptions and undermined fund-raising narratives. I was disappointed, however, that State Department and White House officials left me to fend for myself when members of Congress publicly rebuked me and even ridiculed my efforts in Congressional hearings.[7] It was hard to listen to Senator Sam Brownback say he did not understand how I could call myself a Christian and still deal with President Bashir and the evil murderers in Khartoum. It was frustrating to have senior US politicians in Congress[8] question why I needed to travel to the "center of evil" so often.

Of course, it would have been easier to limit my travel to Sudan's neighbors, but how could we have ended the Chad-Sudan proxy war without going to Khartoum? How could we have reached agreements on Darfur without spending time in Sudan's capital? How could our team have supported a successful election in Sudan and a credible referendum in Southern Sudan without shuttling between the north and the south of the country?

My professional mandate, as well as my personal desire, was to save lives and improve living conditions for all Sudanese in an effective and expeditious manner. My obligation was to serve our nation as directed by the Commander-in-Chief and President of the United States. I don't believe I could have accomplished these without first building solid relationships with members of President Bashir's government.

Facilitating National Elections

As we neared the critical administrative and logistical deadlines leading up to the April 2010 election, the continued lack of progress between the north and south put the viability of free elections and credible referenda severely at risk. The United States and the international community had no choice but to become more involved in making more miracles happen in Sudan.

Sudan planned to hold its general elections over three days beginning on April 11, 2010. A critical milestone of the CPA, this election would be Sudan's first national polling since 1986. It would be the first time people younger than forty-one years old had voted in a multiparty democratic election. More than 10,000 candidates from seventy-two different political parties registered to run for executive offices and for positions in the state and national legislative assemblies. By law, women would hold more than 25 percent of the 1,841 legislative seats. It would certainly take a miracle to pull this off.

Sudan's National Elections Commission faced several major challenges. There was a serious initiative by the opposition candidates and the Sudan People's Liberation Movement to boycott the election. In addition, there was continuous pressure to delay the election for six months. Several Sudanese opposition groups, international organizations, and advocacy groups pushed hard for a postponement—the International Crisis Group and John Prendergast's Enough Project were among the most vocal. I understood their legitimate reasons for wanting a delay. Still, I knew that a 180-day deferment would make it almost impossible to conduct the Southern Sudan Referendum by January 9, 2011.

In my view, there was only one path to a successful referendum, which was to hold free, fair, and credible national elections on time in April 2010 before the annual rainy season and then begin the voter registration four months later in August.

I discussed the national election timing, the challenges of the polling process, ways to improve the credibility of the election and referendum, and other issues with former President Jimmy Carter at every opportunity. He had so much experience with elections in Africa, keen insights about the political process in Sudan, and was well-connected with the international community. I trusted my sage mentor and was grateful for his wise counsel.

The USSES team believed that holding the referendum on Southern Sudan's independence in January 2011 was a pass-fail item—we were convinced the south and the north would go to war again if we missed this date by much. A six-month slip in the national election date was out of the question.

The first ten days of April were extremely hectic as our team worked with the election commission. We also coordinated with National Congress Party and Sudan People's Liberation Movement representatives, Sudanese opposition leaders, leaders from the United Nations missions in Sudan, international technical advisors on elections, and international monitors from the Carter Center, European Union, and the African Union. I made numerous calls back to the State Department and White House, and remained in constant contact with representatives of the international community to set up the conditions for another miracle.

On April 10, while my staff and I were having dinner with members of several pro-democracy organizations in Sudan, my telephone rang. It was a White House number. I quickly excused myself and walked outside. On the line were Tom Donilon, deputy national security advisor, and Denis McDonough, chief of staff for the National Security Council.

"Scott, we need you to return to Washington immediately," Denis said. "We think you're getting too involved in the election. . . ."

I could not believe what I was hearing.

"You're too close to things in Sudan and need to distance yourself a bit," he continued.

I knew it would be futile to protest, but I did manage to respectfully convey my shock and disappointment before saying I would be en route as soon as logistically possible.

Walking back to the table, it was difficult to hide my emotions from the dinner guests but I felt I must. I had not expected a call like that. What did Washington mean by "too close" to this election, and who was the driving force behind such an unfounded conclusion? I had my suspicions, but they were only speculation at that point.

I may have been the special envoy but I was leading a professional team, and we *all* were very hands-on and committed. Our USSES team believed we were doing the right things with the National Elections Commission to ensure a good election and support miracle number seventeen. Not only would 10,000 Sudanese candidates compete for elected office, but this was an excellent opportunity to rehearse the 2011 Southern Sudan Referendum. Polling preparations would not be happening on time nor would they even have a chance of meeting international standards if our international team of technical experts and high-level envoys had not been deeply involved with our Sudanese partners on the ground. I departed, but left our dedicated team in place to continue our work.

What did Washington see that I was missing? Did some in Washington believe my efforts could be construed as an endorsement for Bashir if he won the presidential election as predicted? Not much was said in Washington about my abrupt recall from Sudan and I chose not to pursue the reasons behind it.[9]

Monitoring the election from Washington a few weeks later, I was very satisfied to see that our efforts paid off. The voting process came together to produce polling results across Sudan that citizens accepted as an expression of their will. Miracle number eighteen on my list did happen.

On April 26, the National Elections Commission announced the outcome—as expected, it confirmed President Bashir and Salva Kiir as the presidential winners in the north and south respectively. This election was not only a key CPA milestone, but it provided critical lessons and a useful template for the Southern Sudan Referendum fewer than nine months away.

Not looking at the bigger picture, several key officials in the State Department and the White House were troubled that the Sudanese people had elected President Bashir in the north. There was a move to boycott his inauguration ceremony. I was more concerned about all the unaccomplished checklist items remaining before January 2011, knowing that President Bashir—like it or not—held most of the keys to our success.

I am extremely pleased that our team helped make this election happen on time—even if I did become "too involved" by Washington's standards.

Supporting the Referendum on Independence

I returned to Sudan after the April election and shifted our team's focus toward the January 2011 poll on Southern Sudan's independence. I was concerned that the referendum would not only create the first new country in Africa in more than two decades, but a nation only marginally prepared for autonomy and self-sufficiency. In my view, economic survival of the south depended largely on a continued relationship with Khartoum and the north. We therefore needed an "amicable divorce" where oil would continue to flow through the current pipeline to Port Sudan, where trade would continue along the Nile River between the two countries, and where commerce would continue along the roads and railways linking the two nations.

President Yoweri Museveni of Uganda probably said it best in one of our meetings, "Whether you're in a marriage, business partnership, or in a trade association, you can't be successful if your partner is dead."

Isolating Khartoum with crippling sanctions would damage the north's economy and hurt South Sudan in the short term. If the South failed politically, economically, and socially, the results would be disastrous for Africa. Not only did we have to get this referendum right to prevent further conflict, but our team also had to help the South develop quickly and appropriately to avoid an implosion into civil war and tribal anarchy along the long-standing ethnic fault lines. We needed another miracle.

We would have to foster an integrated approach to north-south relations. Therefore, our office focused on ensuring a credible referendum and a national development plan for the south. At the same time, we had to find a pathway for Khartoum to access international financial institutions in order to ease the economic transition necessitated by the impending dramatic loss of oil revenue. This would also give the National Congress Party more confidence to let the South leave peacefully if the southern Sudanese chose to do so in the referendum.

By October 2010, the Southern Sudan referendum appeared to be generally on track. The White House continued to convene regular meetings on Sudan and it also sent Senator John Kerry to carry a presidential message to Khartoum and Juba, the capital of Southern Sudan.

"President Obama has made it clear that if the referendum proceeds peacefully and, if the other issues of the Comprehensive Peace Agreement are resolved and we move forward peacefully and continue to work on Darfur, he is prepared to submit to the Congress the lifting of the designation on terrorism in writing."

Senator Kerry made this statement in a press conference after talks with the Secretary of the ruling National Congress Party for political affairs. "I personally support doing that. I think we are on a very positive track on that. The United States is interested in a stable and peaceful north. We are interested in Sudan's future for all of its citizens," he added.

Senator Kerry further reiterated the United States' desire to establish normal relations with Sudan, saying, "President Obama is very committed to restoring the relationship with Sudan that allows our countries and our peoples to work together, travel together, visit together, and begin to build the future together."

There were, however, significant internal divisions within the Bashir regime over how to handle the referendum, the related post-referendum negotiations with the Sudan People's Liberation Movement, and this new US rapprochement spelled out by Senator Kerry.

One senior Sudanese official told me, "We are ready to let the south go to achieve peace. We're concerned about letting the south go and continuing to have border conflicts and sanctions."

Ultimately, the decision resided with President Omar al-Bashir. He finally told National Congress Party officials that the referendum would move forward and Khartoum would respect the south's decision. It appeared he had accepted the US pathway to normalized relations.

Yes! Another miracle.

Senator Kerry said in November 2010 that as long as the intelligence review found no National Congress Party support for terrorism, the United States should fulfill its roadmap commitments. Khartoum was now on board—it wanted to shed the State Sponsor of Terrorism designation, exchange ambassadors, and normalize US-Sudan bilateral relations.

Preparing for Possible Independence

While a new relationship between Khartoum, Juba, and Washington was critical, I was concerned that the fierce anti-Khartoum rhetoric mouthed by southerners over the past decades would be redirected on Juba if the new government did not take swift steps to improve social-economic conditions in the South. We therefore introduced numerous initiatives to improve agriculture, education, and healthcare, in accordance with the objectives of Miracle 20.

I got along well with President Salva Kiir Mayardit, the first vice president of Sudan and the president of Southern Sudan. Knowing that he always wore a giant Texan cowboy hat in public and to official meetings, I wore my wide-brimmed hat to our first meeting in his Juba office.[10] He loved it and we immediately forged a warm diplomatic relationship that went beyond our job titles.

A strong Catholic, President Kiir invited me to join him in church which I always did. If he noticed I wasn't keeping up with the readings, he would nonchalantly reach over, turn the page, and point to the proper section. It was good to share a common faith in God as we tried to bring peace and stability to Sudan.

My late-night meetings with Salva Kiir included long sessions on what the Juba government could do to demonstrate to its people that life after independence was much better than a continued union with the north. The bold agenda we discussed would require drastic reforms, harsh penalties for corruption, and an adjustment in spending priorities away from the military. Most importantly, it would require the international community to hold the South's leaders accountable and to levy consequences for bad governance. I prayed that Kiir would have the fortitude to implement the agenda.

Speaking both publically and privately about the negative trends and potential implosion in the south, my warnings were unwanted and unheed-ed in Washington as pre-independence euphoria and unchecked optimism became the prevailing context for decisions regarding South Sudan. Mine was a lonely voice, often dismissed as being too pro-Khartoum. Regardless, the intractable Abyei dispute, regular cross-tribal cattle rustling, the abys-mal education and healthcare systems, rampant and gross corruption, and proliferation of weapons were the swamp in which we were trying to build a new nation.

Without proper buttressing, I believed South Sudan would self-de-struct due to tribalism and greed—causing even more suffering and hard-ships for its citizens. Unless we could prevent an internal implosion, the implications for South Sudan, its African neighbors, and the international community would be extremely challenging. Paraphrasing the Humpty-Dumpty nursery rhyme, "all the king's horses and all the king's men" would have a very difficult time getting the country back together again. We needed more miracles. The United States and its international partners needed to act urgently with "tough love" to prevent this gloomy scenario.

My voice continued to be a lone one as I cautioned of the subsurface but potentially significant tribal cracks in the south's political alliance. Few listened when I opined that the anti-Bashir slogans were a more powerful unifying force than southern identity. My colleagues in Washington, the US church leaders moved by the number of Christians killed, and the advocacy groups that blamed Khartoum for the years of suffering all bristled when I advised against coddling the fledgling government too much. Many still viewed southern Sudanese as "victims" and themselves as the "saviors."

Moving the Goal Posts . . . Again?

On January 9, 2011, the international monitors judged the Southern Sudan's referendum on self-determination to be free, fair, and credible—98 percent of the voters wanted to become an independent country in six months. It was rewarding to witness the long lines of eager voters and to watch the disciplined process in the polling stations. This was number twenty-three of the twenty-four consecutive miracles we had set out to achieve. The referendum on Abyei's future remained elusive.

President Bashir was the first national leader to congratulate President Kiir and South Sudan's citizens. I believe he did this because both Senator Kerry and I carried the US message that Khartoum could be removed from the State Sponsor of Terrorism list if the north peacefully endorsed the referendum results. Why else would the north allow the south to split peacefully with 33 percent of the population and land mass, 75 percent of the oil, and significant oil revenues?

After a successful referendum, the United States backtracked on the State Sponsor of Terrorism agreement again. Eight US dignitaries and senior leaders had offered to remove the north from the State Sponsor of Terrorism list from 2005 to 2011, including Senator John Danforth, Deputy Secretary of State Robert Zoellick, former special envoys Andrew Natsios and Rich Williamson, and Assistant Secretary of State Jendayi Frazer. On eight occasions, the government of Sudan believed Washington reneged and moved the goal posts farther away.

Washington had placed Sudan on the State Sponsor of Terrorism list in 1993 when it was indeed harboring and sponsoring terrorists. I was led to believe we had an agreement in Washington for a dual-tracked sanction program on Sudan. Sanctions resulting from the Darfur genocide and imposed under the Darfur Peace and Accountability Act of 2006 would remain in place until those conditions on the ground were corrected. Sanctions resulting from the 1993 State Sponsor of Terrorism decision could be lifted if Khartoum met President Obama's conditions. That was also the message Senator Kerry conveyed to Sudan's government officials.

I was already the US Ambassador to Kenya when the United States decided not to remove Sudan from the State Sponsor of Terrorism list. I privately felt frustrated and betrayed. Senator Kerry's and my promise to the north had not been kept after Khartoum fulfilled its side of the bargain. No doubt there were good reasons for Washington's decision to move the goal posts again to which I was not privy, but August 18, 2011, was a very sad day for me.[11]

Twenty-Three Miracles Accomplished

Our Sudan team in the State Department did a magnificent job and I will always be indebted to each one of them for demonstrating the initiative and innovation that it took to succeed in this complicated domestic and international environment. The day-to-day operations in our office to settle tough matters like visas, business licenses, and policy differences often went unnoticed, but our staff officers (some on their first assignments) were vital to setting the tone and foundation for the successes we shared in resolving major challenges in Sudan.

The in-country US representatives also deserve much credit for our success, as does the NSC-sponsored working group on Sudan led by Denis McDonough. They ensured that our policy challenges were resolved expeditiously and that US engagement in this region was targeted and effective.

While my emotions roller-coastered between excitement, frustration, elation, and disappointment during my two-year tenure, I was very proud of what we were able to accomplish. Our team, along with prayers, pulled off twenty-three consecutive miracles—against overwhelming odds—to save lives and safeguard peace.

Unfortunately, the first five years of independence in South Sudan have been marred by political and ethnic rivalries, rampant corruption at all levels, and alleged war crimes by both government and rebel security forces. I have been most disappointed by the selfish behavior of many South Sudanese politicians who at independence time seemed to be committed to doing what was best for their new country and its citizens. In the end, we accomplished the task given by President Obama—one that many said was impossible.

It was a distinct and special privilege to serve as the President's Special Envoy to Sudan and thereby help Africa become more peaceful and prosperous, despite the difficult days and the significant sacrifice of family time. It is not often that one is able to save so many lives and be a birth attendant for a new nation. I am deeply grateful to President Obama and Secretary Clinton for giving me this unique opportunity to serve America.

The Obama Legacy

It has now been over eight years since I was deeply involved with the 2008 Obama presidential campaign. My colleagues and I had such high hopes that the Obama-Biden administration would change America profoundly

Hillary Clinton and Scott meet at the State Department. (Courtesy of the US State Department)

Scott- Thank you for your years of service to our country, especially the tough assignment as our Special Envoy on Sudan. All the best to you and your family - Hillary

for the better. I knew the first four years in office would be tough. Having already worked in Washington, DC for ten years in various jobs in the executive branch, I had the opportunity to witness the bureaucratic process of governance up close. I knew that it would be difficult for any president to make significant change within our political system, especially with the partisan gridlock we were experiencing.

As he prepares to leave office in January 2017, I believe the Obama administration will be viewed kindly by history. The United States is better today than it was the day he took the oath of office in January 2009. Our economy is much stronger, the jobless rate has come down significantly, and millions of previously uninsured persons now have access to healthcare.

I appreciated Obama's personal effort as president to restore relationships with Muslims and Arabs, and I agreed with his efforts to reduce US conventional forces in Iraq and Afghanistan. Along with most Americans, I applauded the President's decision to stop Osama bin Laden and to fight al-Qaeda. He made significant progress on relations with Cuba and on the nuclear deal with Iran. President Obama greatly improved America's standing in the world.

A couple of items I wrote about in my ARISE paper for the then-Senator Obama during our 2006 trip to Africa have not been completely accomplished.[12] My document included a discussion on asymmetrical threats, such as cyber attacks and the information security issues. While there has been some progress, I believe the United States is still very vulnerable to cyber attacks and our battles with the Islamic State of Iraq and Syria (ISIS) show that America still struggles with asymmetric challenges.

In my view, the administration mishandled its intervention in Libya and should have removed Sudan from the State Sponsor of Terrorism list as it promised Khartoum in 2010. I believe America and its international partners must find ways to address the root causes of instability and insecurity. Toppling dictators and killing known terrorists might be satisfying in the short term, but America must add a strong socio-economic component to its foreign policy if we are to reduce the pool of potential criminals and terrorists that could continue to threaten Americans and US interests around the globe. A good place to start would be for the United States to negotiate an economic trade agreement with Africa, similar to the ones it has with North America, Europe, and the Far East.

Our country will always need a non-partisan foreign policy and national security agenda that will protect America, our national interests, and future generations. President Obama laid a strong foundation for continued progress and the next president must continue to do what is right for the United States, not just what the political base of the party desires.

President Obama's legacy will likely emerge more clearly as we better understand his commitment to the fundamental values of our nation. I know he shares the vision of the founders of our nation and guards the rights that are guaranteed by our Constitution.

In addition to his well-crafted policy speeches, I am grateful for the words from his heart that healed our nation's soul when we needed it most. I will never forget that moment in Charleston when Obama began to sing *Amazing Grace* at the funeral service for one of nine people killed at Emanuel African Methodist Episcopal Church. This is the Barack Obama I became friends with in Africa and have respected ever since. I am confident Americans will one day understand him better and appreciate him more.

20

America's Representative in Kenya

Character cannot be developed in ease and quiet.
Only through experiences of trial and suffering can
the soul be strengthened, vision cleared, ambition
inspired, and success achieved.

— Helen Keller

WALKING INTO THE CONFERENCE ROOM of Embassy Nairobi at exactly 9:00 a.m. on May 28, 2012, fourteen months after becoming US Ambassador to Kenya, I took my chair at the end of the elegant long table. My senior staff was seated on one side of the table. Members of the Office of the Inspector General (OIG) sat on the other. After my opening comments, Ambassador John McCarthy, the chief inspector, gave us a presentation on the draft OIG report and its findings, and then invited comments from embassy personnel.

I felt like someone had whacked me with a baseball bat. My heart was racing, and I could barely breathe. This had to be a nightmare.

The lies and twisted allegations accusing me of divisive leadership, low morale, damaged cohesion, and lost respect broadsided me. The room shrunk to a dark circle as my mind felt like an F-15 spinning out of control. What had been an expected evaluation of the US Mission's previous five years had turned into a targeted attack on my character and performance.

I had to say something into the cold silence.

"Thank you for your team's evaluation of my one-year tenure as ambassador," I began. "We appreciate your fresh set of eyes on our programs. We will begin today to fix those items you've identified that require more attention—"

The OIG chief inspector said bluntly, "You'll have fourteen working days to submit your comments on our draft report before it will be finalized in Washington for publication."

No one said anything else as we dispersed from the cold, quiet room.

Making my way back to my office, I put the draft OIG Inspection Report in my inbox and turned to my top priority for the day: working with the protocol team and escort officers to finalize details for the four-day visit of Christopher Coons, the US Democratic Senator from Delaware. He and his delegation would be in Nairobi in less than twenty-four hours.

I would later find it ironic to receive a thank-you letter from Senator Coons after his visit, saying "You have a detailed and nuanced grasp of the many issues facing Kenya, and I believe you are doing a great job as ambassador promoting US interests and policy."

Chief of Mission

When I returned to Kenya as ambassador, I was given a new Masai name: *Olomunyak*. This name means "blessed" or "the lucky one." This was true—I was lucky and blessed. Being ambassador to Kenya, a country I loved and felt at home in, was my dream job. I also felt privileged to be working in the State Department.

Throughout all my years as an Air Force officer, I had viewed the State Department's embassies and consulates around the globe as critical components to America's foreign policy and diplomatic relationships. I admired the career diplomats and the men and women who worked in all of the agencies that comprised the US Embassy's "country team."

When President Obama nominated me to serve as the next US Ambassador to Kenya on February 10, 2011, my wife and I were thrilled. We were going back to Kenya again—this time as America's top representative in the country. Following my formal hearing before the Senate Foreign Relations Committee, the full Senate confirmed me for this prestigious position on April 18.

In his appointment letter, President Obama wrote,

As Chief of Mission, you have full responsibility for the direction, coordination, and supervision of all US executive branch employees in the Republic of Kenya, regardless of their employment categories or location, except those under command of a US area military commander or on the staff of an international organization. With these exceptions, you are in charge of all executive branch activities and operations in your Mission.

He further stated in that letter, "I expect you to take direct and full responsibility for the security of your Mission and all the personnel for whom you are responsible, whether inside or outside the chancery gate."

In his guidance, President Obama provided clear direction on what he wanted me to accomplish in terms of leading the embassy, protecting US interests, and promoting American values. I wanted to achieve another objective. Nairobi already was the largest US diplomatic mission in sub-Sahara Africa and one of the largest in the world; I believed we could become the State Department's premier diplomatic post.

Judy and I attended the ambassador seminar where our class received training on our new duties and responsibilities. During her talk to us, Secretary Clinton told our group that we were to be the CEOs of our missions. On April 19, 2011, she administered my oath of office at a warm ceremony in the Secretary's Treaty Room Suite on the seventh floor of the State Department. I was now officially Ambassador Gration.

Ambassador Johnnie Carson, the assistant secretary of state for African affairs whom I was to report to as ambassador, said Washington regarded Nairobi as the "most significant diplomatic posting" in Africa. I wanted to help make our Mission superb in addition to significant.

Representing America

Arriving in Nairobi on a cool early morning in May, I was filled with a sense of excitement at what lay ahead. I remember waking up early the next morning all fired up and ready to go. Climbing into the back seat of an explosion-proof black Chrysler 300 with an American flag flying on the left front fender, I took my place on the left side hidden behind darkened windows. A Kenyan bodyguard sat in the front seat and two more armed guards followed in a Toyota chase car as we traveled the fifteen-minute route from the ambassador's residence to the US Embassy in Gigiri.

A large crowd of State Department employees and well-wishers greeted me as I entered the stately, modern three-story embassy. After a few remarks in the reception area, the deputy chief of mission (DCM) escorted me upstairs to my new office. Two maintenance workers were there as requested to help me remove my office door.

As we unscrewed the last screws from the bottom hinge, I smiled and told my small audience, "Some leaders tell their subordinates, 'my door is always open.' I want all our employees to know I don't even have a door."

I wanted my first message to be unmistakable and genuine—everyone was welcome to see me without discrimination if they had an issue that required my attention.

On my second day in Kenya, I presented my credentials to President Mwai Kibaki in a very cordial meeting. We had been together in New York City during the previous year's United Nations General Assembly session and it was nice to be able to converse with him in Kiswahili. Officially approved by Kenya, I went right to work as the ambassador.

My priorities were to first work with the Kenyan media to get Judy's and my story about coming back to Kenya on the streets. I asked the embassy's public affairs specialist, Katya Thomas, to help me connect with Kenyans right away. My office secretary, Sue Heckman, would then schedule meetings with the government officials I knew, and I would reach out to those I needed to meet. With Kenya's elections and preparations for devolution (i.e., devolving political power and a share of national budget to the county governments) on the immediate horizon, I wanted to establish a solid foundation of relationships, credibility, and influence throughout the country.

We would enhance America's presence and influence within Kenya and around the region by focusing on three areas. The first was to strengthen partnerships with the government of Kenya and its people based on mutual interests and respect.

"We are friends," I told Samson Ongeri, Kenya's minister of foreign affairs. "Friends don't embarrass their friends in public without first trying to work things out in private."

It was well-known that America had the reputation of being heavy handed in Kenya. We were known for using the media as a bully pulpit to get the government's attention or to make a political point. Early in my tenure, I assured Kenyan officials that although I would always do what was in the best interest of the United States, I would try to do it in a way that would benefit both of our nations.

On several occasions when government forces wrongfully curtailed the Kenyan constitutional rights of assembly or free speech, I went immediately to the government and to the media to register our concerns.

There were many times I called a counterpart to explain the US position and to resolve an issue as professionals and friends. There was no mention of our interaction in the Kenya press or even back in Washington—my objective was to get positive results, not credit or recognition.

Two other priorities were top on my list. One was to implement outcome-based programs to support the Kenyan government and to assist and empower the Kenyan people. Another was to ensure our embassy personnel had the leadership, resources, security, and work and living environment to be effective, efficient, and happy. One of my first challenges would be to unify the diverse work force and bridge the gap between Americans in the US Embassy and the Kenyan personnel who were also a vital part of our team. I was off to a good start as the deputy chief of mission and the front office staff were still very friendly and helpful.

Once a month, Judy and I traveled with our Kenyan body guards to different parts of the country, usually by car to show the American flag around the countryside. I also used these trips to meet with Kenyan district leaders, civil society and community groups, and business representatives. We visited US mission activities and toured US Agency for International Development (USAID) and Peace Corps projects to interact with Americans working in Kenya. These journeys gave me an opportunity to see and hear firsthand what was happening at the grassroots level. They were also great opportunities to communicate US policy objectives and to build better relationships between Kenyans, Americans, and the US Embassy.

On August 25, 2011, while on a road trip to Kenya's western region, Judy and I stopped in to visit President Obama's grandmother at Kogelo. We had a wonderful time with Mama Sarah and members of her family. While there I took a cursory look at the protective fences, entry-control points, and the small police station located near the Obama homestead.

I saw obvious security vulnerabilities that I believed should be addressed, especially with al-Shabaab operating in the region.

Knowing that the embassy could not expend US funds to protect a Kenyan citizen, I worked with the Kenya police to improve the overall security environment and asked the embassy's regional security officer to evaluate what else could be done legally. On January 13, 2012, I notified the White House of Mama Sarah's security issues and informed Denis McDonough that State Department diplomatic security and the US secret service could not improve the physical security at her compound.

Because Judy had been born in Nairobi and her parents were buried at Kijabe, she was connected well with Kenyans. In addition to supporting my ambassadorial activities, she cut ribbons to open new facilities, spoke on gender-based issues, and worked with the disabled, poor, and vulnerable. As a mother and grandmother, she related especially well to Kenyan moms and their children.

Judy and I became very involved with the diplomatic community and made many personal and professional friends. We were out three to four times a week representing our government and establishing stronger relationships in and around Nairobi.

I would later discover that the State Department was grading my performance more based on an undisclosed count of internal diplomatic cables rather than what I had accomplished with my Kenyan counterparts.

Doing the Right Things Right

I have always been an outcome-focused and results-oriented leader. I am also passionate about making a difference in the lives of those who have been marginalized, who are less fortunate than we, and who deserve a better and longer life. That's why I decided my first priority as the chief executive officer of the US Embassy would be to work with my senior staff to determine the "right things" for us to do and then concentrate on doing the "right things right." I regret that the OIG didn't take the time to realize that the embassy's exercise to develop our mission-essential tasks was a critical "right things" step in preparing our annual Mission Resource Request.

As a former military commander, I knew it was not my job to be popular—I was leading the US Mission to accomplish our US mission. My predecessor had given a great deal of responsibility for management of the embassy to the deputy chief of mission and to the management counselor while he chose to work on his political and social agenda. This, however, was not my style of leadership. I took Secretary of State Hillary Clinton's direction to "be the CEO of the embassy" very seriously.

It is true that many politically appointed ambassadors (as opposed to career diplomats) are not very knowledgeable about government procedures and the inner workings of the State Department. However, my situation was different. I had been in government service for three and a half decades and had just spent the last two years in Foggy Bottom, working in the State Department.

My assessment upon my arrival was that the embassy was a sprawling organization staffed by highly competent and dedicated individuals but lacking a chief executive focused on outcomes and the effective use of resources. In other words, Team Kenya needed someone willing to question whether the Mission was focused correctly—someone ready to take on the tough issues.

In addition to being a political appointee, I was a retired general officer from the Department of Defense. While it did not come up in conversations with the deputy chief of mission and other senior embassy officials, I sensed an unspoken interagency rivalry between career military officers and career diplomats right from the start.

One senior embassy officer later confided to me, "You had two strikes and a hanging curveball coming at you upon your arrival in Kenya."

I knew he was correct about the two strikes—being a political appointee and a retired general officer. But I did not see the hanging curveball coming . . . deliberate attempts to undermine my authority.

Two Strikes

When I first arrived in Nairobi, I was politely told, in effect, "As a political appointee, your job is to do the external and 'face of the embassy' events. We'll run the internal affairs and other diplomatic functions."

My result-oriented style of leadership did not mesh well with the State Department's hierarchical and rigid management processes. During my first month at the embassy, I had a question concerning one of our initiatives. I told my secretary that I was departing to get some information directly from the program expert on the second floor. Walking down the steps, I was intercepted by this individual's supervisor.

"What are you doing in this section? Do you need some help?" he asked politely, but with a slight tone of confrontation.

I replied that it was my management style to visit staff officers at times instead of writing an email. It was a nice break from my desk and it helped connect faces to electronic signatures.

"Next time you want more information, just ask me and I'll make sure you get the answers you need," he said. I thanked him for his help and continued to the expert's office.

I replayed the conversation in my mind and concluded either I had met a misguided supervisor or I had just seen the tip of an iceberg.

One of my initiatives was to transition our internal processes from output-based measurements (such as keeping track of the number of cables each political officer sent to Washington) to outcome-focused evaluation of our activities. For me, it was about achieving desired results in Kenya for the United States.

This new approach meant I would have to ask the hard questions and, at times, I would likely have to rock the boat. Despite some indications of discontent with my leadership style, I knew I had to prioritize doing the right things above being popular. I was fully aware that my bottom-line leadership might initially cause more discontent among a few high-level embassy managers, but I hoped to win them over with better outcomes and improved results.

As time went on, I chose to become more involved in the day-to-day issues. To my face, the deputy chief of mission and other senior staff were very cordial and seemingly agreeable with my efforts and approach. Yet I sensed a growing resistance just "below the surface" when dealing with a couple of senior managers and sometimes detected a negative spin on my efforts.

For example, several senior embassy leaders resented my chairing the Emergency Action Committee as we reviewed changes to our security posture and took corrective action. They wanted to hold these meetings at the deputy chief of mission level and then make recommendations for my approval. This would work in many embassies, but I had three decades of security experience and wanted to know all the intelligence information, hear the discussions, and be involved in shaping our response.

On another occasion, I wanted to make the protocol office more efficient by moving a few people, redefining some duties, and consolidating some of the embassy's databases. I had years of experience dealing with protocol issues and had developed shared interactive databases in the past. A few days after I chaired a meeting with all the relevant stakeholders in the conference room, I learned that my deputy held a subsequent meeting in his office in which he directed protocol personnel to "slow roll" the new plan and continue doing business as usual.

A week later, I asked my staff assistant, whose official title was special assistant to the ambassador, to do a task for me.

He responded, "I'll have to check with the deputy chief of mission."

I was taken aback at this reply and realized I had a bigger problem with some of my senior staff than I had previously realized.

Conflicts over Security

While Embassy Nairobi appeared to be running well on the surface when I arrived, I perceived that we needed better and broader relationships with Kenyan leaders. On June 5, 2011, I told Assistant Secretary of State Carson that building relationships would be a priority for me and the US Embassy leadership.

The second area of my concern was security, especially given my background as a military officer and my first-hand experiences with terrorist attacks on Khobar Towers in 1996 and the Pentagon on 9/11.

Kenya was the only country in Africa rated critical for both terrorism and criminal activity. We had the same terrorism rating as Afghanistan, Iraq, and Pakistan. This rating was justified based on the grenades, bombs, and improvised explosive devises that were claiming the lives of Kenyans and a few expatriates in Nairobi, Mombasa, and in the country's northeastern region.

Despite this potential danger to US personnel and American interests, I had detected a complacency and "business as usual" attitude among some embassy leaders and our supervisors in Washington. Kenya had become a sought-after family post. The State Department encouraged officers to "safe haven" their dependent families in Kenya while serving in the high-threat areas of Afghanistan, Iraq, and Pakistan.

The practice of safe-havening dependents in a highly unsafe environment such as Kenya without specific guidance from the State Department did not make much sense to me. I elevated my concerns to Washington. It was clear that many in Foggy Bottom were uncomfortable with my not-so-subtle requests for direction; I received few useful responses.

From my perspective, I needed to be able to tell a congressional inquiry that I had done everything possible to protect Americans in Kenya. Clearly, I had nothing against non-essential family members; in fact, the opposite was true. But what would I say if a wife, husband, son, or daughter being "safe havened" was hurt or killed in a violent terrorist or criminal attack?

I asked the Bureau of African Affairs in the State Department to take responsibility for this policy decision and officially direct our embassy to house the growing number of unaccompanied dependent spouses and children. Assistant Secretary Carson would not.

On my next trip back to Washington, I raised my security dilemma with Under Secretary for Management Patrick Kennedy. He explained the safe-havening program was important to Secretary Clinton as she tried to fill the empty State Department billets in combat zones. After hearing me out, Under Secretary Kennedy reluctantly promised to testify with me if a dependent family member was killed in Kenya. I still believed there were safer places for these non-essential personnel to live than Nairobi, but I cared for them in the same manner we looked after the other individuals assigned to our Mission.

As part of ensuring that we had the best possible security posture, I conducted a "no notice" exercise on September 20, 2011, to see how our embassy personnel would respond to a terrorist attack. The scenario consisted of terrorist fighters storming over the embassy walls in two places and eventually taking control of the USAID building. In hindsight, it was almost identical to the actual attack in Libya a year later where terrorists breached the perimeter defenses of the US diplomatic facility in Benghazi and killed US Ambassador Christopher Stevens and three of his civilian security contractors.

Our embassy's US Marine guards reacted perfectly during the exercise, but it was clear some Mission personnel had grown complacent after operating under high-threat conditions for so many years. Several senior officers did not know where the alternate command post was located and some embassy personnel did not comply with our "duck and cover" procedures when the alarm sounded. During the exercise, we identified several significant issues that hampered efforts to secure the embassy perimeter. Our engineers and technicians quickly corrected all the physical deficiencies and we introduced security training to increase our personnel readiness.

My greatest challenge, however, arose over staffing levels in our regional security office. As spring approached and members prepared to depart for their next assignment, I discovered that two assistant regional security officers would depart at the same time for training, leaving concurrent two-month gaps.

We were already at high alert because terrorists were throwing grenades and bombing targets in Kenya virtually every week. Our intelligence analysts were very concerned about the safety of Americans and the security of US facilities. We had reported this to Washington. I was informed of criminal and terrorist activities in the country, including threats on my life. I made my daily routines even more unpredictable and embassy security professionals removed the red diplomatic license plates from my personal and embassy vehicles in an attempt to lower my profile.

In this threatening environment, and already shorthanded in the regional security office, the State Department decided to send the embassy's chief security officer to Washington, DC, for seventy-one days of French language training—leaving us with a 50-percent manning level in the regional security office during this period. I wrote many emails to Ambassador Carson in Washington and to the Office of Diplomatic Security. We offered to provide French language training in Nairobi so that our security supervisor would be in-country until his replacement arrived and the two replacement assistant security officers were present for duty in the embassy.

My requests for more adequate security were denied by Eric Boswell, the assistant secretary for diplomatic security in Washington, with an arrogant and dismissive email on March 28, 2012. The message concluded by saying, "Should an emergency situation develop, you have my promise that we will provide additional personnel if asked."

I was not impressed with his answer. Two days later, I replied, "We appreciate your promise, but we don't need your help when we're already bleeding and dying. Here in Kenya, we are in the business of preventing 'emergency situations.'"

Only four months after my email exchange with Boswell, Ambassador Christopher Stevens was killed in a firefight in Benghazi, Libya.[1] Ambassador Stevens had repeatedly asked for more security from the same assistant secretary for diplomatic security. His requests for more protection were also denied.

I do not fault Secretary Clinton for denying my multiple requests to improve security for Americans in Kenya. As in Ambassador Stevens' case, my pleas probably did not reach her desk. She likely didn't know that her "diplomatic security professionals" in Washington had dismissed an ambassador's request with a hollow promise to provide additional security in an emergency.

I do, however, squarely blame the State Department's "diplomatic security professionals" in Washington for my and Ambassador Stevens' security gaps. While I understand why Secretary Clinton needed to defend the State Department's security officials in her October 22, 2015, congressional testimony about the Benghazi incident, it is disappointing to me that these individuals have not been held accountable for their arrogance, faulty judgment, and poor leadership.[2]

Would I "rock the boat" again on this issue? Yes, absolutely!

Leadership Challenges and Rewards

Despite all of the leadership challenges, I believed that our embassy integrated diplomacy, development, and defense just as Secretary Clinton had directed us to do. In addition, our US Mission adopted the organizational changes concerning the Somalia Unit[4] and dealt with the rising threats emanating from Somalia in a coherent and proactive way. I was proud of our embassy teams that helped the Kenya government and non-governmental agencies meet the humanitarian needs of hundreds of thousands of Somalis after the world's largest drought in sixty years forced them to find refuge and sustenance in Kenya.

Our embassy was the operational platform in the region for a host of State Department and presidential initiatives, including Feed the Future, the Global Health Initiative, the Global Climate Change Initiative, and the National Export Initiative. We were the only embassy in the world tasked to pilot all four programs at once. I was very proud of our strong team of professionals.

We were improving our embassy security posture and our interactions with Kenyan leaders concerning their crime and terrorism challenges. I felt we were now moving in the right direction. While doing all these daily tasks, we also planned and hosted numerous high-level congressional and White House-sponsored trips to Kenya. Each one was highly productive and very enjoyable for the visiting delegation.

While serving as the US Ambassador to Kenya, I celebrated my sixtieth birthday. Around the table were dear friends Judy and I had known from our childhood, from my time of flying with the Kenya Air Force at Nanyuki, from our Kenya visits when I was CEO of Millennium Villages, and from this assignment. The celebration was not just about being back in Kenya with great friends, it was a celebration of four decades of service as a military officer, diplomat, and humanitarian. Being the ambassador to Kenya was just our most recent blessing to celebrate.

It was wonderful to look back on the special seasons of life and to thank God for each one. At the time, we did not realize how much faith we were going to need to get us through our next experience.

You Need to Move On

"Scott, the inspector general just briefed me on the inspection and I believe you'll have to move on."

I looked at my watch: 4:45 p.m. local time, June 5, 2012, less than a week after the OIG inspector had stunned me with his biased report and told me I had until June 19 to refute it.

Cheryl Mills, Secretary Clinton's chief of staff at the State Department, was calling from Washington. I thought she had called to congratulate the embassy on the superb work two of our duty officers had done to save the life of an American tourist. Not so. After she laboriously read a list of allegations, she concluded by saying that the report would be published on the Internet in a few days.

I was shocked. "This is unreasonable, Cheryl," I objected. "I haven't even had a chance to rebut the inaccurate statements and allegations."

I asked for three more days in which to meet with my supervisor, Ambassador Carson. He would be visiting Nairobi on Friday, June 8. Cheryl agreed.

I hung up the phone and sat quietly in my office for a few minutes. My mind was racing as I gazed at the collage of signed pictures of me with each of the last eight presidents of the United States—Richard Nixon to Barack Obama. I'd had wonderful experiences serving in our government. Yet the State Department chief of staff had just told me I was being fired from my dream job—two weeks before my formal response to the report was due in Washington.

I liked Cheryl; our interactions had always been warm. From my experiences in the Presidential Personnel Office, I knew she could be a tough negotiator, and her loyalty to Secretary Clinton was unquestionable. My memory of her office on the State Department's seventh floor was that it was always about ten degrees above my comfortable temperature. Even on balmy spring days, her space heater was glowing and Cheryl had a shoulder wrap nearby.

Why had she now made a snap decision after hearing an informal IG briefing? Why didn't she want to hear my side of the situation? Had the decision been made before the OIG inspection began?

As a warrior I had survived multiple close encounters with enemies "out there." Now I was being attacked from within a secure perimeter. My government reputation as a leader was being ruined and I was being railroaded out of the assignment of a lifetime. Why?

At first, I was in denial—I just could not believe this was happening. Then I became angry at those I believed had engineered the negative OIG report. I wanted to fight the manipulated information and allegations that I knew were clearly false.[5] But most of all, I wanted a fair hearing—the chance to have my side of the story heard. I was being denied the sacred right American justice gives to every accused individual—the right to be heard before being punished.

Then my life went dark. People in the State Department and White House would not return my telephone calls or answer my emails. In the space of one month, I had become a political pariah. I felt very alone.

I had no option but to turn to my foundation—my integrity and values, my family and friends, and my belief in God's ultimate control of my life's circumstances. I didn't know why this was happening, but I remained convinced that things would work out in the end. They always had in the past.

At 7:00 a.m. on Friday, June 8, I met with Ambassador Carson for a private breakfast at Serena Hotel in Nairobi. Sitting at a quiet table on the dining patio, I ordered a cup of coffee as Johnnie went through the breakfast buffet line. As he began to eat, I thanked him for meeting with me and I detailed my telephone call with Cheryl three days ago. He said that he wasn't aware of the call, but he was obviously well-prepared for this meeting—he had all the State Department's talking points in his head.

"You've rocked the boat too hard by raising security issues to Pat Kennedy's level, by confronting Diplomatic Security on manning issues, and pushing the personnel system on the summer transition gaps," he said as he munched on his toast.[6]

Ambassador Carson alleged I had been too tough in public forums and had demanded actions that called into question my ethical standards. *What's he talking about?* I thought to myself as I continued taking notes. *My whole life has been lived on ethical principles.*

Continuing, he said he had been told I limited my staff meetings to senior leaders and would not speak to their deputies. My boss stated that I had reduced the number of country team meetings to twice a month and did not speak with agency heads, although he knew I met with fourteen senior leaders in an embassy staff meeting three times per week.

Then he said, "Some believe you've been using your Gmail account to send classified information."

I found the allegation about my Gmail account demeaning. After serving in the United States government for thirty-five years, including seven years as a general officer and two as the Joint Staff's director of information operations, I was essentially being accused of sending America's secrets to an unauthorized person using an unsecure network. I understood the OIG had an obligation to investigate serious allegations like this, but it was insulting.

"This is preposterous, Johnnie. Sending classified information to whom?" I objected. He made no reply.

At the conclusion of this one-way conversation, I asked Ambassador Carson what *he* thought of my performance as chief of mission in Kenya. As my immediate supervisor, why had he not informed me about these issues or counseled me even once in the past year about these problems?

I also raised my primary question: Why wasn't the State Department giving me the opportunity to present my side in these allegations?

He did not answer my questions.

Ambassador Carson concluded the fifty-minute breakfast meeting by saying I would continue to be the ambassador until I was formally removed. He added that he did not expect the OIG report to be published as soon as Cheryl Mills had indicated.

A week later at 8:30 p.m. on June 15, I received another telephone call from Secretary Clinton's chief of staff. Cheryl said she had spoken to Johnnie Carson about his observations during his visit to Kenya and said, "I'm still convinced you have a compromised ability to lead the mission."

"But Cheryl, again, you're firing me without listening to my side of the story," I said. "I'm preparing my response to the OIG report; I'll send it to you before the 19th. It will answer every OIG write-up in detail—I'll include all the supporting documentation."

Cheryl replied that my response would be included as part of the published formal report. I knew this would not be the case. I was right; it was not included.

She concluded by adding this specific accusation: "Your pressuring of US personnel to protect the president's grandmother is a political embarrassment for the administration. You should think of moving on by mid-July."

This was an outlandish accusation. I didn't pressure anyone to protect Mama Sarah Obama in Kogelo. I just wanted to do everything we could to protect her without spending a dime of US money. But Cheryl had stopped listening and the phone conversation was over.

I submitted forty-one pages containing my side of the story to the Office of the Inspector General, and I sent a courtesy copy of my response to Cheryl Mills and Johnnie Carson on June 19. The appendix contained over 250 pages of supporting documents. These, I believed, would clearly and logically refute the biased conclusions of the OIG inspection and would substantiate the "railroading" I had perceived from the beginning.

On the 19th, again at 4:50 p.m., Cheryl called with her final decision. She had met with members of the OIG inspection team, Under Secretary for Management Pat Kennedy, Assistant Secretary Johnnie Carson, and representatives from State Department's Human Resources. Nothing had changed her mind.

"You need to move on," she declared firmly.

Still not ready to give up, I asked Cheryl if she had read my counter responses to the accusations. "I looked at your responses, but the IG is confident they followed standard inspection procedures," she relayed without emotion.

"What are my options?"

"You can resign or be formally asked to leave," she responded.

Warriors and/or Diplomats

It is very true that warriors and diplomats have different approaches and distinctive terminologies. Because of my background as a warrior and recent experience as a diplomat, I had to mesh two contrasting mindsets and merge two unique institutional cultures. In the military, I was used to getting things done as soon as possible and pushing my subordinates to meet compressed timelines. The diplomatic community was used to having meetings, developing consensus, and distributing meeting notes. In hindsight, I should have adjusted my expectations downward and made a greater effort to perfect the unusual warrior-diplomat amalgamation.

I had approached the ambassadorship believing that my primary job was to implement the mandate the President of the United States and the Secretary of State had given me. Looking back I now realize that my hands-on enthusiasm for embassy operations while resisting the limited role of "chief political officer" or a public goodwill ambassador was misinterpreted by some embassy and State Department staff. I should have communicated my vision more clearly.

I also missed clues about the growing resistance among a few senior leaders who did not appreciate my "intrusion" into their assumed duties. While things continued to be cordial and smooth on the surface, I did not root out the passive-aggressive dissent when I first detected the subtle signs. Eventually it was too late.

I am pleased to say that most of my senior managers and members of the country team were extremely supportive. In addition, junior officers provided me with expeditious answers and high-quality research whenever I needed this type of assistance. The Kenyan members of our embassy team were consistently kind and courteous—they were always ready to stop and converse in Kiswahili with their boss. Overall, I was extremely impressed with our team and admired their dedication to making America successful in Kenya.

There is no question that I made mistakes in dealing with my State Department colleagues. I should have been more accepting of the State Department's consensus-building methodology, its emphasis on diplomatic cables and historical documentation, and the "management by talking about it" approach.

That said, as an experienced leader I should not have tolerated the negative undercurrent, passive-aggressive behavior, and near-insubordination that some Foreign Service officers propagated. I let the "political appointee versus career diplomat" friction fester much too long without intervening decisively.

As a new ambassador, I should have reached out to Ambassador Carson, my boss and a career diplomat, for advice on specific embassy or personnel issues. At the same time, I believe that Ambassador Carson, or whoever was getting the duplicitous complaints from those who wanted to undermine my appointment, should have given me a heads-up about the growing clash. I did not get a warning from the Africa Bureau or guidance on how to lead the mission better. It would be a logical assumption to say that no one had my back in Washington.

I Will Tell the Truth

The last thing I said to Cheryl was, "I've appreciated the opportunity to serve the Obama administration. You can count on me to keep telling the truth."

My integrity would keep me from saying in a resignation letter that I was "leaving to spend more time with my family," as she suggested. I had done nothing immoral, unethical, or illegal. I would be tactful, but I could not and would not distort the facts.

I didn't know all the facts, though. While I believe the OIG "threw me under the bus," I could not understand why my friends in Washington— who knew my background, my character, my integrity, and my passion for justice and fairness—were not standing up for me. I had a history of risking my career to ensure subordinates were treated fairly, and now my supervisors and friends in high places were ignoring my sinking hand when I needed to be rescued from bureaucratic injustice.

I resigned on July 28, 2012, and issued the following comments in a news release:

> It has been a great honor and a profound privilege to be a part of the US State Department team for the past three years and to serve as the US Ambassador to Kenya and as the CEO of Team Kenya since May of 2011. However, differences with Washington regarding my leadership style and certain priorities lead me to believe that it's now time to leave. Accordingly, I submitted my notice of resignation last Monday to the Secretary of State and to the President of the United States of America, to be effective as of 28 July 2012.
>
> Being the US Ambassador Extraordinary and Plenipotentiary to the Republic of Kenya has been a dream job for my wife and me. This assignment has been the perfect opportunity to use my deep-rooted knowledge of Kenya—its people, its language, and its culture—and

my diplomatic, development, security, and humanitarian experience. Judy and I have been extremely honored to lead Team Kenya, and we wish all of you the very best as Kenya implements its Constitutional reforms, holds elections next year, and proceeds with the devolution of political and economic power.

I am very proud of my 35-year career of dedicated and honorable service to our great nation, leading at all times with integrity first and the highest ethical standards. Judy and I are looking forward to returning to the work about which we are so passionate. But as we depart, we will deeply miss Kenya, the Kenyan people, our partners in the diplomatic corps, and our colleagues in the US Mission. Our hearts will remain here with you and true friendships will endure until death.

Proud to Have Served

Two months after I was fired, the formal investigations into the OIG's allegations were completed and the charges against me were subsequently dropped. I was fully exonerated, but, alas, it was too late. And the uncorrected OIG report containing the baseless allegations is still online for the world to see.

What no one saw were the numerous letters that came from members of the government of Kenya and from my counterparts in the international community. No one saw the extensive network of professional relationships I had worked hard to develop with Kenyan leaders. In addition, no one heard the telephone calls both Judy and I received for several weeks thanking us for our personal friendship and professional accomplishments. It didn't really matter as these were for us to see, know, and hear. The kind words were very meaningful and helped considerably to heal the wounds that were so fresh and deep.[7]

Three weeks before my last day in the State Department, the US Embassy hosted its Fourth of July reception at our residence. Judy and I knew this would be one of our last official events as "Ambassador and Mrs. Gration." We were determined to make it special despite the deep sorrow we would feel as our friends filed through the reception line for the last time.

It was hard to watch our residence staff putting out flowers, cleaning, and making everything perfect for this event. They had become like family

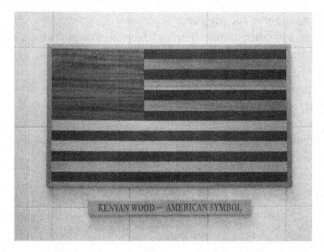

*The American flag
Scott constructed
with Kenyan wood.*

to us and we appreciated their kind gestures and friendly smiles so very much—it would be so sad to say good-bye to these very special friends.

After passing by the row of the fifty US state flags along the front walkway, our guests would enter the gorgeous "America House" that had been our home for almost a year and a half. Constructed in 1916, elegant design features accompanied the thick walls, high ceilings, and parquet flooring.

On the left side of the foyer was a collage of Joseph Sohm's exceptional photographs, each prominently featuring the American flag in a different US setting. There was a picture of President Obama with the flag in the background and photographs of flags in Arlington National Cemetery, at a baseball game, on the Iwo Jima memorial, on the back of a motorcycle, and flying on the front porch of a typical American home.

We had mounted these meaningful pictures around a 3- by 5-foot wooden flag that I had constructed with six different types of Kenyan wood. I used dark mahogany, mvuli, and teak for the red stripes and the blue field, and lighter camphor, cedar, and cypress woods for the white stripes and the flag's frame. I called the piece, *Kenya Wood – American Symbol*, and believed it was a strong representation of US-Kenya partnership.

Visitors, stepping out onto the back porch, were greeted by the stately trees, and green carpet lawn that enhanced the US ambassador's residence and made it the envy of other diplomats. Off to the left was an enormous 80-foot flag, suspended between two beautiful jacaranda trees, waving gently behind the stage. Another large flag brought color and a sense of patriotism to the other side. American volunteers staffed the drink tables while other embassy personnel prepared and served grilled hamburgers and chicken, US hot dogs, homemade potato salad, and other goodies as our gift to the Kenyan and diplomatic guests.

The event included a joint honor guard of Kenyan and US servicemen to post the colors, and the world-class Nairobi chamber chorus singing the national anthems. The Rift Valley Academy Jazz Band provided first-class entertainment after the formal ceremony. Everything was perfect.

At the completion of America's 236th birthday celebration, we dedicated the expanded memorial to those who lost their lives in the 1998 bombing of the American Embassy in downtown Nairobi. With the State Department's knowledge and despite the OIG's criticism, I had refurbished the existing memorial for US employees and had added another section that recognized the two hundred eighteen Kenyans who also died in the bomb blast.

After everyone had gone, Judy and I sat together on a wooden bench in the backyard watching the sun rest behind the American flag. As its colors dimmed to hues of grey, we reflected on the rich blessings of the past fifteen months. We had lived the special opportunity to serve the United States—the land we love. We had strengthened the US relationship with Kenya—the land of our roots. We thanked God.

I did what I believed was right and in accordance with the president's guidelines. While no leader is perfect and there are things I could have handled better, my conscience was clear and my integrity was intact. Judy and I would move on with pride in our efforts, love for our country, and faith that God's plans are always sovereign.

When everything seems to be going against you,
remember that the airplane takes off against the
wind, not with it.

— Henry Ford

21

A Double Standard?

When you forgive, you in no way change the past—
but you sure do change the future.

— Bernard Meltzer

"Mr. Ambassador, given that which has now been revealed about Secretary Clinton's use of a private e-mail account, in retrospect, do you believe that your firing represents a double standard?"

It was March 8, 2015, a hot day in Nairobi. Michael Smerconish, a guest host of CNN's *State of the Union* program, was interviewing me from Washington, DC.

I answered honestly but diplomatically. "As I look back, it may have," I said, gazing straight into the camera. "As I was going through it, I did not perceive that it was a double standard because I did not know of Secretary Clinton's use of a commercial e-mail account. But as I've reflected on it in the last couple of days, it does appear like there was a different standard that was used in my case from that which has been used in hers."

Since then, we have learned a lot more about former Secretary of State Hillary Clinton's use of her private email account and home server during her time in the State Department. But back during the spring and summer of 2015, Republican candidates and various journalists and commentators used my abrupt dismissal from the US ambassador posting, in part for using my Gmail account, to contrast Hillary Clinton's use of State Department computer systems and her lenient treatment by high-level officials in the Obama administration.

As new information has been uncovered, yes, it is clear that I was treated very differently. Based on the emerging facts, it is also evident I was judged by harsher criteria throughout the entire OIG inspection.

The question is, why? Why did the State Department use a double standard in dealing with me?

Some say it is because I was an Obama supporter in a Clinton State Department. Others have speculated that it was because I was a military man in a career-diplomat world. Finally, I was told that some in the State Department resented a political appointee taking one of Africa's plum postings that had historically been given to a career diplomat. As of 2013, President Obama had nominated a record 135 non-career candidates for ambassador positions. The American Foreign Service Association, the labor union and trade association for career diplomats, implies in its website that the lower number of career diplomats getting ambassadorships is unacceptable.

Maybe these mismatches were a factor, but my get-it-done leadership style was probably the major contributing factor to my ouster. My assertive efforts to improve security that irked State Department leaders in Washington, coupled with my efforts in the embassy to make management practices more efficient and information-technology procedures more effective, likely fomented the lightly disguised effort to rid the State Department of my perceived boat-rocking tenacity.

In retrospect, I don't believe my firing had anything to do with the relationship between Secretary Clinton and President Obama. I perceived their rapport was genuinely solid. In addition, Mrs. Clinton was always very friendly and extremely supportive of my efforts when I served as the US Special Envoy to Sudan. Although I didn't speak with her after my ambassadorial swearing-in ceremony, I always got along very well with the Secretary of State in our meetings, appreciated her backing, and respected her leadership.

That said, there was a palpable friction between some State Department political appointees and some officials in the White House—subtle abrasion that had its roots in the 2008 campaign for the Democratic Party's presidential nomination. Many of the State Department's senior managers had come from the Clinton campaign and were fiercely loyal to the Secretary of State. As someone with strong connections to the president and the Obama campaign, I was never accepted as a State Department insider by the Clinton camp.

I would hope that political rivalry had nothing to do with my abrupt and unfair departure from the US Embassy, but this subtle political divide probably didn't help my case.

It is true that my military background influenced my approach to problem solving, my passion for American values, and my patriotism. I admit that my warrior mindset was not appreciated by some of my State Department colleagues and I should have tried harder to mask it in my dealings with senior career diplomats. Only I am to blame for the undue friction this may have produced during my ambassadorship.

An Independent Inspector General?

I received several expressions of kindness after my departure directly attributed to President Obama.[1] On his July 2012 visit to Kenya, Michael Froman, the deputy national security advisor for economic affairs, relayed one such message from the president.

"President Obama has been paying lots of attention to your situation. The president asked that I relay he's very sad about your departure, especially that Judy had to go through the pain of leaving early," said Froman. "He's praying for Judy and you."

I had worked with Mike during the presidential campaign, so I felt I could share with him a question I was hoping to have an answer to. After thanking him for the president's message, I bluntly asked, "What is the president going to do to help me?"

Froman wasn't encouraging. "The president can't force the IG to change its words," he said. "They represent an independent body in the Department. He can't interfere—it would be politically impossible."

"I understand, Mike, but here's the issue someone needs to address. Who inspects the IG? Who can demand a redress of an IG wrong?"

Froman had no answer. I was disappointed but not surprised. I had queried a number of senior leaders in the Obama administration and asked the same question. When faced with perceived unfairness and a double standard originating from the Office of the Inspector General, what was one's official recourse? No one answered my emails or returned my telephone calls.

I understood that President Obama's hands were proverbially tied—and even more so by the pressures of the upcoming 2012 election. I appreciated his kind sentiments. At least the most powerful man in the world had not given me the cold shoulder, as had many friends I worked closely with on the 2008 campaign trail and in the White House.

Still, I wondered, why hadn't senior administration officials at the State Department or the White House stepped in to allow me to present my side of the story?

The next month, August 2012, I was at the State Department to complete my termination paperwork. I sought out several legal officers and government officials and asked the same question: Who inspects the OIG inspectors?

The answer I received most often was that the Office of Inspector General is "self-policing." I learned the OIG is a congressionally mandated "independent and objective unit" within the Department of State, headed by an inspector general (IG) appointed by the president and confirmed by the US Senate.

I also learned that by law, the State Department's IG is not permitted to be a career member of the Foreign Service.

What? If the IG had to be an individual appointed by the president and confirmed by the US Senate, and could not be a career member of the Foreign Service, why was this not the case in the State Department while I was the US Ambassador to Kenya?

It appears that State Department leaders and White House officials overlooked this flagrant noncompliance with US law and administration policy year after year. The State Department's Office of the Inspector General did not have a presidentially nominated, Senate-confirmed inspector general from January 16, 2008 to September 30, 2013—more than five and a half years!

During Secretary Hillary Clinton's entire tenure at the State Department, Ambassador Harry Geisel was the acting inspector general. Geisel was a retired career Foreign Service stalwart with forty years of experience in the State Department's bureaucracy. Many of his inspectors were from the same career Foreign Service officer pool. He used his friend, Ambassador McCarthy, to inspect me and our US Embassy in Nairobi.[2]

This discrepancy was obvious to people outside the State Department. US Congressmen Ed Royce (R-CA), the chairman of the House Committee on Foreign Affairs, and Eliot Engel (D-NY), the ranking Democrat, wrote letters dated February 2013 to the new Secretary of State John Kerry and President Obama concerning this problem.[3] One letter noted

> That gap of more than 1,840 days is the longest vacancy of any of the 73 Inspector General positions across the federal government. While this would be problematic under any circumstances, the repeated criticisms of the independence and effectiveness of that office by the Government Accountability Office heighten the need for an appointment.

According to a letter sent to President Obama in November 2010 by the nonprofit Project for Government Oversight, the absence of a Senate-confirmed IG at State was a major problem.[4] The letter highlighted the longtime personal friendship between the Acting Inspector General Geisel and State's Undersecretary for Management Patrick Kennedy, who is "responsible for the people, resources, facilities, technology, consular affairs, and security of the Department of State."

The Government Accountability Office reported, "The appointment of management and Foreign Service officials to head the State OIG in an acting capacity for extended periods of time is not consistent with professional standards for independence."[5]

A quick search of the Internet reveals stories about external manipulation of OIG investigations—mostly by senior officials in the State Department. Based on my experience at the US Embassy in Kenya and reports I have heard from other inspections, the State Department OIG was clearly neither a self-policing nor an independent body.[6]

The Government Accountability Office also stated "the use of Foreign Service officers at the ambassador level to lead OIG inspections resulted in, at a minimum, the appearance of independence impairment." Of course I completely agree. In addition to appointing an independent Inspector General in 2009, the Obama administration should have cleaned up the OIG that was led by career insiders and staffed by many recruited from the "good old boy" network.

My case aside, I believe this biased inspection and investigatory system significantly damaged the State Department and careers of some good Foreign Service officers and political appointees. During this period, the OIG was sometimes used as a tool for the State Department's inner circle to purge their ranks of those branded as "boat rockers" and others that did not fit the mold.

Unfortunately, government servants who have been forced out of service unfairly do not have a convenient mechanism for redressing their grievances. In fact, most maligned high-level government officials choose to accept the injustice and depart quietly without making political waves.

An Inspection or a Weapon?

There appeared to be two different objectives and standards used by the State Department's OIG to conduct inspections while I served as an ambassador—one to evaluate a US Mission and the other to justify or force a personnel change. In my case, I believe the OIG was focused on the latter.

In the end, I believe the part-time chief OIG inspector that evaluated the US Embassy in Nairobi was simply obeying his instructions from the State Department in Washington. Ambassador McCarthy and his team of inspectors likely arrived in Nairobi with their premise in hand:

> Ambassador Gration's willingness to elevate issues of disagreement up the chain of command within the State Department is tantamount to "insubordination."

Ambassador McCarthy wrote as much on my evaluation: "His failure to follow Department instructions constitutes insubordination." The entire report suggests to me that the State Department expected me to be a compliant ambassador, accepting the security shortfalls and other problematic pronouncements from Washington without a murmur—and I was unacceptable because I was not compliant.

I learned subsequently that the perception of insubordination in Washington was fueled by a damaging campaign of back-channel emails and discreet telephone calls. A few of the embassy's disgruntled managers who disliked my hands-on approach and bold leadership style which focused more on results than rhetoric had been sending disparaging reports about me to their colleagues in Foggy Bottom. I got wind of these after the damage had been done.

During the OIG inspection and after the report was made public, many embassy personnel came to me privately to tell me about the underhanded campaign against me in the embassy. Others sadly told me how they were naively used to support some of the allegations against me. Several broke down in tears as they recounted the manipulation.

On June 22, 2012, I informed Denis McDonough at the White House in an email that "the OIG inspection was biased against me and was focused on gathering negative antidotes and one-liners to build a case that I was ineffective, unethical, and demoralizing. Many embassy staff members have reported to me accounts of inspectors forming questions to get the negative information they wanted or digging until they found something that could be construed as a shortcoming." This approach had hardly been objective fact finding . . . it was cherry-picking to support the OIG's predetermined desired outcome.

One very senior-ranking State Department officer in the Mission confided to me and to others in my office after the OIG team departed, "We wanted a 20 percent change, but we got 200 percent." I took that to mean that there were practices and decisions in the embassy that he disagreed with and wanted changed. But he and whomever he was working with had not intended for me to be fired and my reputation destroyed. Although he offered no apology, his tone was remorseful. His admission confirmed the existence of a dissident undercurrent in some offices of the embassy that I should have resolved, but regrettably did not.

The Important Differences

That CNN interview with Michael Smerconish on March 5, 2015, included a follow-up question. He asked whether I thought Cheryl Mills, the State Department chief of staff and the woman who fired me, knew that our boss, Secretary of State Hillary Clinton, had been using a commercial email system to conduct her official government business. I answered cautiously, saying I could not say for certain but it would have seemed unlikely for Cheryl not to know.

It is now certain that Cheryl had to be fully aware that Secretary Clinton was using a commercial email account supported by her own home server to conduct official government business. We now know, applying the same language that the OIG report did in my case, that this was "ignoring State Department instructions." Clearly, Secretary Clinton "willfully disregarded State Department regulations concerning the use of commercial email for official government business," to quote the OIG again.

Of course, this was disheartening. Why was I berated for using Gmail while no one questioned the Secretary's practice?

I was well-aware of the background events leading up to that accusation. Soon after becoming Ambassador in May 2011, I pushed hard to have my unclassified State Department emails and my Gmail messages displayed as separate accounts on the same State Department Blackberry. After four months of trying and the request still being turned down, I gave up and agreed to carry two devices to read my unclassified email traffic, even though it could have easily been displayed on one device. I realize now that I irritated some in the State Department's information security community by my efforts to do what I believed made perfect sense.

My second confrontation with the information security professionals had to do with a special document-handling procedure that was called Sensitive But Unclassified (SBU).[7] In reading the State Department's instructions and regulations concerning SBU information, I realized that US Embassy personnel in Kenya had been inadvertently violating the SBU procedures as they were currently written. Embassy personnel had been lulled into using SBU as a quasi-classification of information above "Unclassified"—which it was not.

I invited a State Department cyber specialist from the diplomatic security's regional office to spend a week in Nairobi to help our embassy team rewrite the instruction so it would be clearer and so we could comply with the letter and intent of the special-handling procedures. I adopted these upgraded SBU procedures for use in the embassy, as they provided more information protection than did the Department's instruction. Of course, our team recommended that the State Department's diplomatic security office formally change to the Foreign Affairs Manual to reflect the improved wording.

During this time, I continued to question the "no Gmail policy" because I couldn't get technical answers to my basic questions. For example, if I was prohibited from sending a Gmail message to a State Department computer except in an emergency, why were Department of Defense dot mil accounts, USAID accounts, and every Kenyan account authorized to send emails to OpenNet users when these emails passed through the same routers and security firewalls as a Gmail account?

It didn't make sense to me that the State Department would ban my unclassified "gmail.com" while letting all other commercial and foreign accounts through its computer firewall. I tried to understand why the State

Department's computer firewall couldn't stop a malicious "exe" code in a Gmail message while it professed to stop similar worms and virus-executing commands in other commercial email messages. The State Department won its tug-of-war with me over information and communications technology (ICT) policy in August 2012 when I was forced to resign.

While the email issue was not the only unsubstantiated allegation forcing my resignation, it was a major argument in the OIG's case against me. Therefore, it is useful to point out the important differences between my use of Gmail and Mrs. Clinton's exclusive use of her home email server when she was Secretary of State. The following truths are presented without the "political spin" often associated with the 2016 presidential campaign. They are just the simple facts.

First, I did not send any classified information at any time on any unclassified computers, including the State Department's OpenNet system and email accounts on my personal computer. I always used the State Department's classified communications system to transmit anything that was classified by either designation or content. State Department investigators examined my unclassified email records in the months after the OIG inspection. They found no evidence that I had ever processed classified information on the OpenNet or that I processed classified information via my commercial email account. The case was closed.

Second, I did not use any personal Blackberries, laptops, or computer servers while I was the US Ambassador to Kenya. All of the mobile devices and computers that I used belonged to the State Department, and all programs and systems were installed and maintained by State Department employees.

Third, my official business was conducted on State Department computers to the maximum extent and these email messages were captured and stored in State Department databases. I used the Department's OpenNet for my routine official business as I had full access to this unclassified government computer system at my US Embassy office and in my ambassador's residence. There was no need to use a commercial email account to conduct official business.

Fourth, I would not and could not try to permanently delete emails in the State Department computer system. My emails, along with email messages from all State Department personnel, were routinely backed up in Washington and saved as a part of the US government's historical recordkeeping system.

Just the Facts, Please

As the Clinton email saga began to gain national interest, my name was increasingly drawn into the discussion, along with the OIG report and its many false and misleading statements.[8] I have no interest in Hillary Clinton's communications when she was the Secretary of State; however, it may be useful to point out the true and false statements in the OIG report concerning my use of commercial email.

It is false that I ignored State Department instructions and willfully disregarded State Department regulations concerning the use of commercial email for official government business.[9] I used Gmail for unofficial business. While the definition of "official business" is still open for debate, it is true that I used my Gmail to communicate some unclassified information to State Department personnel in circumstances authorized by Department regulations (for example, when I needed to communicate while traveling and an OpenNet terminal was not available).

It is true that I used my Gmail account to access my alerts and unclassified personal emails. I had subscribed to "alerts" to get breaking news stories, analysis of important events, and Africa-related articles. These Gmail-accessed services were not available on the State Department's OpenNet computer network. Over the previous years in government service, I had also built a network of professional contacts that were linked through my Gmail address book. I wanted to have access to these capabilities and contacts while at work.

It is true that the only "unclassified area" in the ambassador suite was an unused bathroom. This area was renovated by US Embassy personnel to accommodate a desk, printer, and two unclassified State Department computers so I could access my OpenNet and Gmail accounts. This small office was not used as a bathroom after the US Embassy's modifications to the room. The ambassador's office continued to be used for classified discussions and "Secret" communications.

It is true that I used a government-owned and issued laptop to do my email in the US Embassy (not a personally procured laptop) and this computer was not physically or electronically connected to the Department's OpenNet network.

It is true that I challenged State Department ICT policy and was frustrated when I could not get technical answers to my questions on the "firewall" capabilities, encryption, and other aspects of the OpenNet system and Blackberry server. When I was continually stonewalled, it is true that I became directly involved in the ICT process—and this irritated some State Department personnel in the US Embassy and in Washington, DC.

It is true that the US Embassy cyber policy document (drafted by State Department cyber professionals) authorized the ambassador, deputy chief of mission, and department directors to classify and declassify information as appropriate and to determine the correct level of classification to transmit, manage, and store this information (for example, classified; sensitive, but unclassified; unclassified). It is very misleading for the OIG report to state that I drafted and distributed a mission policy authorizing US Embassy personnel to use commercial email for daily communications of official government business. I did not.

It is true that I contacted the State Department in Washington on several computer and communications-related issues. It is also accurate that I kept pushing back when I was given the cryptic answer, "Because we said so," to my queries. It is likely that my efforts to get satisfactory answers irritated the State Department's ICT office as well as my supervisors.

I probably should not have been surprised that the OIG came after me during their inspection. However, it is still disappointing that senior leaders in the State Department used one standard to punish me for using Gmail to supplement the State Department's OpenNet and a different standard to exonerate others in the Department for exclusively using their commercial email systems to conduct official business. That sure looks like a double standard to me.

After the State Department OIG released its report on May 25, 2016, criticizing Hillary Clinton's use of a private email sever during her time as Secretary of State, many reporters made false statements about me in their stories.[10] For example, Lisa Desjardins, PBS NewsHour's Political Director, erroneously declared in her May 26 article,

> In 2011, Jonathan Scott Gration as the new US Ambassador to Kenya wrote a memo to his staff authorizing them to use private email for daily communication. The inspector general report says the State Department dispatched a security adviser to tell the ambassador it was against agency policy.
>
> Gration continued to use private email, and as a result of that and other problems, the State Department initiated a disciplinary hearing. But Gration resigned before any penalty was imposed.

While several dozen lower deputies at the State Department used personal email occasionally, the report said Gration was the only other official to exclusively use a personal account for regular department business."

I understand that Lisa simply reported the story she believed to be true. Unfortunately, she gathered her egregious, baseless claims from the Nairobi Embassy's OIG inspection report to write a story about me that was totally false. Her article then became the foundation for similar stories and blogs that made their way around the Internet without any hope of correction.

Even though my name has been connected with former Secretary of State Hillary Clinton's email controversy in the 2016 general election campaign, I choose not to be defined by a passing political debate. My life is much more than this lone event.

Better, Not Bitter

While it figuratively ripped our hearts out to leave this assignment at such a critical time and under extremely questionable circumstances, we thanked God for the time we had in Kenya and for the positive difference we had been able to make for so many. My wife, Judy, and I again pledged to be better, not bitter. We believe it is how one reacts to a situation that determines its outcome, not the circumstances themselves.

I decided to use this "dismissal" experience, as I have all the experiences in the chapters of this book, to learn more of life's lessons and to become a better person and a stronger leader. I would never sacrifice my solid commitment to America's values, my family, and our nation, and my dedication to serving God and humanity.

In the last thirty-five years, I had been a White House Fellow, had flown more fighter combat missions over Iraq than any other American,[11] served as commander of a combined joint task force, an operations group, and two Air Force wings. In addition, I had senior military assignments in the United States and Europe with worldwide responsibilities. I had also been a chief operating officer, a chief executive officer, a special assistant to the President of the United States, the President's Special Envoy to Sudan, and ultimately the US Ambassador to Kenya.

Scott and Judy's last day as the US representatives in Kenya. (US Embassy photo/ Gilbert Otieno)

In this long record of government service, I essentially had two careers serving America—one in the military as a warrior and one in the Foreign Service as a diplomat. In the US Embassy, I needed to amalgamate two very different mindsets and institutional cultures. While I was very successful as a diplomat in the military, I clearly was too much of a warrior in the State Department.

Through life's exhilarations and challenges, I have been able to hold securely to the things most important to me and for that I'm deeply grateful and very satisfied. Yes, I have kept my reputation of personal integrity, but more importantly, I have maintained my strong faith, nurtured a wonderful family, and made treasured friendships . . . I could ask for nothing more.

My wife continues to be my lifelong best friend. For years, we have worked together, prayed together, and played together. Judy has been my closest partner in the good times and she has been a rock of support and a fountain of encouragement in the tougher times. I love my family. My children are a constant source of pride and joy, and my grandchildren continue to make me so happy—I am indeed most blessed.

My enduring and valued friendships are a significant part of my wealth. Judy and I are extremely "rich" and grateful for God's many blessings over the past six and a half decades . . . and the flight path continues.

22

Reflections

*What lies behind us and what lies before us are
tiny matters compared to what lies within us.*

— Ralph Waldo Emerson

I HAVE SPENT THE MAJORITY OF MY TIME looking forward out of life's large windscreen. There were many times when I could not see very far ahead, but that did not really matter. My passion for making a difference through service and my strong belief that all things come into our lives for a purpose have kept me pressing on, despite the challenges.

Fortunately, I also have a small rear-view mirror on life which has given me perspective. Our memories permit us to look backward to see how each experience has taught us a lesson and has prepared us for the future. After six decades of living forward, I have aggregated the significant lessons flowing from my life's stories. My hope is that this summary will be of benefit to readers with more future than past.

Make Your Priorities Your Priority.[1]

After nearly losing my life over San Antonio, I realized that position, awards, and accomplishments were not a priority compared to making a lasting positive difference in my world. Crossing the border from Congo as a refugee taught me that possessions were not a priority compared with life, family, and friends. My time in Uganda in 1979 showed me that my wants and desires were not a priority compared with the needs of others. I had accepted as a child that things in this life were not a priority compared with my relationship with God.

I purposed as a teenager to put God, my health, my family, my friends, and my country on my life's priority list—in that order. In combat situations, I had to reorder the list a bit, when my health, family, and friends had to take a back seat to defending the United States and the freedoms we cherish. Nevertheless, I've tried to make these five priorities the defining values of my life.

Balancing priorities to maintain a quality of life is a critical skill to learn early in one's career. Listen and be sensitive to those closest to you and make the changes they recommend, because it is often difficult to recognize when your life creeps out of balance.

Live As If It's Your Last Day, But Plan to Live a Full Life.[2]

Attending the memorial services for Glenn Hessel, David McCloud, the nineteen victims from Khobar Towers, and many more worthy acquaintances reinforced to me the truth that you and I do not know our last moment of life. None of these people woke up knowing they would pass into eternity later that day.

We must learn to live with short accounts. Say "I love you" often and "I'm sorry" with sincerity. Pay your taxes and bills on time; keep your will up to date. Buy those flowers for no reason. Take the road trip. Ponder that passage in the Psalms. Send the note of appreciation. Smile at the cashier. Don't put off becoming an organ donor so you can help others even in death.

At the same time, plan well for the future. Look for ways to build strong relationships with family and friends, and seek opportunities to make a positive change in your community. Few things are better than helping someone in need or saving a life.

Think about that little dash that will one day be on your tombstone— that little line that separates the birth date and the date of death. What will be its significance? We don't control the beginning and end dates, but we make the choices that determine the significance of our life and the legacy of our dash.

Love Your Family and Friends.[3]

Relations with family and friends, along with life itself, are gifts to be guarded and preserved much more than material treasures. We owe much of the credit for personal success to our spouses, families, and friends who have picked up the things we've dropped and have supported us with consistent encouragement and constructive criticism.

Never miss an opportunity to spend quality time with your parents, your guardians, or whomever shaped your childhood. They've poured their lives into you and crave interaction with you. Take pleasure in children—I can't think of anything that gives me more satisfaction than being a proud and loving parent and grandparent.

Be careful about what you say and how you say it. Sharp words can cut deeper than the sharpest knife and are just as deadly as poisoned arrows. They can leave invisible wounds that take years to heal. At the same time, don't be afraid to express sincere appreciation to your colleagues, even if you're a hardened warrior in a combat zone or in a very conservative work environment. Kind words and encouraging expressions can heal the soul faster than modern medicine ever could.

Protect your friends and allies, even if there is a personal cost for doing so. Sharing tough times makes relationships stronger. Don't take your special friends for granted. Nurture friendships over your lifetime—as my Masai brothers say, "The only thing that can separate friends is death."

Be Thankful For Everything.[4]

Gratitude is an attitude. Recognize and be grateful for life's little blessings which we sometimes overlook and often take for granted. For example, our government offices, local stores, garages, and other service organizations are filled with professionals who demonstrate technical expertise, dedication to excellence, and a positive attitude every day—give them a smile and tell them "thank you for your service" when you have the opportunity.

I'm deeply grateful for each man and woman who has volunteered to serve in the US Armed Forces and who has willingly gone into harm's way when directed by their Commander-in-Chief to protect our nation's freedoms and ideals. Military spouses and families are the unsung heroes of the military—they make the significant sacrifices for our country, yet their enormous contributions are often overlooked and underappreciated. Help them when you have the opportunity.

Take the time to express your appreciation to the military personnel, veterans, fire fighters, and law enforcement officers who have dedicated their lives to make America safer and more secure. Independence Day, Memorial Day, and Veterans Day are not just three-day weekends with big sales and beautiful fireworks; they are an opportunity to show you are grateful for the significant sacrifice of these dedicated professionals.

Be Humble and Tolerant.[5]

The biblical proverb is still true today: a proud heart often precedes a big downfall. Learn to listen and listen to learn. Don't just hear what you want to hear, especially if you don't speak the local language.

Seek opportunities to expand your world view by visiting new places and learning about other cultures. We have lots to learn from other cultures about kindness, generosity, and work ethic.

Your professional colleagues, co-workers, and staff don't all think the same way you do—be tolerant of diverse personalities and different standards of excellence. Even though pragmatists and ideologues see solutions to the same problem in very different ways, they both get up in the morning trying to do the right thing for their organization and for our country. Appreciate different points of view for they will make you and your decisions better.

Keep Learning and Honing Your Skills.[6]

Discover what you do well and learn to do it even better. Develop your strengths in a way to compensate for your known deficiencies. Remember that everything is easy if you know how to do it, so develop the positive mental attitude to get out there and learn new skills.

Learn how to plan by paying attention to the execution of complicated events—you never know when you'll be called upon to orchestrate a complex activity. Use every opportunity to listen and learn about new subjects. The more you learn about a subject, the more you will realize that there's much more to learn, so be careful about calling yourself an expert. While information and knowledge are good, judgment is better and wisdom is best—if you do not possess the latter two competencies, then find mentors who do.

One can finish successfully, even after faltering at the start. However, sometimes hard work, determination, perseverance, and priorities can't make dreams come true—you must learn to cope with major disappointment and significant loss . . . and move on.

Leadership Matters; Make a Difference by Doing the Right Things Right.[7]

When leading, make sure your team understands the organization's vision, mission, and objectives. Remember Niccolo Machiavelli (the Italian Renaissance historian, politician, diplomat, philosopher, humanist, and writer) and do not be afraid to make big plans that have the power to move men's minds. If there is a question about the unit's mission, resolve it immediately. If the unit isn't doing the right things, change its direction if you can. It is critical to have the correct authority over all units in one's area of responsibility and for what one will be held accountable.

Don't be too proud to ask for assistance and to build a team of trusted partners. An African proverb says: "If you want to go fast, go alone; if you want to go far, go together."

Understand that things will go wrong and fail, so think through the contingencies and have a back-up strategy. Plan ahead and be mentally prepared for the unlikely and unexpected—when a crisis happens, take charge until others can assume their leadership roles.

Be a good manager of the organization's resources and assets. Encourage unit pride. Catch people doing the little extra so you can recognize them. Strive to improve the lives of your subordinates and to help them be successful.

Keep innovating and improving, even when change is hard and resistance is personal. Don't forget Henry Ford's reminder that you've got to change the process if you want a better outcome. In the end, your job is to be efficient and effective and to make a positive difference—not to be popular. It is all right if everything you've worked to accomplish for two years is destroyed in a week; we are called upon to do our best every day whatever the final outcome. While we strive for success, the only things we really control are the amount and quality of our effort.

Practice Principled Behavior,
Even to the Point of Resignation.[8]

Compromise and deal-making is perfectly acceptable, except when it comes to your principles. Think now about what characterizes you and what principles regulate your behavior. Whether you use teachings from your faith, cultural norms, society's standards, or national regulations to define your principles, have them seared in your mind.

Have a strong moral compass and well-founded convictions so you're not swayed by attractive exceptions or "situational ethics." Always do what you believe is right, even if you are humiliated and punished for your actions—never give up your integrity to keep your job.

Keep Your Integrity.[9]

If you have integrity, nothing else matters. If you don't have integrity, nothing else matters. No one can give you integrity—you must live it. No one can take your integrity—you must give it.

"Integrity first" is an Air Force core value and one of my personal core values as well. Integrity—being fair and honest; adhering to your code of ethics—is absolutely essential in leadership. I've always wanted people around me who had integrity, who could be trusted to do the right thing—even when no one was watching, and even when it hurt. I could tolerate mistakes, misunderstanding, and miscalculations, but not dishonesty and willful wrong behavior.

In Diplomacy, Build Relations First and
Do the Work Second.[10]

If you live in a foreign country or work with people who are not from your nation of origin, make sure to cultivate a personal relationship if you expect to get anything accomplished professionally. Begin by establishing friendships based on honest respect and mutual understanding. Maintain these relationships, for you may need them again in the future.

Trust is a prerequisite for successful negotiations, and it begins with a personal relationship—not a PowerPoint presentation. Any agreement can be negotiated if one first establishes a relationship, makes a genuine effort to understand the views of the other side, and thinks of innovative ways to accommodate divergent positions. Enemies shouldn't remain enemies forever and fighting is not always the best way to resolve conflicts.

Be Fair and Equitable to Everyone, for the World is Inherently Unfair.[11]

Try to think about others and how your actions make them feel. Imagine yourself in the situation of other global citizens as you think less about benefiting yourself. This doesn't mean you always have to be doing something for others—just have a caring attitude about life's events and a compassionate approach toward daily activities and the "doing" will happen.

Seek opportunities to serve family, friends, coworkers, community, and mankind. Share or give something away every day, even if it's just a pretty flower. Giving away haircuts and cookies was a source of great joy and satisfaction for my wife and me. Be generous—share your abundance and give away your excess.

Be a Servant Leader and Your Legacy Will Happen.[12]

The prayer of Saint Francis of Assisi is a good starting place for making this world a better place. Accept challenging tasks that could make a difference and don't regret failing after trying your best to succeed. Don't give up hope or lose courage, even when the odds are not in your favor. Life is lived by taking one step at a time; success is making methodical progress toward a goal—not necessarily reaching the destination.

Final Reflections

I wouldn't want to relive the terrifying dash with my family to the Congo border ahead of angry soldiers. I wouldn't want to relive those thirty seconds in my single-seat fighter that dark night over San Antonio—thirty seconds that seemed like an eternity. I wouldn't want to relive that bomb blast in Dhahran where I lost eighteen men. I would not want to relive the aircraft crashing into the Pentagon where one hundred eighty-four people had their dash closed out at 9:36 a.m. I wouldn't want to retrace my steps through dark times as a diplomat either. But I'm thankful for those events because they were life-changing and reorienting experiences.[13]

We only get one chance to live today and to make a difference in our communities and for mankind. Life's daily choices are ours alone to make. Make them count.

Aim for service and success will follow.

— Albert Schweitzer

Epilogue

*"Do not follow where the path may lead. Go
instead where there is no path and leave a trail."*

— Ralph Waldo Emerson

I'M STILL BULLISH ON AFRICA. After resigning from my position as
United States Ambassador to Kenya, Judy and I chose to remain in East
Africa to continue making a difference in the region we loved. We wanted
to help the chronically underemployed, those living in poverty and squalor,
and those historically marginalized.

In my role as the executive chairman of Champion Afrik, my partners
and I are working with international groups, the national government,
and county leaders to bring significant investment and development to
the region. We are convinced that Kenya is the new "front door" to Africa
and its significant number of the world's fastest growing economies.[1] Our
company is dedicated to pushing this front door wide open by building
world-class enterprises in Kenya that incorporate the best management
philosophies and principles.

Culminating my working years with this third career is my hope for a
lasting legacy before I have to say "gear down, last stop" and move back to
the United States.

Aging, Wiser, and Still Optimistic

Ups and downs. Highs and lows. Bright days and dark days. Happy times
and sad times. Victory and humiliation. Accolades and embarrassment. My
careers as a warrior, diplomat, and entrepreneur have seen them all.

Scott with President Obama in Nairobi, Kenya.
(White House photo/Pete Souza)

Several people have asked me the obvious questions that arise from reading this book. For example, why did the State Department's chief inspector misrepresent the facts to damage your reputation? Why did Cheryl Mills fire you without listening to your side of the story? And if your relationship with the White House personnel was so good, why did they abandon you in Kenya? Frankly, I don't know the answers to these questions and the many more that I have been asked.

It took a couple of years to get beyond the pain, but I was finally able to forgive all the people who hurt me while I was the US Ambassador to Kenya. The "why" questions do not matter to me anymore because I have moved on. While the scars of this event will always remain, the emotional wounds have mostly healed and my attitude is positive.

When President Obama visited Kenya in July 2015, I had the opportunity to meet with him in Nairobi. We had a warm conversation and I departed with the same good feeling I had when we last met in Washington, DC. The Masai chief was correct when he said, "The only thing that can separate true friends is death."[2]

As I reflect on this memoir, a few things are wonderfully obvious. God blessed me with loving parents, an awesome and beautiful wife, and a family that makes me proud. He has given me friends and colleagues that, with their support and encouragement, made me look good even in the dark times. I've awakened almost every day excited to serve and ready to make a difference. I'm truly grateful to have served the United States as a warrior and diplomat.

I now enjoy greeting each day fired up and ready to go as an *aging* warrior, a *wiser* diplomat, and an *optimistic* business executive working to help overcome the underlying socio-economic and security challenges in East Africa.

My unlikely journey has taken me far beyond a warrior and a diplomat. On the next leg, I will look for opportunities to tell my stories, share my perspectives, motivate with my reflections, and serve those in need. I cannot think of a better landing to my flight path.

"For I know the plans I have for you," declares the LORD, *"plans to prosper you and not to harm you, plans to give you hope and a future."*

Jeremiah 29:11
Holy Bible, New International Version®

Acknowledgements

First and foremost, I would like to thank my wife, Judy, for allowing me to take on yet another challenge that decreased the time I could spend with her. But more than that, she has stood beside me throughout my life. She has made significant sacrifices to further my career and she has been a constant source of encouragement. I am deeply grateful for both.

I've dedicated this book to my father who encouraged me to keep good notes and to write the book. However, I also owe an enormous debt of gratitude to my mother, Dorothy. Not only did she give me more details about stories I remembered, but she also recounted childhood events that were not part of my memory. She and my father forged my personality and allowed me to follow my dreams. My parents modeled a daily Christian lifestyle and taught me about character and values from an early age. I've become more appreciative of their significant input with the passing of time.

I would like to express my thanks to my family who provided input on personal stories and family events as they were a significant part of my life's journey. In addition to Judy, I'm grateful to my children, Jonathan Gration, Jennifer Yoder, David Gration, and Katherine Gration, for their understanding and assistance. Other members of my family provided very useful comments on grammar and style. These include Judy's sister, Jocelyn DeYoung, and my sisters, Barbara Harbert and Judy Kohl.

My supervisors, co-workers, and subordinates in my military and diplomatic careers deserve great credit for making me look good and for helping me to achieve my lofty objectives and sometimes impossible dreams. Thank you all.

I am very grateful to former President Jimmy Carter for writing the Foreword for this book. I have long respected President Carter's integrity and moral courage and have admired the work he and the Carter Center have done to make our world a better place. The kind endorsements for the back cover from General John Abizaid and the Cabinet Secretary for Foreign Affairs of Kenya, Dr. Amina Mohamed, are also deeply appreciated.

For those who critiqued the sections of this book for its professional content, I am truly grateful. Those who contributed to the accuracy of the stories include DeVere Crooks, Doc Cabayan, Marti Flacks, Terry Schwalier, Scott Swanson, and Jim Traister.

I sincerely thank the superb efforts of my professional team whose perceptive inputs shaped the book and made the stories easier to read. These experts include Blake Arensen, front cover design; Saija Autrand, cover and interior designer; Diane Omondi, final proofreader; Anita Palmer of the Strong Word Services, consultant and line editor; and Sally Rushmore, editor.

My friends were invaluable. I can't thank Josh and Judy Weston enough. In addition to sound mentorship and warm friendship over the years, they kept on encouraging me with great advice and useful connections during the early days of writing. Other friends provided superb support, talked things over, read, offered comments, and assisted in the editing, proofreading, and finding a publisher. These special people include Jonathan Alter, Sandra Angelo, Shel Arensen, Peter Beren, Doug Cress, Lanny Davis, Ken Emerson, Elizabeth Frost, Richard Frost, Ranjit Krishna, Paula Lacombe, Jack LeCuyer, Duncan Mitchell, Lynda O'Connor, Pete Ondeng, Britt-Marie Seex, Steve Strasser, Ruth Van Reken, and Justin Westre.

Without the assistance of these special individuals, this memoir might still be just diary entries and a pile of notes. I am deeply grateful that together we produced *Flight Path: Son of Africa to Warrior-Diplomat.*

End Notes

Chapter 2: African Roots

1. The *African Lightning* was built in 1947 and sailed as part of the Farrell Lines fleet between New York and Mombasa, making multiple port calls in southern Africa along the way.
2. On January 8, 1953, the ocean liner *Klipfontein* struck a foreign object off the coast of Mozambique in uncharted waters, sinking in three hours. All 234 passengers and crew were saved by the ocean liner *Bloemfontein Castle*.
3. My mother recounted this story to me.
4. See Ken Ringle, "Risking Life and Limb for Love," *The Washington Post*, January 9, 2011, B6. Grogan wanted to marry Gertrude Watt, a match disapproved of by her stepfather. To prove his character and seriousness, Grogan became the first man known to walk from Cape Town to Cairo, reaching his destination after two and a half years in 1900 at the age of 24. He published his tale in *From the Cape to Cairo: The First Traverse of Africa from South to North* (1902). In 1947 he founded Gertrude's Children's Hospital in memory of his wife.
5. Belgium was consistently criticized for failing to develop social programs for the Congolese people before independence; instead it concentrated on extracting minerals and growing cash crops (cotton, coffee, and groundnuts) destined for the European market.
6. My mother recounted the story, which was corroborated by other sources.
7. Another story from my mother and corroborated by other sources.
8. See Stephen Kinzer, *The Brothers: John Foster Dulles, Allen Dulles, and Their Secret World War* (New York Times Books, 2013). Independence leader Patrice Lumumba and two ministers from his newly formed independent government were lined up against a tree and shot. The execution probably took place on January 17, 1961.
9. Benoît Verhaegen, "Les rébellions populaires au Congo en 1964," *Cahiers d'études africaines* 7 (26), 345–359, 1967.
10. Anthony Lukas, "Fall of Stanleyville to Rebels Reported," *New York Times*, August 6, 1964 (archive).

11. I reconstructed the story from my vivid memory of these days, plus interviews with my parents and the recollections of others who experienced the evacuation from Congo.
12. Rift Valley Academy (RVA) is a Christian boarding school in Kijabe, Kenya, founded in 1906 by Charles Hurlburt. After meeting Hurlburt in the White House in 1905, President Theodore Roosevelt visited Kijabe in 1909 shortly after leaving office and laid the cornerstone for Kiambogo, the main school building that remains the centerpiece of RVA's campus.

Chapter 3: Out of Africa

1. My mother recounted the story, which was corroborated by other sources.
2. Corroborated in a letter from Mrs. Edythe DeYoung to her relatives in Dunkirk, New York.
3. Landry's Palsy is also known as Guillain–Barré–Strohl syndrome. The disorder often begins with a flu-like illness that brings on general physical weakness, but is then characterized by rapidly progressing paralysis that starts in the legs and arms, and may move on (ascend) to affect the breathing muscles and face. In February 2016, the US Center of Disease Control publicly linked Landry's Palsy with the Zika virus.
4. My mother recounted the story, which was corroborated by other sources.

Chapter 4: Wearing Green to Work

1. There is no question about the details in this story—I remember Captain LeBlanc's "chewing out" as if it happened yesterday!
2. Rod Bishop retired as a lieutenant general. His last assignment was as commander, 3rd Air Force, United States Air Forces in Europe, Ramstein Air Base, Germany. Tom Kane retired as a major general. During his final assignment, Tom served as the director of strategic plans, requirements, and programs, Headquarters Air Mobility Command, Scott Air Force Base, IL.
3. During the Vietnam conflict, the Selective Service National Headquarters in Washington, DC, instituted a lottery draft system. Birthdays of nineteen-year-old men were matched with numbers from 1 to 365. As the selection board needed more men, it activated men having birthdays corresponding to the next number. In 1970, my birthday corresponded to number 156.
4. I'm joking. Beards have been uncommon in the US Armed Services. Admiral Zumwalt allowed them in the Navy from 1970 to 1984, and the coast Guard permitted facial hair until 1986. But beards have never been permitted in the Air Force.
5. Formally named "Prince of Denmark's March" when English baroque composer Jeremiah Clarke wrote it around 1700, the piece was attributed to Henry Purcell until the 1940s.

6. The Northrop T-38 Talon is a two-seat, twin-engine supersonic jet trainer. It was the world's first supersonic trainer and has been in service for over fifty years.

7. One of the most enduring military aircraft designs ever introduced, Northrop Grumman Corporation's F-5 tactical fighter is an agile, highly maneuverable, reliable supersonic fighter, combining advanced aerodynamic design, improved engine performance, and low operating costs.

8. The number of people killed as a result of Idi Amin's regime is unknown. Estimates by international observers and human rights groups of civilian deaths range from 100,000 to 500,000 out of a total population of 12 million, and most sources put the number closer to the high end.

9. Kiswahili spread as a trade language, thanks to Arab caravans during the eighteenth and the nineteenth centuries. As it reached the Democratic Republic of the Congo, the locals introduced many words from the Bantu dialect; the Kiswahili variant then became known as Kingwana.

10. My mother recounted the story, which was corroborated by other sources.

11. On June 27, 1976, West German terrorists forced a French airliner to fly to Entebbe, Uganda. Israel responded on July 3 by sending a special operations team to Entebbe. After flying some 2,500 miles, the Israeli force rescued the 103 hostages within an hour. The Israeli unit commander, Lt Col Yonatan Netanyahu (Benjamin Netanyahu's brother), was killed during the operation, as were three hostages. All seven of the militants were killed.

12. Mengo Hospital, established by Sir Albert Cook in 1897, is the oldest hospital in Uganda. It was one of the few medical facilities in Kampala that remained open during the 1979 conflict.

Chapter 5: Back to Our Roots

1. The Ten Outstanding Young Americans program (sponsored by the United States Junior Chamber, also known as the Jaycees) exists to recognize and honor ten Americans each year who exemplify the best attributes of the nation's young people, aged eighteen through forty. Prior to 1985, the program was known as the Ten Outstanding Young Men program. Members of the 1981 class included Thomas Carey, Thomas Daschle, Ronald Darnell, Alan Page, Roger Porter, Christopher Reeve, Willie Register, Darryl Stingley, Brandon Tartikoff, and me.

2. White House Fellowship (WHF) classes range from eleven to nineteen per Executive Order 11183 (as amended). The first class had fifteen fellows—one for each cabinet officer and four for senior White House staff. President Johnson (LBJ) made sure that WHF enjoyed the status he had envisioned for them as fellows. The non-partisan/bi-partisan WHF program has endured across nine presidential administrations and just celebrated its 50th anniversary in 2014. The program has more than fulfilled LBJ's vision for fostering a lifetime commitment to public service, often at the highest levels of government.

3. In 1959, movie star and film director William Holden stayed at the Mawingo Hotel with his friends Ray Ryan and Carl Hirschmann. In the middle of a shooting safari, Ryan sustained a cut in the eye from a gun recoil and needed to recuperate. The three succumbed to Mawingo's charm, bought the property, and turned it into one of the most unusual and exclusive clubs in the world: the Mount Kenya Safari Club.

4. The 1982 Kenyan coup d'état attempt was a failed effort to overthrow President Daniel arap Moi's government. At midnight on 1 August 1982, a group of soldiers from the Kenya Air Force took over the Voice of Kenya radio station and announced that they had overthrown the government. Air Force fighter pilots were forced to fly to the State House at gunpoint. The pilots pretended to follow the orders, but dropped their bombs over Mount Kenya's forests. Hezekiah Ochuka, a low-ranking airman, ruled Kenya for about six hours before escaping to Tanzania. Extradited back to Kenya, he was tried and found guilty of leading the coup attempt; he was hanged in 1987.

Chapter 6: View from the Top

1. Members of our class went on to become distinguished leaders in their fields. Positions held including a judge, attorney general, director of the Center for Disease Control, two ambassadors, three deans, three chief executive officers, three general/flag officers, and four college professors.

2. Shenzhen Special Economic Zone was established in May 1980 as China's first special economic zone. Shenzhen's gross domestic product is now over $240 billion and its container port is one of the busiest in the world.

3. Perkin-Elmer Corporation developed the optical system for the Hubble Space Telescope in Danbury, Connecticut in 1981. Lockheed Missiles and Space Company of Sunnyvale, California integrated the telescope into the spacecraft in 1985 and the telescope was launched on April 24, 1990. In 1983, NASA designed a transportation canister to move the fifteen-foot diameter telescope by air because the spacecraft was too large to be transported by rail. In the end, the risks associated with the ship transportation through the Panama Canal could not justify the high costs for a one-time-use container to ferry the Hubble Space telescope from California to Florida.

4. NASA and the US Air Force wanted to use the Space Shuttle to put satellites into a polar orbit—this would necessitate a northerly launch from Cape Canaveral in Florida cross heavily populated South Carolina and the Great Lakes. Since this was not possible, NASA and the Air Force developed a shuttle launch pad at Vandenberg Air Force Base (midway between Los Angeles and San Francisco, California) to enable a lower-risk launch into higher-inclination polar orbits. Without nature's assistance from the earth's rotational velocity, NASA would now have to increase the power of the engines and reduce the weight of the space shuttle to achieve the required thrust-to-weight ratio. The filament-wound solid rocket boosters were designed to reduce about 8,000

pounds of weight from the space shuttle, but these had never been rated for manned operations. NASA's challenge was to test the structural integrity of the boosters without damaging the carbon fibers and epoxy resins during the evaluation process. After the Challenger accident in January 1986, the Air Force decided to use expendable rockets to launch payloads into polar orbits and terminated the Vandenberg effort in December 1989.

5. "C-9B Flight Trajectory" (jsc-aircraft-ops.jsc.nasa.gov), March 17, 2009. NASA's reduced-gravity-program aircraft gives its occupants the sensation of weightlessness by following a parabolic flight path. After the aircraft climbs with a pitch angle of 45 degrees, nose is pushed over to maintain zero-G flight and the weightless sensation. Weightlessness begins while ascending and lasts all the way "up-and-over the hump," until the aircraft reaches a downward pitch angle of 30 degrees.

6. The F-16 Fighting Falcon is a single-engine multirole fighter aircraft originally developed by General Dynamics. The Fighting Falcon has key features including a frameless bubble canopy for better visibility, side-mounted control stick to ease control while maneuvering, a seat reclined 30 degrees to reduce the effect of G-forces on the pilot, and the first use of a relaxed static stability/fly-by-wire flight control system, all of which help make it a very nimble aircraft. The F-16's official name is "Fighting Falcon," but "Viper" is commonly used by its pilots.

Chapter 7: Office in the Air

1. When I was flying the F-16, the typical fighter squadron was commanded by the squadron commander. The second officer in charge was the operations officer—the individual responsible for day-to-day operations and overseeing the activities of fighter pilots assigned to four or five squadron flights. Each flight commander managed the daily activities and professional development of pilots in his flight. He was also responsible for monitoring Air Force-related personal issues of his assigned pilots to ensure each one was ready physically, mentally, and emotionally to fly our demanding missions.

2. During combat maneuvering in the F-16, the pilot may experience a combination of acceleration forces up to nine Gs (nine times the force of gravity). Pulling high Gs pushes the blood in your body towards your feet and fights your heart's attempts to pump it back upwards. Each fighter pilot wears a personally fitted "anti-G-suit." This tightly-fitting garment is worn over the flying suit and is connected to the aircraft compressed air system. During high-G maneuvers, the G-suit's bladders inflate to restrict blood flow to the legs and midsection. When combined with the pilot's straining maneuver, the G-suit enables the pilot to push more blood to the brain and sustain high-G turns without losing consciousness. One of the first indications of an impending "black out" may be a progressive loss of vision as the aircraft enters the maneuver. If the rapid onset of G forces continues, the end result maybe G-induced

loss of consciousness (GLOC). In the F-16, the G-onset rate can be so rapid so as to reach GLOC without visual symptoms of warning. This has been the cause of far too many military and civilian aviation fatalities.

3. The missing-man formation is a flyby aerial salute at a funeral or memorial event in memory of a fallen pilot. Four combat aircraft in tight fingertip formation (V-shape with the flight leader at the point and one wingman on his left side and a two-ship element on his right). The formation flies over the ceremony low enough to be clearly seen and the second element leader abruptly pulls up out of the formation while the rest of the formation continues in level flight until all aircraft are out of sight. The aircraft performing the pull-up is honoring the fallen fighter pilot and represents his departure to the heavens.

4. I use the male gender in referring to fighter pilots for literary convenience. While I did not have a female fighter pilot in any of my flying squadrons, women began to pilot US fighter aircraft in 1993 when Jeannie (Flynn) Leavitt became the first female USAF fighter pilot.

5. The Aldeburgh Festival of Music and the Arts is an English arts festival devoted mainly to classical music. It takes place each June in Snape, a village just outside Aldeburgh in Suffolk. The festival was founded in 1948 and eventually moved into the Snape Maltings Concert Hall, converted from one of the largest mid-nineteenth-century maltings in East Anglia. The Queen of England has attended numerous Aldeburgh festivals at Snape Maltings over the years.

6. The Advanced Medium-Range Air-to-Air Missile (AMRAAM) is a beyond-visual-range air-to-air missile capable of all-weather day-and-night operations. Its "fire-and-forget" feature enabling the aircrew to aim and fire several missiles simultaneously at multiple targets and to perform evasive maneuvers while the missiles guide themselves to the targets.

7. Niccolò Machiavelli is quoted as saying, "Make no small plans for they have no power to stir the soul." Oscar Wilde said, "Dream no small dreams for they have no power to move the hearts of men." It appears that Mr. Beggs' version is a combination of these two famous quotes.

Chapter 8: Combat Operations

1. After the American-led international coalition drove Saddam Hussein's forces from Kuwait in 1991, rebellious Kurds in northern Iraq, whom Saddam had brutally suppressed with chemical weapons three years earlier, launched a new uprising in early March. When the Iraqi government's troops defeated the rebellion a month later, more than one million Kurds fled to Iran and Turkey. Hundreds of thousands more gathered on cold mountain slopes on the Iraqi-Turkish border. Lacking food, clean water, clothing, blankets, medical supplies and shelter, the refugees suffered enormous mortality rates. On April 3, the United Nations Security Council authorized a humanitarian relief effort for the Iraqi Kurds. Two days later, the UN passed United Nations Resolution 688, calling on Iraq to end repression of its population. On April 6, Operation

Provide Comfort began to take humanitarian relief to the Kurds. American, British, and French aircraft established a no-fly zone north of the 36th parallel. USAF C-130 cargo airplanes operating from Incirlik Air Base, Turkey began air-dropping relief supplies directly to Kurdish refugees in the mountainous Iraqi border area on April 7.

2. USAF airplanes transported more than 7,000 tons of relief supplies. The combination of Provide Comfort's air cover and ground forces in the security zone, along with a promise of some degree of autonomy from Baghdad, persuaded most Kurdish refugees to return to their homes by mid-July 1991.

3. We always removed our patches to "sanitize" before heading into a combat zone—we obviously did not want the enemy to have any useful information about us should we become prisoners of war.

4. During a search of the Internet for Todd Reed, I was delighted to read several articles about him and his life after the military. I learned that he spent six weeks recovering at Walter Reed Army Medical Center in Washington, DC followed by six months of rehabilitation. During that time, Todd was fitted with an artificial limb and worked his way back to a normal life. After spending twenty-one years as a police officer in Mesa, Arizona, Todd retired to take up other pastimes and to enjoy his three grandchildren. I am very proud to have known Todd Reed for a brief moment and to say thanks for his most positive example and service to our nation in so many ways.

5. U.S. Code § 663—Joint Duty Assignments after Completion of Joint Professional Military Education states, "The Secretary of Defense shall ensure that each officer designated as a joint qualified officer who graduates from a school within the National Defense University specified in subsection (c) shall be assigned to a joint duty assignment for that officer's next duty assignment after such graduation (unless the officer receives a waiver of that requirement by the Secretary in an individual case). I was one of only a handful of officers to receive waiver from joint duty after graduating from the National War College and the only one to be given a waiver in 1993.

6. Unified Task Force (UNITAF), later called UNOSOM, was a United Nations-sanctioned multinational force that operated in Somalia between December 5, 1992 and May 4, 1993. The United States, operating under its Operation Restore Hope, played a major role in helping UNITAF create a protected environment for conducting humanitarian operations in the southern half of the country as specified in United Nations Security Council Resolution 794. Turkish Army Lieutenant General Cevik Bir was appointed commander of the UN force, with US Army Major General Thomas Montgomery as his deputy. General Montgomery also retained his position as commander of US Forces in Somalia (USFORSOM) under Marine Corps General Joseph Hoar, CENTCOM's Commander-in-Chief. Thus the US forces retained their own national chain of command while inserting themselves into the UN structure. Only if the forces were committed to any combat operation would US units

fall under the tactical control of the United Nations. This all made sense, except the US Special Forces did not report to General Montgomery, the US commander on the ground in Somalia. Instead, Major General William Garrison, the Special Forces commander, report directly to General Hoar at CENTCOM. After an initial misstep, General Garrison worked to ensure that he coordinated all Special Forces operations with General Montgomery. That said, the disconnected lines on the organizational chart and the multiple lines of authority connected by dotted lines of coordination were problematic. Unfortunately, there was no single person in charge of all US military operations in Somalia—a lesson that was not lost on me.

7. In addition to the 4404th Composite Wing (Provisional) that was in the vicinity of Dhahran's international airport, the city has a major port and is the administrative center for the Arabian American Oil Company (Aramco) that is now fully owned by the Saudi government.

8. When I decided to introduce the desert-tan flight suit, I used my credit card to buy five from a supplier in the United States. When they arrived, I put desert nametags and patches on the desert-colored flight suits and gave one to Brig Gen Schwalier, 4404th Wing commander; Lt Gen Jumper, 9th Air Force commander; and General Ralston, the commander of Air Combat Command (ACC) in Langley Virginia. While my bosses endorsed the tan flight suits, they were disapproved because the brass zippers could be seen at night when viewed with night-vision goggles. Working with the manufacturer, I bought additional flight suits with black zippers for testing. The tan flight suits were finally approved and added to the Air Force supply system. In just three months, arriving units were issued with tan flight suits and desert combat boots. Within a year, tan flight suits had become the standard uniform for aviators deploying to desert locations.

Chapter 9: Warrior Commander

1. The Khobar Towers bombing was a terrorist attack on part of a housing complex in the city of Khobar, Saudi Arabia, on June 25, 1996. (While some eye witnesses have slightly different recollections of the timing, no one disputes the sequence of events that occurred that night.) At 9:50 p.m. local time, a team of terrorists drove a sewage tanker truck to a parking lot adjacent to Building 131, an eight-story structure housing US Air Force personnel assigned to a deployed rescue squadron and deployed fighter squadron. The bomb exploded at approximately 9:53 p.m. local time and heavily damaged six high-rise apartment buildings in the complex. Windows were shattered in buildings up to a mile away. In the minutes following the blast, residents of the complex evacuated severely injured US military personnel from the area. With no electricity in many of the buildings near 131, the scene was chaotic and tense as little was known about the possibility of further attacks. In all, nineteen US servicemen

were killed and approximately 500 were wounded. On December 22, 2006, a federal judge ruled that Iran and Hezbollah were responsible for the attack, stating that the leading experts on Hezbollah presented "overwhelming" evidence of the group's involvement and that six captured Hezbollah members detailed the role of Iranian officials in providing money, plans, and maps.

2. Doctors and ambulances from local Saudi hospitals arrived soon after they were alerted. Many of our more seriously injured personnel were taken to Saudi medical facilities where they received excellent trauma care before being air evacuated to Landstuhl Regional Medical Center in Germany.

3. I wrote a letter to General Ronald R. Fogleman, chief of staff of the Air Force, when he refuted claims that Brig Gen Schwalier was to blame for perceived security lapses in Khobar Towers. The text follows:

> Sir, having read the news accounts of your recent testimony before the Senate Armed Services Committee, I want you to know how much I appreciated your defense of Brigadier General Schwalier. During the 11 months I worked for him in Dhahran last year, I was privileged to witness his daily emphasis on the mission, force protection, and readiness. He worked particularly hard to build closer relations with host nation officials—especially his military counterparts. He also dedicated himself to improving our living conditions, dining facility, and dorms. Every one of General Schwalier's efforts reflected his deep concern for his troops—their morale, quality of life, and safety. My most enduring impression of General Schwalier was that he is more than just the sum of his accomplishments; he is one of the finest men and leaders I have worked for or with during my Air Force career. He demonstrated daily our core values—integrity, service before self, and excellence—not only because they are important to the Air Force, but because they are deeply ingrained in his character. Many of the leadership tools I use today as commander of the 39th and 7440th Wings, I learned from General Schwalier. I believe adversity brings out the best or worst in people. After the cowardly bombing of our Dhahran compound, I saw General Schwalier at his best. Leading by strong example, he helped us pick ourselves up, bandage our wounds, honor our fallen comrades, and re-engage the mission with excellence and pride. Your statement to the Senate was a powerful expression of your confidence in all Air Force men and women in the field. Your defense of this fine officer was also an important step toward healing our Air Force and refocusing us on the mission.

4. The following are the names of those who lost their lives on June 25, 1996 at the Khobar Towers Barracks: Capt Christopher J. Adams, SSgt Daniel B. Cafourek,

Sgt Millard D. Campbell, SrA Earl F. Cartrette Jr., TSgt Patrick P. Fennig, Capt Leland T. Haun, MSgt Michael G. Heiser, SSgt Kevin J. Johnson, SSgt Ronald L. King, MSgt Kendall K. Kitson Jr., A1C Christopher B. Lester, A1C Brent E. Marthaler, A1C Brian W. McVeigh, A1C Peter J. Morgera, TSgt Thanh V. Nguyen, A1C Joseph E. Rimkus, SrA Jeremy A. Taylor, A1C Justin R. Wood, A1C Joshua E. Woody.

5. I understand Victor Hugo's full quote—"Change your opinions, keep to your principles; change your leaves, keep intact your roots"—is referring to one's character and not to a change of command ceremony. However, I still believe his image of changing leaves and not roots is powerful and appropriate to the military ceremony.

6. Headquarters Air Force decided that all of its forces would have a USAF administrative chain of command even when deployed in support of a joint (multi-service) or combined (multi-national) operation. This deployed command and control structure was designated as "expeditionary." Under the new system, I was still commander of the 39th Wing which was not deployed and therefore not expeditionary. However, I was now also the commander of the 7440th Air and Space Expeditionary Wing and had administrative control of all the USAF units deployed to Incirlik in support of Operation Northern Watch. I was responsible for organizing, training, and equipping USAF forces for combat operations. In addition, our Wing was in charge of providing an operational airfield; maintaining the logistics pipeline and communications infrastructure; and managing all the personnel support facilities.

7. The Revolutionary People's Liberation Party/Front (*Devrimci Halk Kurtuluş Partisi-Cephesi* or DHKP/C), a Marxist-Leninist party in Turkey, was designated as a terrorist group by Turkey, the United States, and the European Union. During the 1990s, DHKP/C attacked US military and diplomatic personnel and facilities, assassinating two US military personnel.

8. The Air Force Chief's Creed is as follows:

> Chief Master Sergeants are individually to be regarded as people who cannot be bought; whose word is their bond; who put character above wealth; who possess opinions and a will; who are larger than their vocations; who will not lose their individuality in a crowd; who do not hesitate to take chances; who will be honest in small things as in great ones; who will make no compromise with wrong; whose ambitions are not confined to their own selfish desires and interests; who will not say they do it, "because everybody else does it"; who are true to their friends through good report, and evil report, in adversity as well as prosperity; who do not believe that shrewdness, cunning, and hardheadedness are the best qualities for winning success; who are not ashamed or afraid to stand for the truth when it is unpopular, who can say "no" with emphasis, although all the world is saying "yes."

Chapter 10: Making a Difference

1. Aungelic L. Nelson with Kathryn A. Wilcoxson, *The Best of the Best: A Brief History of Air Mobility Command's Air Mobility Rodeo, 1989-2011* (Office of History, Air Mobility Command, Scott Air Force Base, Illinois, 2012) 26-29, http://www.amc.af.mil/shared/media/document/AFD-131018-051.pdf.
2. 3rd Wing awards included Best Short-field Landing Aircrew, Best Airdrop Crew, Best Airdrop Wing, Best C-130 Aircrew, and Best C-130 Wing. "3rd Wing Grabs Top Honors at Rodeo," *AMC News Service*, July 1, 1998.
3. The Yakovlev Yak-54 is a two-seat acrobatic and sport competition aircraft. Its high thrust-to-weight ratio and good maneuverability make it perfect for a full set of aerobatic maneuvers.
4. Activated as the Army Surveillance Group on July 1, 1919, the group was a loosely organized band of World War I veterans and newcomers serving on detached duty at scattered outposts along the Rio Grande—from Brownsville, Texas, to Nogales, Arizona. The 1st Army Surveillance Group was inactivated on September 15, 1921, and the unit subsequently became the 3rd Attack Group—the numerical designation and mission that remains intact today.
5. The Lockheed P-38 Lightning was a World War II American fighter aircraft with distinctive twin booms and a single, central nacelle containing the cockpit and armament. Because the P-38's guns were mounted in the nose rather than on the wings, a Lightning could reliably hit targets at ranges up to 1,000 yards. The P-38 was used most successfully in the Pacific theater of operations and was flown by America's top aces—Richard Bong (40 victories) and Thomas McGuire (38 victories). The P-38 was also the first fighter to fly faster than 400 mph.
6. Interested readers can find the story by visiting www.hlswilliwaw.com/aleutians/Aircraft/html/p-38-recovered.htm.
7. Staff Sgt Sheila deVera, JBER Public Affairs, "*Elmendorf street names carry a lot of history these days*," Joint Base Elmendorf-Richardson, Alaska, website, September 10, 2014, http://www.jber.af.mil/news/story.asp?id=123427832. Douglas Beckstead, 3rd Wing History Office, Elmendorf Air Force Base, Alaska, "*The Streets of Elmendorf Air Force Base, Alaska*," 2007, http://www.jber.af.mil/shared/media/document/AFD-080425-113.pdf

Chapter 11: Finding Osama bin Laden

1. On August 7, 1998, suicide bombers used trucks laden with explosives to almost simultaneously bomb the US embassies in Dar es Salaam and Nairobi. The Nairobi blast killed 218 people (including 12 Americans) and wounded an estimated 4,000. Another 11 were killed in Dar es Salaam and 85 wounded. The attacks brought Osama bin Laden and al-Qaeda to the attention of the

American public for the first time, and resulted in the US Federal Bureau of Investigation placing bin Laden on its ten most-wanted fugitives list.

2. *The 9/11 Commission Report* (Thomas H. Kean and Lee H. Hamilton, The National Commission on Terrorist Attacks upon the United States, 2004) on p. 188 ascribes this quote to a military officer. However, Admiral Fry and other sources found via the Internet attribute this statement to President Clinton.

3. The RQ-1 Predator is an unmanned aerial vehicle (UAV) built by General Atomics. Initially conceived for reconnaissance and forward observation roles, the RQ-1Predator carried cameras and other sensors. In 2002, it was modified and upgraded to carry and fire two Hellfire missiles; this variant was designated the MQ-1 Predator. In addition to three UAV aircraft with their sensors, the Predator system includes a remote ground control station and a satellite-link communications suite.

4. Ahmad Shah Massoud was an Afghan political and military leader who was a powerful military commander during the resistance against the Soviet occupation and in the following years of civil war. He was assassinated on September 9, 2001, probably at the instigation of al-Qaeda, in a suicide bombing at his home just two days before the September 11 attacks in the United States.

5. The Economy Act provides authority for federal agencies to order and to pay the actual costs of goods and services from other federal agencies. An Economy Act order can be used when 1) funds are available, 2) the head of the ordering agency determines that it is in the best interest of the government, and, 3) the head of the ordering agency decides that ordered goods or services cannot be provided as conveniently or cheaply by contract with commercial enterprise.

6. C-band was the first band to be used for satellite communication systems. However, when the C-band became overloaded (due to the same frequency being used by terrestrial microwave links), satellites were built for the next available frequency band, the Ku-band. While Ku-band is now the primary frequency for satellite communications, C-band is still performs better in areas with adverse weather conditions.

7. Kean and Hamilton, *The 9/11 Commission Report*, 190.

8. *Ibid.*, 190.

9. On the morning of October 12, 2000, the *USS Cole* docked in the Yemeni harbor of Aden for a routine fuel stop. A small craft approached the port side of the destroyer and blew up, creating a 40-by-60-foot gash in the ship's port side. The explosion hit the ship's galley, killing seventeen sailors and injured thirty-nine.

10. Richard Whittle, *Predator: The Secret Origins of the Drone Revolution* (New York: Henry Holt, 2014). On May 1, 2000 General Jumper, commander of Air Combat Command (ACC), announced his intent to configure the Predator with Hellfire missiles. After receiving a briefing from the commander of the reconnaissance program office at Wright-Patterson Air Force Base which oversaw Big Safari on June 21, General Jumper directed his staff to come up with

a detailed plan for arming the Predator with the Hellfire. ACC gave formal
authorization to proceed on July 28, 2000, subject to Congressional approval.
11. *The 9/11 Commission Report*, 212, 2004.
12. *Ibid.*

Chapter 12: International Influence

1. The September 11 attacks were a series of four coordinated terrorist attacks
   by al-Qaeda in New York City and Washington, DC. American Airlines Flight
   77 with a crew of six and fifty-three passengers, not including five hijackers,
   crashed into the Pentagon, leading to a partial collapse in its western side of the
   building.
2. Official DOD letter signed by Doug Feith and dated October 30, 2001; Subject:
   Lead for DOD's Information Strategy.
3. Psychological Operations (psyops) are planned operations designed to convey
   selected information and indicators to foreign audiences to influence their
   emotions, motives, objective reasoning, and ultimately their behavior in a
   manner favorable to the originator's objectives. There are three different types
   of psyops: white, gray, and black. White psyops are official statements or acts
   of the US government, or emanate from a source associated closely enough
   with the US government to reflect an official viewpoint. The information is
   true and factual, and is identified as coming from US official sources. Gray
   psyops are deliberately ambiguous and the true source (US government) is
   not revealed to the target audience. Black psyops activities appear to emanate
   from a source (e.g., government, party, group, organization, or person) usually
   hostile in nature. While I believe psychological operations are very useful in
   winning the hearts and minds in conflict area or combat zone, the United
   States must always be vigilant to carefully segregate white and black psyops. It
   is critical that the target audience of a white psychological operation does not
   perceive that the truth is being manipulated to manage perceptions and influence behavior. In my view, blending white and black psyops can undermine the
   credibility of the military's public affairs reporting or legitimate media sources.
4. Black propaganda is false information and material that purports to be from
   a source on one side of a conflict, but is actually from the opposing side. It is
   typically used to vilify, embarrass or misrepresent the enemy.
5. Gerry J. Gilmore, *"Strategic Influence Office 'Closed Down,' Says Rumsfeld,"*
   American Forces Press Service, February 26, 2002.

Chapter 13: Stopping the Scuds

1. The US-led coalition forces invaded Iraq on March 20, 2003, kicking off
   Operation Iraqi Freedom. On May 1, 2003, President Bush announced the end
   of major combat operations from the deck of the aircraft carrier USS *Abraham
   Lincoln.* The combined invasion force consisted of troops from the United

States, the United Kingdom, Australia, Denmark, and Poland. In the north, the coalition forces were supported by Iraqi Kurdish militia troops. The Bush administration briefly used the term, "Coalition of the Willing," to refer to the forty-nine countries who supported, militarily or verbally, the military action in Iraq and subsequent military presence in post-invasion Iraq since 2003.

2. The 4th Infantry Division was scheduled to take part in the Iraq War in the spring of 2003 by spearheading an advance from Turkey into northern Iraq. On March 1, 2003, the Turkish parliament dealt a heavy blow to the Bush administration's plans by refusing to grant permission for the operation. American officials had been counting on Turkey's support to bring as many as 62,000 American troops into the country to create a northern front. Planners had to find new bases in which to bed down the 4th Infantry Division forces.

3. President George Bush, transcript, televised address, March 17, 2003 ("Bush: 'Leave Iraq within 48 hours," CNN.com), posted March 18, 2003, 0234 GMT, http://edition.cnn.com/2003/WORLD/meast/03/17/sprj.irq.bush.transcript.

4. A humanitarian assistance coordination center is a temporary center established by a geographic combatant commander to assist with interagency coordination and planning. Such a center operates during the early planning and coordination stages of foreign humanitarian assistance operations by providing the link between the geographic combatant commander and other United States government agencies, non-governmental organizations, and international and regional organizations at the strategic level.

5. Air Force Capt Eric Das was the pilot of an F-15E that went down during a combat mission in Iraq. Eric was born in the Netherlands where his family was serving as missionaries, but grew up in Texas. He graduated from the Air Force Academy in 1995 with a degree in civil engineering. Eric volunteered to serve in Iraq to be close to his wife who was deployed there. He was remembered as a deeply religious and humble man who led an extraordinary life.

6. There were many emails waiting in my inbox upon my return to Washington, DC. Among them was the following citation for a Bronze Star medal:

> Major General Jonathan S. Gration distinguished himself by meritorious achievement as Commander, Combined Joint Task Force-West, while engaged in ground combat operations against an enemy of the United States from 20 January 2003 to 1 May 2003. During this period, in support of Operation IRAQI FREEDOM, General Gration was integral to the planning, coordination, insertion, and execution of Joint Special Operations Task Force personnel and supporting air and space power conducting counter theater ballistic missile operations in western Iraq. As a result, over 1,085 Coalition special operations forces were inserted and 40,000 supporting combat sorties flown with over 8,000 munitions dropped, servicing 1,500 targets. As the Unified Commander's direct link to the western area of responsibility, he facilitated coordination between Host Nation governments and military

command structure, the Component Commanders, the Forward Headquarters' staff, and the Combined Air Operations Center for the activities of 9,800 Coalition personnel and 140 combat aircraft. He coordinated and facilitated all aspects of the reception, staging, and onward integration during the rapid deployment and redeployment of air defense artillery assets, special operations forces, and tactical combat aircraft in the western region, as well as the medical evacuation of personnel wounded in action. His efforts in support of the ground campaign and coordination of air assets providing close air support and air interdiction led to the absolute denial of theater ballistic missile launch opportunities in the western theater of operation. The exemplary leadership, personal endeavor, and devotion to duty displayed by General Gration in this responsible position reflect great credit upon himself and the United States Air Force.

Chapter 14: Military Diplomacy

1. As the senior military officer in SAF/IA, I served as the US representative to the Five-Power Air Senior National Representative meetings where senior leaders from France, German, Italy, the United Kingdom, and the United States collaborated to develop technologically superior and interoperable weapon systems essential for improving coalition war fighting. Another of my duties was to lead the regularly scheduled bilateral discussions with Air Force leaders from Australia and Japan. I also represented the US Air Force at air and trade shows where American companies were demonstrating their newest products. At least once a month, I traveled to speak at conferences and symposia, to promote US military products, and to foster closer bilateral relations with our allies and partners. My job was to overcome technical, scheduling, and financial challenges and to make sure the foreign customer's requirements closely matched US suppliers' capabilities in a way in which our two governments could agree to in a formal bilateral contract.

2. If I could do one thing over again as senior leader of a large staff, I would be more tolerant of imperfections in documentation. Now I realize that my high standards were hard on some who worked for me. Looking back, I sincerely appreciate my staff's' dedicated efforts and quiet tolerance of my intolerance— and wish I could express my continued gratitude to each one of them.

3. The unified command plan (UCP) assigns areas of responsibility or combatant command alignments to nine unified combatant commands. Six have regional responsibilities, and three have functional responsibilities. Before October 7, 2007, EUCOM, CENTCOM, and PACOM had responsibility for various countries in Africa.

4. Morón Air Base's massive flight line, in-ground aircraft refueling system, long runway, and prime location close to the Mediterranean and the Middle East makes this base a vital link in any operation moving people and equipment

across the Atlantic. In 2003, Morón was a key pillar in the air bridge for airlift and fighter deployments in support of Operation Iraqi Freedom.

5. My negotiation experience at Rethy Academy can be found in chapter 3.

6. The officer corps of United States Armed Forces is grouped into broad categories that reflect the officers' level of responsibility. The Army, Air Force, and Marines categorize 2nd lieutenants, 1st lieutenants, and captains as company-grade officers. Majors, lieutenant colonels and colonels are field-grade officers. Brigadier generals, major generals, lieutenant generals, and generals are general officers. The Navy refers to the corresponding officer ranks as junior-grade officers, mid-grade officers, and flag officers.

7. The 1986 United States bombing of Libya, code-named Operation El Dorado Canyon, was carried out by the Air Force, Navy, and Marine Corps. The attack began at 2:00 a.m. Libyan time, lasted about twelve minutes, and dropped 60 tons of munitions. Eighteen F-111 bombers supported by four EF-111 electronic countermeasures aircraft flying from the United Kingdom bombed Tripoli airfield, a frogman training center at a naval academy, and the Bab al-Azizia barracks in Tripoli. Twenty-four A-6 Intruders and F/A-18 Hornets launched from aircraft carriers bombed radar and antiaircraft sites in Benghazi before bombing the Benina and Jamahiriya barracks. An American F-111 was shot down by a Libyan surface-to-air missile over the Gulf of Sidra, resulting in the death of two airmen.

8. The *Intrepid* was loaded with more than 100 barrels of powder and set to blow up in the midst of the enemy fleet anchored near the walls of Tripoli. The explosives on the vessel were set to detonate fifteen minutes after the fuses were lit, giving the US sailors an opportunity to escape before the blast. Before the *Intrepid* could get to its final position it exploded, killing all on board. The remains of the thirteen sailors on the ship washed ashore the next day and were buried in an unmarked mass grave outside Tripoli. In 1949, the Libyan government moved the remains to their current resting place in a small cemetery by the sea.

9. Seumas Milne, "If the Libyan war was about saving lives, it was a catastrophic failure (NATO claimed it would protect civilians in Libya, but delivered far more killing)," *The Guardian*, October 26, 2011.

10. While I will never wear them again, my eighty-three medals and ribbons highlight the milestones of my thirty-two years of service to our nation. These included the Distinguished Service Medal with one oak leaf cluster, Defense Superior Service Medal, Legion of Merit with one oak leaf cluster, Bronze Star Medal, Purple Heart Medal, Defense Meritorious Service Medal, Meritorious Service Medal with five oak leaf clusters, Air Medal with ten oak leaf clusters, Aerial Achievement Medal with seven oak leaf clusters, and the Air Force Commendation Medal with valor device and two oak leaf clusters.

Chapter 15: Obama Goes to Africa

1. Barack Obama was elected in November 2004 to the United States Senate as a Democrat from Illinois. He received considerable national attention in July of that year after his keynote address at the Democratic National Convention.
2. Robben Island is an island about five miles west of Cape Town, South Africa. It has been used for many years to incarcerate political prisoners.
3. Although he was initially committed to nonviolent protest, Nelson Mandela co-founded the militant group *Umkhonto we Sizwe* in 1961, leading a sabotage campaign against the apartheid government. In 1962, he was arrested, convicted of conspiracy to overthrow the state, and sentenced to life imprisonment. Mandela served twenty-seven years in prison, initially on Robben Island, and later in Pollsmoor Prison and Victor Verster Prison. He was released in 1990.
4. Picture available on http://blogs.cfr.org/campbell/2012/03/30/south-africas-apartheid-museums/
5. Desmond Tutu is a South African social rights activist and retired Anglican bishop who rose to worldwide fame during the 1980s as an opponent of apartheid. Tutu received the Nobel Peace Prize in 1984.
6. Before attending Harvard Law School, Barack Obama visited his relatives in Kenya. He recounts part of this experience in his memoir, *"Dreams from My Father: A Story of Race and Inheritance,"* first published in 1995.
7. See chapter 11, end note 1, for information about the US Embassy bombing in Nairobi.
8. Kibera is a neighborhood of Nairobi about three miles from the city center. It is the largest urban slum in Africa. Most residents live in extreme poverty, earning less than a dollar per day, and the unemployment and illiteracy rates are high. Diseases caused by poor hygiene are prevalent, HIV cases are numerous, and crime including assault and rape is common.
9. Wangari Maathai was a Kenyan environmental and political activist. She founded the Green Belt Movement, an environmental non-governmental organization focused on the planting of trees, environmental conservation, and women's rights. In 2004, she became the first African woman to receive the Nobel Peace Prize for "her contribution to sustainable development, democracy, and peace." Wangari Maathai died in September 2011 of complications from cancer.
10. Camp Lemonnier is a United States naval expeditionary base, located at Djibouti's international airport. The only US military base in Africa, it is home to the combined joint task force—Horn of Africa (CJTF-HOA) of the US Africa Command. The camp, as well as a nearby airport and port facilities, was established as a base in the region for the support of combat operations. It is used to facilitate US humanitarian, demining, and counter-terrorism efforts.
11. The conflict in Darfur began in February 2003 when the Sudan Liberation Movement/Army and Justice and Equality Movement (JEM) rebel groups (recruited primarily from the non-Arab Muslim Fur, Zaghawa, and Masalit

ethnic groups) took up arms against the government of Sudan. They accused Khartoum of oppressing Darfur's non-Arab population. The government responded to attacks by carrying out a campaign against Darfur's non-Arabs, orchestrated by Sudanese military, police, and the Janjaweed (a Sudanese militia group recruited mostly among Arabized indigenous Africans). This resulted in thousands of civilian deaths from either combat or starvation/disease and mass displacements that forced millions into refugee camps or across the border, creating the humanitarian crisis.

Chapter 16: Service, Faith, and Family

1. Friedman and Rosenman (both cardiologists) developed their theory of personality types based on an observation of the patients with heart conditions in their waiting room. People with *Type A personality were generally* more ambitious, rigidly organized, highly status-conscious, sensitive, impatient, anxious, proactive, and concerned with time management. They were often high-achieving "workaholics," with a propensity for high blood pressure and a greater risk of heart disease.

2. "Love languages" pertain to a system devised by psychologist Gary Chapman to understand how people prefer to express or receive expressions of love. The five categories are words of affirmation, acts of service, receiving gifts, quality time, and physical touch. More information at www.5lovelanguages.com and *The 5 Love Languages: The Secret to Love that Lasts* (Chicago: Northfield; reprint ed., 2015),

3. Saint Francis of Assisi (b. 1181 or 1182; d. 1226), perhaps the most universally loved of Christian saints, was known for following the teachings of the Lord Jesus Christ and walking in his footsteps. While the prayer is attributed to Francis, researchers cannot trace it further back than 1912, when it was first printed in a small spiritual magazine called *La Clochette* (The Little Bell). That said, I am grateful to whoever wrote these words, for the guiding principles and worthy objectives have become my daily prayer.

4. The Millennium Development Goals (MDG) were fifteen-year targets for addressing extreme poverty in its many dimensions—income poverty, hunger, disease, lack of adequate shelter, and exclusion—while promoting gender equality, education, and environmental sustainability. The worldwide program was to be achieved by 2015.

5. Schistosomiasis, also known as Bilharziasis, is a disease caused by parasitic flatworms of the *Schistosoma* kind. The disease is spread by contact with water that is contaminated with parasites released from infected freshwater snails. In developing countries, the disease is especially common among those who fetch water and among children who play in contaminated water. In tropical countries, schistosomiasis is second only to malaria among parasitic diseases with the greatest economic impact.

Chapter 17: Trek to the White House

1. Senator Barack Obama (D-IL) visited Afghanistan and Iraq, accompanied by
    Senators Chuck Hagel (R-NE) and Jack Reed (D-RI) on a government-funded
    congressional delegation trip—known as a CODEL. This trip was designed to
    give lawmakers firsthand knowledge of matters relevant to their legislation. A
    secondary benefit for Senator Obama was to bolster his foreign policy creden-
    tials by having substantive discussions with military and Middle East leaders.
2. The Brandenburg Gate is an eighteenth-century neoclassical triumphal arch in
    Berlin and one of the best-known landmarks of Germany. During the post-war
    partition of Germany, the gate was isolated and inaccessible immediately next
    to the Berlin Wall, and the area around the gate was featured most prominently
    in the media coverage of the opening of the wall in 1989. Throughout its exis-
    tence, the Brandenburg Gate was often a site for major historical events and is
    today considered a symbol of the tumultuous history of Europe and Germany,
    and also of European unity and peace.
3. The Landstuhl Regional Medical Center (LRMC) is an overseas military hospi-
    tal operated by the Department of Defense. Located near Landstuhl, Germany,
    LRMC is the largest military hospital outside of the continental United States.
    It serves as the nearest treatment center for wounded soldiers coming from
    Iraq and Afghanistan as well as a medical stop-over for serious casualties from
    Iraq and Afghanistan being flown to the United States.
4. The Plum Book is a publication of the federal government that lists more than
    7,000 civil-service leadership and support positions in the legislative and exec-
    utive branches that are subject to political ("noncompetitive") appointments.

Chapter 18: "Save Lives," Said the President

1. On March 4, 2009, Sudan's President Omar al-Bashir became the first sitting
    president to be indicted by the International Criminal Court (ICC) when the
    court issued an arrest warrant for him on counts of war crimes and crimes
    against humanity. The court initially ruled that there was insufficient evi-
    dence to prosecute him for genocide. The Sudanese government retaliated by
    expelling thirteen international aid agencies for allegedly cooperating with the
    court in its investigation of President Bashir, including CARE, Ireland's Goal,
    International Rescue Committee, *Médicins Sans Frontières* (Doctors Without
    Borders), Mercy Corps, Oxfam, and Save the Children. On July 12, 2010, the
    ICC issued a second arrest warrant of arrest which added three counts of
    genocide. As of this writing, President Bashir has yet to be arrested.
2. The Bureau of African Affairs, part of the US Department of State, is charged
    with advising the Secretary of State on matters related to Sub-Saharan Africa.
    It is headed by the assistant secretary for the Bureau of African Affairs who
    reports to the under secretary of state for political affairs. Carving Sudan out of

the Africa bureau's historical sub-Saharan responsibilities created an uncomfortable situation for some.

3. When the British established an East-West administrative border through Sudan, the area south of the border was called southern Sudan or the south. Following the First Sudanese Civil War, the Southern Sudan Autonomous Region was formed in 1972 and the ten southern states of Sudan became known as Southern Sudan. When this region gained its independence on July 9, 2010, Southern Sudan was renamed, South Sudan.

4. The Comprehensive Peace Agreement (CPA), also known as the Naivasha Agreement, was a set of agreements signed in January 2005 between the Sudan People's Liberation Movement and the government of Sudan. The CPA was meant to end the Second Sudanese Civil War, develop democratic governance countrywide, and share oil revenues. It also set a timetable by which Southern Sudan was to hold a referendum on its independence.

5. President Reagan used his "trust, but verify" slogan during the Cold War to describe the basis for transparency in political relationships.

Chapter 19: Serving in Sudan

1. Darfur, a region in western Sudan approximately the size of Spain, was an independent sultanate for several hundred years until it was incorporated into Sudan by Anglo-Egyptian forces in 1916. Because of the conflict between Sudanese government forces and the indigenous population in Darfur, the region has been in a state of humanitarian emergency since 2003.

2. While I was the US Special Envoy to Sudan (USSES), our team fluctuated between fifteen and thirty members. I initially inherited the staff of the Sudan Program Group, including Jimmy Clarke, Mike Christian, Josh Drake, Marti Flacks, Kemi Yai, Kathryn Nash, Leslie Robinson, Dave Rogers, Rob Satrom, Tim Shortley, and Wanda Curry. Then I went to work recruiting staff for our new office from the within the State Department and from other departments and agencies in the executive branch. During my tenure, the following individuals were part of the USSES team: Sean Brooks, Kathy Crewe, Trampes Crow, May Doherty, Brian D'Silva, Jessica El Bechir, Mark Emblidge, Miriam Estrin, Mark Flemming, Dana Francis, Ibrahim Gambari, Omid Harraf, Cameron Hudson, Raja Jandhyala, Kristina Johnson, Brian Kelly, Jonathan Lalley, Allison Lombardo, Andy Loomis, Summer Lopez, Lee Martinez, Cash McCracken, Gail Morgado, Marie Nelson, Marvin Nicholson, Susan Noblick, Shirlene Ostrov, Alexis Prieur, Peter Quaranto, Chris Runyan, Nazik Salih, Karim Smither, Bart Stokes, Margo Sullivan, Colin Thomas-Jensen, Joe Tucker, Melis Tusiray, John Zavales, and Beth Ryley.

3. The Justice and Equality Movement (JEM) is an armed opposition group in the western region of Darfur that was founded and led by Dr. Khalil Ibrahim. Because it was more disciplined than other rebel groups, JEM emerged as the leading force after 2005, escalating the war with significant support from

Chad. Chadian President Idriss Deby is widely believed to have supported JEM because he is from the same Zaghawa ethnic group as Ibrahim. In early 2010, Mr. Deby visited Khartoum and both sides agreed to stop supporting each other's rebels. Ibrahim was killed in a December 2011 aerial bombardment while living in Libya. The group has been led since January 2012 by his brother Gibril Ibrahim.

4. A US State Department démarche to a foreign official can be a request for support of a policy or a protest about the host government's policy or actions. The US government issues démarches to foreign governments through "front-channel cable" instructions sent from the Department of State in Washington, DC to the appropriate US mission. Upon receipt of démarche instructions, posts make every effort to deliver the démarche to the appropriate foreign government official(s) as soon as possible. Diplomatic démarches are usually delivered by the US ambassador or designated representative to his or her host-nation counterpart. The demarche concerning Sudan's President al-Bashir that was sent to the US Embassy in N'Djamena in February 2010 carried the full weight of the US government and, if delivered, would have seriously undermined our efforts to achieve peace in Darfur.

5. John Garang was a prominent Sudanese politician and leader. From 1983 to 2005, he led the Sudan People's Liberation Army during the Second Sudanese Civil War and briefly served as first vice president of Sudan from July 9, 2005. Dr. Garang was killed on July 30, 2005, in a helicopter crash that was caused by pilot error. A developmental economist by profession, John Garang is widely considered the single most influential person in the history of South Sudan, having led the rebellion that led to the independence of his country.

6. The most powerful active rebel groups are the Justice and Equality Movement (JEM) and two Sudan Liberation Army factions: one led by Abdel Wahed Mohammed al-Nur (SLA-AW) and one led by Minni Arcua Minnawi (SLA-MM).

7. I was disappointed with the Obama administration's response to the imbalanced and inaccurate *Washington Post* article by Stephanie McCrumman. I have yet to understand why I did not get much political top cover when I was repeatedly derided by congressmen and advocacy groups based on the *Post* story. Taking matters into my own hands, I wrote the following email to Rich Verma, the assistant secretary of state for legislative affairs, advising him that negative things were happening and I was ready to fight back. It stated:

> First, by not challenging the numerous personal attacks, my advocacy friends have been able to significantly damage my credibility. Based on administration advice, I didn't correct the record when the Washington Post grossly misrepresented my statement about pressure and incentives with a terrible misquote about "gold stars" and "cookies" that was reinforced by an Administration official. If I'm to

be effective as the US Envoy to Sudan, if I'm to be the point man for shaping the domestic debate for the President and Secretary Clinton on Sudan's challenges, then I must be perceived as credible when I speak. Listen to the way Representative Chris Smith speaks about me on YouTube or read the comments he made about me in Panel II of the December 3 hearing—you will get a small taste of the tone we must challenge. We can't allow elected or appointed officials in high offices to pass off unsubstantiated allegations concerning Sudan as the truth. These individuals must be asked to produce the evidence for their unsupported claims. We have the facts on our side to challenge the arguments made by advocacy groups and vocal members of Congress that have too long been accepted as undisputable truth. I'm ready to take this one on. Thanks, Scott

I did take on those who were spreading falsehoods and misleading statements about me and Sudan with formal responses to congressmen and calls to advocacy group leaders. I did not, however, get much help from the national security staff at the White House, from Ambassador Rice's staff at the US mission to the UN, or from the State Department to support my efforts.

8. Representatives Frank Wolfe, Chris Smith, and Donald Payne were the hardest on me in congressional hearings and they used tough language about me in the media and in their letters to senior Obama administration officials. Several years later, I had a private meeting with Frank Wolfe in which he apologized for misunderstanding my motives in negotiating directly with Khartoum about Southern Sudan's independence. This kind gesture was very meaningful to me.

9. While I didn't personally witness the "No Drama Obama" from the president himself, it appeared that high-level staff members in the administration often avoided internal confrontations in an attempt to present an exterior image of collegiality and cohesiveness.

10. President George W. Bush presented Salva Kiir a large cowboy hat as a gift during the South Sudanese liberation leader's 2006 visit to the White House. Apparently, Salva Kiir liked it so much that he purchased several of his own. Since then, the Texan cowboy hat has become a significant part of the South Sudan leader's persona.

11. Jonathan Schanzer and Laura Grossman, "Pariah State: Examining Sudan's Support for Terrorism," *Fighting Terrorism and Promoting Freedom*, July 5, 2012. Conveying the position of the US government, Kerry promised: "If [Sudan] allows a politically sensitive referendum to go ahead in January, and abides by the results, the US will move to take the country off its list of state sponsors of terrorism as early as next July [2011]." On August 18, 2011, the US Department of State released its annual terrorism assessment, *Country Reports on Terrorism 2010*, which concluded that terrorist groups, including "Al-Qaeda-inspired terrorists remain in Sudan as gaps remained in the

Sudanese government's knowledge of and ability to identify and capture these individuals as well as prevent them from exploiting the territory for smuggling activities." Many nations not on the State Sponsor of Terrorism list have unidentified terrorists within their borders. I believe political pressure from advocacy groups in the left-wing base and some Obama administration ideologues kept Sudan on the State Sponsor of Terrorism list despite US government promises to the contrary.

12. ARISE was my 2006 think piece for then-Senator Obama on foreign policy concerns and national defense priorities (see chapter 15). "A" was on the need to rebuild and reshape the United States ARMED FORCES and its capabilities to meet asymmetrical threats and cyber attacks. "R" was for the RELATIONSHIPS we had to restore around the globe. "I" was about reestablishing America as a nation of global INFLUENCE. "S" was for ways to increase SECURITY to protect Americans and US interests at home and around the world with a special emphasis on addressing the root causes of instability and insecurity. "E" contained my thoughts for an EXIT strategy to disengage safely and prudently from Iraq.

Chapter 20: America's Representative in Kenya

1. On December 19, 2012, Eric Boswell, assistant secretary of state for diplomatic security, resigned under pressure less than a day after a report blamed poor leadership and management failures in his bureau for many of the security lapses at the US diplomatic mission in Benghazi, Libya. The US Ambassador to Libya and three other Americans died when the Benghazi mission was attacked by militants on September 11, 2012.

2. Even during her October 22, 2015, testimony to the House Select Committee on Benghazi, former Secretary Clinton strongly defended the State Department "security professionals" on multiple occasions. Even when Eric Boswell was pressured to resign after the independent Benghazi Accountability Review Board highlighted his poor leadership as head of diplomatic security, she permitted him to stay at the State Department with full pay.

3. After incumbent President Mwai Kibaki was declared the winner of the presidential election held on December 27, 2007, supporters of Kibaki's opponent, Raila Odinga of the Orange Democratic Movement, alleged electoral manipulation. Ethnic violence erupted in major cities and in some rural areas of Kenya, causing a major political, economic, and humanitarian crisis. While a mediated settlement and power-sharing government resolved the immediate crisis, some Kenyans still feel the lingering effects of the targeted violence.

4. When I arrived in Kenya as the ambassador, I had responsibility for all of Kenya and Somalia. The Somalia Unit reported to me as the chief of mission and the senior individual in the Somalia Unit acted as a second deputy chief of mission in the US Embassy in Nairobi. In the summer of 2011, the assistant secretary of

state for African affairs, Johnnie Carson, created a new free-standing Somalia Unit and assigned Ambassador James Swan to Kenya as his special representative with responsibility for State Department activities in Somalia. Amb Swan reported directly to Amb Carson, and this formal chain of command bypassed me totally. On June 27, 2011, I met with Amb Swan and we agreed that our embassy would support the Somalia Unit in its efforts to provide leadership on Somalia policy and as it implemented its programs in Somalia. Our mission provided all the support Amb Swan requested to facilitate the Somalia Unit's activities with the international community, regional organizations and partners, and with the Transitional Federal Government within and outside of Somalia. I ensured the Somalia Unit was well taken care of in terms of embassy space, management support and physical security for its personnel, and other administrative support that we normally provided to our tenant organizations. As for lines of authority, I continued to be responsible for US activities in Kenya and Amb Swan handled all of Somalia. Where there was overlap and a clear intersection, our staffs communicated closely—the Somalia Unit was located in the same classified spaces as our political section. My DCM attended the Somalia Unit's staff meetings and a Somalia Unit representative was always invited to my country team meetings.

5. The OIG officially accused me of a) financial conflict of interest, b) misuse of present position, and c) unauthorized use of the State Department's computer systems. OIG inspector, John McCarthy, immediately launched formal investigations into each charge and my first interview with two investigators sent to Kenya by the OIG took place on May 20, 2012 . . . eight days before the OIG inspection was completed. I agreed to testify voluntarily and without legal counsel because I had nothing to hide from the State Department's investigators. Unfortunately, the widely circulated accusations impugned my character and damaged my reputation, even though they were eventually proven untrue. The three nameless and baseless allegations are as follows. First, the OIG alleged that I pushed the Government of Kenya and Kenya Airways to initiate direct flights to the United States for my personal gain. I had never corresponded with a major airline (e.g., Delta, KLM, or United) or any other airline-related company concerning direct flights. My passion about getting direct cargo and passenger flights between the United States and Kenya stemmed from my desire to develop economic markets for Kenyan products, create jobs in the United States and Kenya, and stimulate more economic growth in both countries. This was part of my job as the US Ambassador to Kenya. Second, the OIG alleged that I used my position as ambassador to get a special favor from the Government of Kenya. Specifically, Ambassador McCarthy accused me of requesting a waiver to fly in Kenya (with Kenya Airways) beyond the age of 65. I was 60 years old at the time and had no desire to fly commercially in Kenya. I had not flown military aircraft since January 2000, nor had I piloted a civilian aircraft since September 1980—thirty-two years. While this allegation

was silly and slanderous, it was still taken very seriously by OIG investigators. Finally, the OIG alleged that I used the State Department's computer systems for unauthorized activities. This issue is fully discussed in chapters 19 and 20.

6. I had raised security issues to Under Secretary for Management, Patrick Kennedy, when I didn't get satisfactory answers at Ambassador Carson's level.

7. I received so many personal and professional messages after my resignation. Deeply touching were those from my colleagues at the US Mission. I have chosen three representative messages from senior embassy officials:

One senior Foreign Service officer wrote,

It has been an honor and a blessing to work for you. I have witnessed first-hand the love you have for Kenya, and the warmth with which Kenyans embrace you. Your tenure here has been priceless for our relationship with this beautiful country. Kenyans were willing to hear hard messages from you because they know you have their best interests at heart. I cannot pretend to understand the politics of the Department, but it seems likely to me that DoS wanted to put one of its own people in and used the OIG to do so. It breaks my heart to see you go. But I know there are more important callings in your future.

Eric Whitaker, the embassy's Economic Counselor and acting Deputy Chief of Mission, sent me the following email shortly after I resigned as US Ambassador to Kenya.

Sitting between Judy and Joan this morning came with great difficulty, as we sat in a state of stunned empathy as you courageously spoke to Mission Kenya regarding the present circumstances and your future. I did not envy you for what you had to do, yet I certainly admired you for having the fortitude you demonstrated under duress. Those that know you best know you are a man who values faith and family, as well as country and career, and that you have endeavored to serve your nation well here in Kenya, a land and a people you so clearly love. Thank you again for your guidance and leadership as Chief of Mission.

Dr. Shon Remick, a senior leader from the *Let's Live* campaign, wrote the following

While it's true I am not in the "know," I can't help but feel that there are agendas which have utilized negative momentum to spin events. I guess that is politics. After having served in Kenya under three ambassadors, you are the only one who took a special interest in health. I continue to remember with pride the late nights and push to do more to save lives. Yes, we struggled to keep up with you, but you committed yourself to be in the fray with us. Together we all got our hands dirty. I think we were all amazed at your commitment. Sir, you challenged us. You challenged our procedures. You challenged our process. You challenged our priorities. You challenged our perspectives. You challenged our relevance and most importantly, you challenged the way we think. Isn't that what great strategic leaders do? There are really no words that can describe all that you have taught me as a leader, I am extremely grateful, richer and blessed to have worked for you. I have nothing but respect for you.

Chapter 21: A Double Standard?

1. These expressions from President Obama come in telephone, email, and conversations with friends who know the president or had contact with him. For example, I received the following email from a friend on August 8, 2012:

   Scott, Obama spoke of you with affection. He recognized your friendship—that you were helpful and with him from the beginning. He didn't get into any specifics about your current situation, except to say it was unfortunate and he reinforced that you were a good man. I'm sure no surprise to you, but thought I'd pass along.

2. Joseph Schmitz, "Obama's Inspector General Negligence," *Wall Street Journal*, June 4, 2013.
3. http://foreignpolicy.com/2013/02/05/congress-calls-on-kerry-to-appoint-a-state-department-inspector-general/ and press release, House Committee on Foreign Affairs, February 5, 2013.
4. http://www.nationalreview.com/article/350823/missing-watchdogs-state-joseph-e-schmitz
5. http://www.gao.gov/products/GAO-11-382T.
6. At least two political appointees have come under pressure by a negative OIG report to resign. The OIG report regarding James Rosapepe, US Ambassador to Romania (1998–2001), looks very similar to mine. If the OIG inspectors in Kenya did not actually lift language from the Romanian report, it's pretty suspicious how close the wording is. It is also interesting that it appears to present parallel accusations, according to a newspaper account (Jay Hancock, "A scorching report card for our Romanian envoy," *The Baltimore Sun*, December 22, 1999):

   . . . preferring results over paperwork is the sum of the case against him, and it doesn't amount to much. While Rosapepe may have alienated staffers and failed to pay the home office enough attention, they said, he delivered on basic State Department goals. . . . The report is especially harsh on the Bucharest embassy's failure to send frequent and relevant reports on Romanian affairs and political trends to

Washington. . . . The report criticized Rosapepe for meeting repeatedly with top Romanian officials without filing reports of the meetings
with Washington. . .

Another US ambassador, Cynthia Stroum, who headed the mission to
Luxembourg, was forced to resign in January 2011 after the OIG gave her a
negative report similar to mine. On July 7, 2012, she wrote me a note in which
she said (and I quote with her permission),

But to read the exact same phrases and hear the exact reasons for
your 'poor performance' followed by a negative OIG was just all too
familiar. I KNOW I was thrown under the bus. It sure sounds like you
were, too.

7. Sensitive but unclassified (SBU) information is information in the United
   States federal government that is not classified for national security reasons,
   but that warrants/requires administrative control and protection from public
   or other unauthorized disclosure for other reasons. The SBU label cannot be
   used instead of classification to protect information.
8. At the end of Secretary Clinton's first news conference about emails on
   March 10, 2015, David Shuster from Al Jazeera America asked her about
   my being forced to resign. Secretary Clinton replied, "David, I think you
   should go online and read the entire IG report. That is not an accurate representation of what happened." At that point, all the falsehoods and inaccu-
   racies in the OIG report concerning my ambassadorship were used by Mrs.
   Clinton to discredit me and to justify my forced resignation. The entire
   transcript of the news conference in available at: http://time.com/3739541/
   transcript-hillary-clinton-email-press-conference.
9. In 2009, the National Archives issued regulations saying that agencies allowing
   employees to do official business on nonofficial email accounts had to ensure
   that any records sent on private email systems are preserved "in the appropriate agency recordkeeping system." In September 2013, the National Archives
   issued further guidance to federal agencies that said federal employees generally
   should not use personal email accounts to conduct official business, except in
   limited situations, such as during emergencies when an official may not be able
   to access an official account. In 2014, the federal government placed explicit
   limits on agency officials using private email accounts for official business.
   The new law says agency officials can't create or send a government record on
   a private account unless they also copy or forward the email to their official
   government email address. I was the US Ambassador to Kenya in 2011–12, a
   year before the before the regulations on commercial email were tightened. My
   limited use of Gmail in the State Department was not prohibited at that time.
10. Articles include, Lisa Desjardins, PBS News Hour, May 26,2016, http://
    www.pbs.org/newshour/rundown/5-things-you-might-have-missed-in-

the-clinton-email-report/; Steven Lee Myers and Eric Lichtblau, New York Times and carried in the Boston Globe, https://bostonglobe.com/news/politics/2016/05/25/clinton-criticized-for-private-mails-state-dept-review; and Eugene Kiely, FactCheck.org, http://www.factcheck.org/2016/05/ig-report-on-clintons-emails/.

11. Because combat missions are tracked officially in the US Air Force's flight records database, I had a flight-records technician research the data before I retired. As of mid-2006, no other fighter pilot or aircrew member had flown close to my 274 combat missions over Iraq. In fact, based on available data, the pilot with the next highest number had approximately150 combat missions.

Chapter 22: Reflections

1. The beginning of chapter 5 describes my near fatal accident over San Antonio. Chapter 3 tells about crossing the border from Congo as a refugee. My 1979 trip to Uganda is chronicled at the end of chapter 5.
2. The story about Major Glenn Hessel's F-16 accident is told in chapter 7. The account of Lieutenant General David McCloud's Yak-54 accident is recounted in chapter 10. The terrorist bombing of Khobar Towers is detailed in chapter 9. The 9-11 attack on the Pentagon is briefly recounted in chapter 12.
3. My immediate family tree is described in chapter 16. The special time I spent traveling with my father from Chicago to Washington, DC, is highlighted in chapter 11. My boarding-school experience with an adult's cutting words and the invisible scars is recounted in chapter 3. Examples of expressing appreciation are outlined in chapters 9 and 13. The principle of protecting friends and colleagues is lived out in chapter 10; therefore, I was surprised when my friends in the Obama administration abandoned me when I was fired as the US Ambassador to Kenya (chapter 19). My induction into Masai tribe is recounted in chapter 2.
4. The story of Captain Eric Das's ultimate sacrifice is told in chapter 13. The rescue of a Special Forces soldier who lost a limb in Iraq is relayed in chapter 8. The story of a young airman who used initiative and innovation to change an outcome is relayed in chapter 10. My efforts as a US ambassador to mark special days with meaningful ceremonies is explained in chapter 19.
5. I've benefited greatly from many cross-cultural experiences, including the White House Fellows trip to Asia (chapter 6). One example of arrogance getting in the way of reality occurred in 1982 when Kenya experienced a coup d'état (chapter 4). Examples of bureaucratic conflicts involving dedicated Americans trying to do the right thing include the humanitarian effort in Jordan (chapter 13), Sudan and Libya policymaking (chapter 18), and the different cultural perspectives between the State Department and the Defense Department (chapter 19).
6. My efforts to develop personal strengths and skills that include memorization (chapter 3), manual skills (chapter 3), and teaching skills (chapters 5 and 7) are

detailed throughout the book. Learning from complicated events is illustrated in the two F-16 deployments (chapters 7 and 8). My shaky start in pilot training illustrates that one can finish successfully, even after faltering at the beginning (chapter 4). My elimination from the Thunderbird try-outs proved that hard work, determination, perseverance, and priorities don't always make dreams come true (chapter 7).

7. Making sure organizational charts, responsibilities, and authorities were clear and correct is illustrated with three examples: Washington (chapter 1), Somalia (chapter 8), and Kenya (chapter 19). The story about being humble enough to ask for advice can be found in chapter 7. Mr. Beggs' citation of Niccolo Machiavelli is found in chapter 7. The lesson about having a back-up strategy was first learned in boarding school (chapter 3) and practiced throughout my life, for example in mission planning (chapter 8). My leadership role in the aftermath of Kenya's coup d'état is detailed in chapter 4; unfortunately the Kenya Air Force was disbanded and my efforts to establish a vibrant F-5 squadron were put on hold. Illustrations of promoting unit pride and of pushing innovation are included throughout chapter 10 about my time at Elmendorf Air Force Base.

8. The concept of practicing principled behavior and of always do what is right to keep your integrity, even if you are humiliated and punished for your actions, is illustrated in chapters 7 and 10. Chapter 19 tells about trying to do the right thing as the US Ambassador to Kenya.

9. Integrity is a quality I value and practiced in my professional careers and daily life (chapters 7 and 10). I wished I had seen more integrity while I was the US Ambassador to Kenya (chapter 19).

10. Stories about cultivating personal relationship and trust with foreign nationals and about negotiating significant agreements based on these are found in chapter 4 about Kenya, chapter 9 about Turkey, chapter 11 about the Middle East, chapter 14 about Spain, and chapter 14 about Libya. Chapter 18 discusses the negotiations in Sudan to return NGOs to Darfur, to end the conflict between Chad and Sudan, to resolve lingering issues associated with the Comprehensive Peace Agreement, to unify rebel forces so we could negotiate the Darfur Peace Agreement, and to carry out the referendum on independence of Southern Sudan.

11. Examples of sharing and contributing to the community include Ugandan medical staff (chapter 5), cutting hair at the Lorton Community Center (chapter 12), and starting a new company in East Africa (Epilogue).

12. The prayer of Saint Francis of Assisi can be found in chapter 15.

13. The thirty seconds over San Antonio is in chapter 5, the bomb blast in Dhahran is described in chapter 9, and the story of the 9-11 attack on the Pentagon is told in chapter 12.

Epilogue

1. It is difficult to get a definitive ranking of the world's fastest growing economies, but Ethiopia, Democratic Republic of the Congo, Cote d'Ivoire, Mozambique, Tanzania, and Rwanda are consistently ranked near the top.

2. This quote comes from my induction into Masai tribe that is recounted in chapter 2.

Acronyms, Abbreviations, Aircraft

Acronyms

AFRICOM	US Africa Command
AHC	Aircraft Handling Characteristics
AK-47	*Avtomat Kalashnikova*, also known as Kalashnikov AK
AMRAAM	Advanced Medium-Range Air-to-Air Missile
AOR	Area of Responsibility
AWACS	Airborne Warning and Control System
CENTCOM	US Central Command
CEO	Chief Executive Officer
CIA	Central Intelligence Agency
CPA	Comprehensive Peace Agreement
CSAF	Chief of Staff of the Air Force
CTF	Combined Task Force
DCM	Deputy Chief of Mission
DOD	Department of Defense
DPA	Darfur Peace Agreement
EU	European Union
EUCOM	US European Command
G	Measurement of the force of gravity
GAO	Government Accountability Office
GO/FO	General officers and flag officers
HIV/AIDS	Human immunodeficiency virus and acquired immune deficiency syndrome
HUD	Heads-Up Display
ICC	International Criminal Court
ICT	Information and Communications Technology
IDP	Internally displaced person
IG	Inspector General
ILS	Instrument Landing System

IRRI	Initial Response Readiness Inspection
IOTF	Information Operations Task Force
IV	Intravenous Fluid
J-3	Directorate of Operations
J-39	Directorate of Information Operations
J-5	Directorate of Strategy, Plans, and Policy
J-8	Directorate of Assessments, Capabilities, and Transformation
JEM	Justice and Equality Movement
JP-8	Grade of Jet Fuel
LJM	Liberty and Justice Movement
LRMC	Landstuhl Regional Medical Center
MGB	Four-cylinder British-made roadster
NASA	National Aeronautics and Space Administration
NATO	North Atlantic Treaty Organization
NCO	Non-Commissioned Officer
NCP	National Congress Party
NGO	Non-governmental organization
NOTAM	Notice to Airmen
OIG	Office of the Inspector General
PACAF	US Pacific Air Forces
PACAF/IG	US Pacific Air Forces Inspector General
PEPFAR	President's Emergency Plan for AIDS Relief
PJ	Pararescue Jumper
POW/MIA	Prisoner of War/Missing In Action
ROTC	Reserve Officer Training Corps
SAF/IA	Secretary of the Air Force/International Affairs
SPLM	Sudan People's Liberation Movement
TF-W	Task Force-West
TRA	Temporary Reserved Airspace
UAV	Unmanned aerial vehicle
UBL	Usama bin Laden or Osama bin Laden
UCP	Unified Command Plan
UNAMID	United Nations-African Union Mission in Darfur
USAID	US Agency for International Development
USAFE	US Air Forces in Europe
USSES	US Special Envoy to Sudan
WHF	White House Fellows/Fellowship

Aircraft

A-10   Attack aircraft, nicknamed the Warthog (1970s–present)

C-130   Medium-lift cargo aircraft, nicknamed the Hercules
        (1950s–present)

E-3   Aircraft used for the Airborne Warning and Control System,
        nicknamed the Sentry (1970s–present)

F-5   Multi-role fighter, nicknamed the Tiger (1960s–1980s)

F-15C   Air superiority fighter, nicknamed the Eagle (1970s–present)

F-15E   Multi-role fighter, nicknamed the Strike Eagle (1980s–present)

F-16   Multi-role fighter, nicknamed the Fighting Falcon or Viper
        (1980s–present)

F-22   Stealth fighter, nicknamed the Raptor (2000s–present)

F-86   Air superiority fighter, nicknamed the Sabre (1940s–1960s)

KC-10   Tanker aircraft based on the DC-10 airframe, nicknamed the
        Extender (1980s–present)

KC-135 Tanker aircraft based on the B-707 airframe, nicknamed the
        Stratotanker (1960s–present)

T-37   Subsonic initial trainer, nicknamed the Tweet (1950s–2000s)

T-38   Supersonic trainer, nicknamed the Talon (1960s–present)

U-2   Ultra-high altitude reconnaissance aircraft, nicknamed the
        Dragon Lady (1950s–present)

HH-60G Search and rescue helicopter, nicknamed the Pave Hawk
        (1980s–present)

Yak-54 Light acrobatic aircraft (Yakovlev-54) (1990s–present)

Installations

Columbus AFB   USAF pilot training air base in Mississippi

Nellis AFB   USAF multi-purpose air base in Nevada

Williams AFB   USAF pilot training air base in Arizona

Ramstein AB   US-used air base in Germany

Incirlik AB   US-used air base in Turkey

Vaihingen   Location of the US European Command in Germany

NAS Sigonella   US-used naval air station in Sicily

Operations

Desert Storm	Operation to liberate Kuwait (1991–1992)
Proven Force	Operation to compliment Desert Storm in northern Iraq (1991–1992)
Provide Comfort	Operation to support and protect Kurds in northern Iraq (1991–1996)
Northern Watch	Operation to enforce the UN-mandated no-fly zone north of N36° (1997–2003)
Southern Watch	Operation to enforce the UN-mandated no-fly zone south of N33° (1992–2003)
Iraqi Freedom	Operation to find Iraq's weapons of mass destruction and toppled the government of Saddam Hussein (2003–2011)

Index